The Joseph Communications:
Your Life
After Death

For Jane

The Joseph Communications:
Your Life
After Death

Michael G. Reccia

with thanks to:
Jane, David, Tony and Mark

Band of Light
MEDIA

First Paperback Printing April 2011
Second Paperback Printing Sept 2011
Third Paperback Printing March 2012
Fourth Paperback Printing December 2012
Fifth Paperback Printing June 2013
Sixth Paperback Printing August 2014
Seventh Paperback Printing March 2016
Eighth Paperback Printing November 2016

e-Book edition July 2011

Published by Band of Light Media Limited © 2016
10 Sparrable Row,
Briercliffe,
Burnley,
BB10 3QW
United Kingdom

www.josephspeaks.com

ISBN: 978-1-906625-03-0

Printed in the United Kingdom by Pioneer Print Solutions Ltd.

Contents

Concerning my friend Joseph:
an introduction

It's strange now to think that, just a short few years ago, Joseph and myself hadn't even met...

Correction. This 'concerned observer of mankind'... this 'spiritual scientist'... this 'communicator on behalf of millions of enlightened, discarnate souls' (there are so many appropriate terms I could use to describe him) *had* met me, in a manner of speaking, but I hadn't consciously made *his* acquaintance at that time.

I'd better explain.

My public work as a spirit medium dates back to the mid-eighties, when I first began giving clairvoyant messages to individuals and groups. Fairly rapidly I became an in-demand source of spiritual communication, being booked to capacity two to three months in advance at any given time for personal readings. I travelled the length and breadth of the country to give demonstrations and lectures on various spiritual topics. I should have been happy. After all, I was using the gifts I'd been given. I'd turned my back on a lucrative career in order to do so, and considered what I was doing to absolutely be the one thing I was *meant* to be doing with my life, and of far greater importance than mere pounds, shillings and pence. People were, quite literally, beating a path to my door... so why on earth did I feel so unfulfilled?

Well, the messages that were delivered through me, whilst many and varied, and accurate and detailed, were hardly world changing. True, they gave comfort to the people they were directed to, and there could be little doubt in their minds, due to the amount of information given that could only be known to them, that they were indeed receiving communications from their loved ones and friends 'on the other side', but they left me, personally, aching to achieve so much more as a spiritual worker than circumstance allowed me to deliver at that point.

You see, from the time I first began my mediumistic development, I had wanted to understand not only how the gift of mediumship 'worked', but also *why* it existed, how this world was actually put together from a spiritual point of view, how the spirit 'worlds' or 'spheres' functioned, why things are as they are on Earth, and what awaits us beyond this physical life ...and to share that knowledge with those who were seeking such insights.

Joseph provided answers to all those questions. How I began working with this wise and ancient discarnate spirit from a higher level of being (who had been linked to me 'behind the scenes' since my birth, waiting for that point in physical time when we could connect and challenge certain personal and world views together) and how I then progressed from clairvoyant delivery to trance communication, with Joseph completely taking over my faculties, is chronicled in the introduction to his first book, *Revelation*. I don't, therefore, propose to cover old ground here. Suffice it to say that the type of spiritual communication coming through me changed dramatically as soon as Joseph and I consciously 'linked up' with each other, and that, within the space of a couple of years, he had delivered an extraordinary amount of information. This was gathered together first as *Revelation*, a book that, to my great satisfaction, *actually does* explain who and what we really are, why we are here and what we are capable of spiritually; and next as *Illumination*, a spiritual self-help manual that empowers its readers to apply principles that, when exercised religiously (no pun intended) *actually work* in slowly changing this completely insane and hell-bent world we live in at the moment into that harmonious paradise we dream about but have never quite seemed capable of achieving.

Joseph's third book, the one you are beginning right now, answers the 'biggie' – the single, most scary, *enormous* question that unites all of us, in that at some stage in our lives each of us simply *has* to ask it:

'What, if anything, comes *next*?'

Coming out of trance sessions I find I can remember little to nothing of what has transpired during the time Joseph has been speaking through me, so it is always a joy to read a Joseph transcription (Joseph's words are recorded by the three other members of our 'Band Of Light', as Joseph describes it, the four of us sitting regularly to receive his communications) and to discover that, during the time I have been voluntarily 'taken over' and taken out of the picture, a phenomenal amount of vital information has been transmitted.

It was with particular delight, then, that I read the transcripts for this book. To say that Joseph had once again 'delivered the goods' would be an understatement. Here was a book that, in his characteristic, no-nonsense way, addressed the subject of life after death in illuminating and comprehensive detail, asking and answering the questions we all voice concerning the subject; answering questions we'd never thought of asking, and also turning on their head any preconceived ideas we might have about what actually does lie ahead for us – for *you* – once the physical body has been left behind.

Forget clouds and harps, obviously. Forget Heaven and Hell too. Forget the traditional views of punishment and reward. Forget certain occult assumptions that glibly quote a finite number of 'levels of being' beyond physical life and the reaching of a precise number of heavens, these beliefs confining and restricting the reality of the afterlife by the human need to make everything fit neatly into that fiercely calculating, but rarely comprehending, mental box that is the physical mind. Instead, here is a book that tells it *like it is* from outside of that box – with *heart* and from a high spiritual perspective. Here is a book written by someone who has personally walked and observed the various landscapes 'beyond the veil'; a book suffused with spiritual input that applies to our lives in this world now as much as to the next, and that delivers that information in a succinct, *contemporary* way. There never have been any jarring 'thees' or 'thous', or airs or pretensions threaded through Joseph's words... Nor would I expect there to be from a spirit intending to relate to twenty-first century life. Joseph cares not for himself and his past lives... but for *you* and your present one.

This book has been presented in exactly the way that Joseph delivered it, and where he sometimes hesitates when searching for the right words to illustrate complex concepts his attempts to turn the unseen into the readable and the understandable have been included in the text. This, I feel, makes him more human somehow... this, plus, of course, his sense of humour and obvious limitless love for mankind, which shine through every chapter.

Also, and although this is a very complete book on the subject in its own right, we invariably discover, as he sheds Light (with a capital L) onto more areas that were previously regarded as unfathomable spiritual mysteries, that Joseph has *even more* to tell us (life, the universe and...well... *everything* is a vast topic, after all) and you will therefore, on occasion, note in the text that he refers to topics we have yet to receive from him and which, God willing, will be covered in future communications... Perhaps even in a companion book to this one.

Joseph always invites questions after each address he delivers within our little circle and these have also been included, as his detailed answers to them offer a wealth of further information of vital importance to the spiritual seeker.

Time for me to bow out now, much as I do when Joseph takes up temporary residence in my mind and body – and time for you to, literally, be transported to another world... or *worlds*, as I should more correctly say.

If you are changed in any way by your journey through this book and feel you would like to know more about the *Joseph Communications*, why not keep in touch with us? You can contact us via our website: josephspeaks.com

Michael G. Reccia
March 2011

Terminology: 'the Field', 'the Fall' – a brief explanation

If you are new to *the Joseph Communications* and have not read the other books in this series, allow me to qualify the terms 'the Field' and 'the Fall', which Joseph refers to at points throughout this book.

The Field

When referring to 'the Field' Joseph is describing the conscious field of thought-energy we, as spirits on Earth, are surrounded by and live within. Every second of our lives we project our thoughts and beliefs as to the nature of reality into this energy field. The Field is actually created and maintained *by us*, but we have lost sight of this fact. As a result of us forgetting this, which is in itself as a result of 'the Fall' (see below), the Field is not operating as it was originally intended to. It was supposed to serve us, but at the moment we, in effect, serve it. It exhibits, and seeks to perpetuate in us, a negative charge and outlook, and, because of this and its disconnection with God-Light, is maintaining itself and us via a finite and dwindling amount of energy. The Field in its present state, and therefore also we as human beings existing within it, cannot last much longer. Joseph urges us to re-energise the Field with God-Light and, by doing so, to transform it and take control of it once again for the betterment and continuance of mankind and of the planet.

The Fall

...is a term that Joseph applies to a complex decision and action taken by human souls millions of years ago which resulted in a cataclysmic change in vibration that plunged the Earth into a darkness we and the planet are still suffering from and feeling the effects of. This change in vibration separated us in conscious thought from our God-heritage and resulted in the negative, violent, power-hungry world and society we currently live in.

Chapter One
The Last Chapter

Joseph: The title of the first chapter, beginning this third book, is '*The Last Chapter*', because in beginning this book I have to deal with what happens to the human soul before it is liberated into the higher vibrations.

Most people on Earth do not realise that life is an arc, that there is a burst of vibration that accompanies the birth of the physical being, and that that burst of vibration extends outwards and grows, and becomes stronger up to the midway point. At the midway point in life that vibration then begins to fold in on itself and that tendency, that path, is *built into* the vibration. So, from the moment of birth on Earth as a physical being, the soul is approaching death.

You would expect me to talk about death before talking about the life hereafter, wouldn't you? I cannot simply begin this book by telling you what comes next; I have to tell you what happens *before* death as you approach death so that you can appreciate what happens *after* physical death.

Your vibration (your *physical* vibration – not your soul's vibration) has built into it a timescale which is designed to bring you back to your start-point. It encases the soul at the moment of physical birth. The vibration extends from the soul in strength and then, from the midway point, there is a drawing in and a releasing, little by little, of the bonds

15

that have tied the soul for a very short time to the Earth plane. And those bonds are quite complex – you talk of a 'blessed release' when someone is taken from this life and released from pain, or from suffering, or from a life that is sad and miserable, but automatically built into your vibration – into you, the reader – *is* a 'blessed release'… a blessed release from the bonds of the Earth. The Earth is a very magnetic, attractive place, as I have explained in the other books [*ref. to Revelation and Illumination*]. The Earth pulls at you – pulls at the physical, pulls at the mental – and were you to stay here in this vibration in its present state for longer than a normal lifetime and normal span of years, you could become immersed ever deeper in this vibration to the extent that it would take a great deal of time and effort on behalf of others in the spirit worlds to elevate you to a point where you could be released from the vibration of the Earth. Therefore, built into your vibration as a physical being (because you are also a physical being… are *linked* to a physical being) is a 'release' and a 'release date'.

In the normal course of things there is a 'release date' for you to exit this earthly vibration and that date is known about. Sometimes you go to fortune-tellers and to mediums because you want to know the future, but your future in terms of you returning to your heavenly home is *assured*, is known about, is calculated, is (if you would like an analogy) written up in chalk on a great board, is pre-destined …and *there is nothing you can do about it.*

However, there is a lot that you can do about *how you live your life*, which is why I dictated the first two books. Here I have to get you to confront the *fact* that *you will exit this physical realm.* As you grow older and as you reach the mid-point the vibration of the physical body begins to change. The physical body rejects the Earth – not the other way round. The physical body is subject to a change of vibration that, little by little, alienates it from the physical realm. Changes take place in the cells but changes take place at a spiritual level more than at any other level as your soul (the person, the being, the *consciousness* that you really are) begins to release itself, little by little, from the physical body. It is amusing to hear people say, 'Well, I have ten years left', or 'I have twenty years left', or 'I have thirty years left'. That may be true, but during that time the soul is gradually extricating itself from physical existence and, little by little, the energies from the soul that feed the physical body are cut off. It is the same thing you see in a tree: a tree in autumn and in winter cuts off the supply of energy to its leaves and those leaves fall. But the tree is not the leaves; the tree will produce leaves again and this is an analogy I would like to give you... From your mid-point in physical energy you – you as a *soul* – begin to cut off the energies that feed your physical and mental bodies because on a soul-level you *know* that you have to return. If people were not so preoccupied with the physicality and distractions of this level they would also *intuitively* begin to receive warnings from the soul: 'Put your house in order; tie up those things that need to be tied up; release yourself from those things that need to be released – because the time draws near for you to return home.'

So, little by little, the physical body is starved of the energies that maintain it via the God-centre within the soul. It is not something that is done on an earth-conscious level; it comes from the soul as a mechanism and is an automatic response. This is why the body grows older; this is why the body retreats from the illusion and, not being fed by the soul, the body begins to wither and decompose and to be pulled by the illusion. There are two operations taking place: firstly the body withers because it does not have enough energy to maintain its illusion or projection and, secondly, once you take away the soul-energies the body reacts more and more on a physical level and on the level of the illusion. The illusion then pulls at the body and, because the illusion or 'Field' of the Earth is negatively charged, that negative charge has an effect on the body and increasingly the body decays until it reaches a *point of no return.*

There comes a point where the pull on the physical body from the Earth plane and the lack of sustenance to the physical body via the soul cause the body to cease functioning. At that point things happen very quickly – something that has been going on for years suddenly terminates, suddenly comes to a conclusion, and the soul is released. The body falls away and the soul is projected *instantly* to the vibration that is suitable for it to appreciate, consciously and harmoniously. The soul, in other words, goes to the place that has been prepared for it by its endeavours during its recent stay on the Earth plane plus the culmination of its endeavours during other lifetimes and experiences to this point.

There is a cord that is often talked about in spiritual books and spiritual discussions which connects the soul (which is *also* a casing, of course, for the consciousness that is represented as an individual) to the physical body. That cord allows the soul – for the time that the physical body is on Earth – to be either totally integrated with the physical body or, during sleep-time or trance-meditation or other changes of mind-vibration, to exist at a distance from the physical body and yet still be connected to it. Whilst the cord is connected to the physical body energy flows from the soul and the soul is able to animate the physical body.

At the *point of no return* there is a severing of the cord and, as soon as the cord has severed, the cord retreats; the projection of energy or cone of electro-magnetic energy that the cord represents is reabsorbed into the shell that is the soul and the body undergoes a death. The *soul* does not undergo a death but the *body* undergoes a death because the body has an intelligence that has been fed by the electro-magnetic impulses from the soul via the cord. The body operates, to some extent, autonomously and independently of the soul but needs the soul's connection to it in order to exist. The body has a separate intelligence that is programmed to operate at a certain level of health and to operate at a certain level of instinct. You do not, for example, have to tell your feet to walk or your head to turn or your eyes to focus; that is a separate intelligence – separate to you yet connected to you and tailored individually to you via the energies that emanate from your soul to animate that body.

When the soul severs its connection to the physical body, the physical body's intelligence *truly* dies as an individualisation of energy. The energy that is within the physical body migrates back to a pool of energy from which other physicalities can be drawn. That pool of energy has a separate consciousness to the soul-consciousness. What I am saying is that there is a pool of energy from which physicality is created that is *separate* from the God-energy that the human soul is created from and the intelligence within the physical body migrates back to that pool. That pool in itself is also God-energy (please do not misunderstand me) but it is not the God-energy that is the individualisation that you recognise as the individual soul.

Once the energy from the physical body has migrated back to the pool, the body lacks coherence because the body then is simply a construct within the illusion without any individual identity, and the magnetic attraction of the illusion breaks down that body into the soup of consciousness that we have called 'the Field' in the other titles. The body goes back to the Field. The ancients knew this – the ancients knew that the physical body had a separate consciousness to the soul, not an identity but a conscious, intelligent programme that ran the physical body. This, again, is why, upon physical death, the physical body in ancient times was completely destroyed and taken back to the Earth – usually by fire – to make absolutely certain that the consciousness within the physical body had migrated back to the Field and could not be linked to the body.

Here I must explain that the soul, upon physical death, will sometimes not relinquish the body – particularly if the soul believes *that it is the body* – and the soul tries to re-animate the body on occasions saying, 'Why am I lying here when I can open my eyes but I can't see through my physical eyes? Why can I not lift my hands or move my feet?' The ancients knew that, in destroying the physical body and allowing that energy of the physical body to migrate back to the pool of energy that feeds individualisation on a physical level, they were freeing the soul.

Souls, as you know, become stuck, and they become stuck because they are not ready to acknowledge that there is anything beyond the death of the physical body; they become stuck because they have forgotten that they are Light and that they are spiritual beings. On the death of the body, in many cases, the soul cannot acknowledge and come to terms with the separation of the body from the soul's shell and desperately tries to re-animate the physical body for a time. Many souls actually inhabit the physical body until the physical body is no more, until the strength of the illusion pulling at the physical body overpowers the soul's memory of the physical body. Sometimes bodies decompose at a different rate; sometimes bodies are preserved. Sometimes a body, years after interment, can be as new, and this depends on the strength of the soul wishing to keep that physical body together.

There are many, many souls that inhabit the area of their physical body for as long as possible because they cannot acknowledge anything else. But there comes a point for each soul when their effect on the physical Field is (if you will forgive the expression) *a ghost of its former strength* and, at that point, the physical body gives in to the pull of the illusion; the intelligence of the physical body is fully absorbed back into the individualisation pool that relates to physical matter and the soul is left wondering what to do next.

This does not, of course, apply to a great many souls... yet there *are* a great many souls who will not leave this place, and there are a great many souls, too, who leave *expecting specifics*: expecting upon death of the physical body, for example, to see their Saviour; to be in a specific type of Heaven; to be greeted by saints or holy men and women; to be in a place that is a reward for their past endeavours on Earth.

If only it were so simple!

So, this initial talk, this initial chapter, is about the *Last Chapter*; it is about the need for *you*, the reader of this book, to acknowledge that you are not permanent on a physical level and that there *has never been* a soul on a physical level that is permanent.

You are on a journey. If you were to set out on a holiday you would expect, wouldn't you, to enjoy the journey outwards and to anticipate the days ahead? Then there would come a mid-point in your holiday where there were as many days behind as there were in front, and from that point you would say, 'I only have *x* days left – four days left; three days left; two days left.' Then you would gather your possessions and you would return to your home. The holiday would be over. The journey would be over. In this case *as below, so above* ...this is what happens to the soul. The soul has gone not on a holiday, but on a journey, and has set out into physicality. But physicality is an impermanent state so the soul has to turn around and return to its start-point – bringing with it its experiences.

You are going to die...

...but that is a joyous thing; that is an exciting thing; that is a further journey. I do not open this book to make you sad, to make you miserable. I wish to make you aware of the fact that you will not be *here* for much longer (no matter how young you are as a reader reading these words) and that there is a far more exciting, infinite journey ahead of you. In making you aware of your own mortality (of the mortality of your *physical body*) you will be more interested in what comes next... because the soul always has to have a 'next'. The soul is always moving on to a new experience, to a new integration of itself with levels of energy.

The level of energy that you leave when your soul parts company with your physical body is a low one, is a restrictive one, is a limited one in vision, understanding and experience. So many souls cling on to this experience and return themselves to it. In this book I hope to show you that there is much more ahead for you than you could ever experience on the Earth plane. Also, I hope to change your attitude towards death – not so that you welcome it (you are supposed to be here, you are designed to be here for a certain amount of time) but so that you are not afraid of it, and so that you are given the option, to examine and to consider, **of not coming back here.**

Many of your cultures talk of reincarnation. Reincarnation *does* exist, but *you* are the one who instigates it and you instigate it because either you feel that you have unfinished business on the Earth plane or you feel that the experiences the Earth plane has to give you are worth re-experiencing. You are drawn back to so many things: you are drawn back to physicality, to sex, to food, to *pain*. How can you be drawn back to pain? Because pain becomes familiar and because, when pain stops, you are relieved and feel that you have achieved something (and I am talking not just of pain physically; you also put yourself through mental pain, through spiritual pain and through emotional pain). And you will say: 'Joseph, this is nonsense, I could never return into pain,' and yet you do time and again; you become used to it. Do you not say *better the devil you know*? You become used to it and you blind yourself to the possibilities, to the realities, to the illumination and evolution of the next steps in your infinite journey as a part of God.

So this is 'the last chapter'. Your life and this book begins with your physical death, and it is my intention to explain, scientifically and as precisely as I can, what happens to you upon physical death and to explain to you why it is a far better idea for yourself and for your brothers and sisters in God that you decide to move on when you leave this place.

Joseph [*speaking to David and Jane*]: This book is far more complex than the ones that have preceded it and there are many concepts that will have to be woven together by my words over the coming months. You will have to approach it in a more fluid manner than you have with the previous books that far more easily fit into chapters. I will return to themes throughout the next few months so that we can expand on them and so that we can get everything in its right place. I find myself having to remain calm in bringing through this information because I am excited about it. There is so much to tell and there is only one small beam of communication along which to direct my words.

You must act as monitors of the book that is taking shape and you must ask me questions – and you must remember that I am only presenting one dimension of a multi-dimensional concept and want to present as *full* a concept as I can to your readers. So I will begin this today by asking you to ask me questions if there is anything that you need to expand upon in what has been said in this introduction to the book.

Jane: I am appalled to think that people sometimes stay with their bodies after they have died and try to re-animate them for a while and I just wondered why they don't notice that their bodies are underground, in a grave, rotting? What do they see?

Joseph: They see *themselves*. They identify completely with the body and they are so steeped in and so locked into the idea that physicality is all there is that they (for a time) shut out the possibility of there being more for them than identifying with the physical body. You must understand that there are thousands, millions of souls who look in the mirror and say, 'That is me' and that there is a lifetime of reinforcement of: 'That is me! No matter what goes on within me, that is me. I am this island of flesh and nothing more', and because God grants through the soul whatever the soul desires then that desire and belief is solidified. They are locked into an idea of *that is me*, and so, when they are suddenly not that image of *that is me* they cannot cope with it. They are so identified with their physical image they attempt to re-animate that physical image even though, from the perspective of another soul, they are standing next to their body and looking identical to that body but a good sight healthier. Do you see that?

Jane: I just wondered whether they were trying to re-animate the body that is in the grave?

Joseph: They are in a kind of dream-state (Michael has experience of this through working with souls who have become lost for a time), so it is not a consciousness as you would understand it today from your perspective of being in an earthly body. It is, if you like, an 'un-waking dream'; it is a muddied perception; it is a sense of self projected onto something that they know will not respond any longer. So, if your question is: are they aware of their bodies degrading and are they aware of being underground – not as such because they are not there in effect, but they are making the *link* with the physical in a dream-like state (much as Michael goes into trance). You might call it an 'earthly trance' – a pull back to that perception of themselves that they believe.

You are, unfortunately, living in a time of celebrity, a time when so much importance is given to the physical body... *The physical body must be preserved at all costs* – particularly for women. You therefore have souls who pass having believed for the greater amount of their physical lives that the physical body must be preserved at all costs, so their instinct and their volition forces them for a time (until they realise something else) to buy into that and to continue their expectation that the physical body must be preserved at all costs. And so, of course, they are linked to the physical body until such time as we can convince them that there is more to do and a greater perspective ahead of them. They are in a stupor (as many discarnate souls who are linked to the Earth plane, for a time, are) because they cannot exist in a physical world and they have not yet learnt to exist on a higher vibration. They are 'between'. It is a twilight; it is a dream – as everything is a dream – but they are more aware of it being a dream-like state than the spirit who is in an earthly body or the spirit who has passed on to one of the higher spheres. Does that make sense?

Jane: Yes.

David: When we do go through a physical death and the soul withdraws you say that sometimes a soul forgets that it is a being of Light. Rather than just hanging around the physical plane I presume it can actually plummet even further down the vibrational scales. Is that the case?

Joseph: That is a very good point and it is the subject of quite a few paragraphs. You see how there is so much that needs to be said! In fact I will address this next time, touching on the effects of the Lower Astral on the soul and the effects of this plane on the soul at the point of it being severed from physical death.

We are talking about a *vast* book here and it was mentioned by Michael's mentor, Joan, that there would be difficulty in bringing through the third book. There will be no difficulty but you have to be very precise and I am trying to follow a logical sequence of events. So we have, first of all, the shock and the realisation that must be brought to people that they will leave this plane, that they will meet that point of physical death. It is inevitable. Then I wish to explain what happens next and that is where that attraction via the astral plane and also via the Earth plane (for many souls wander the Earth plane for quite some time, having left their physical bodies) needs to be put under the microscope. I will do it next time. I will talk about the pull of the Lower Astral, and we must also talk about the upper vibrations, the upper desires with each soul and that the desires of the soul, on the point of death, determine what happens to it next and attract like-vibrations that can either be of a higher vibration or a lower vibration than the Earth plane.

In constructing this book we must work together far more than we have done on the first two books and have an interaction to place everything in its correct position in presenting an argument to the people of Earth as to what happens upon death and what happens next and the options that are open to them as they progress.

Does that answer your question? I invite your questions because you will remind me of things and spark off other areas from the text that I have prepared within my aura to deliver at the right time.

We are, as you know, simply progressing ourselves, and this book gives me some nervousness in the weight of truth and fact that I have been entrusted with to bring through. I have *my* facts straight (as I know them) but I then have to transmit them through to you and you have to construct them in the correct order. Joan was wrong saying it would be more difficult – I would say that it will *take more time* because of its nature. In the meantime, to keep the audience interested and growing, I will deliver other lectures and addresses that you can give out to them [*reference to public trance demonstrations*] but this book is the most precise *so far* and is a massive undertaking.

Would that we had more time to spend together (and we are working to ensure that that takes place) but we have to work within the confines of the Earth plane. I could talk to you at great length for hours from *my* point of view but we would exhaust Michael. We are aware of the pulls on his life and, because of his mediumistic ability and status, there are constant attacks on him from all quarters to try and prevent this information coming through. So it is a communication that is difficult under ordinary circumstances that is then made the more difficult by the forces you have just mentioned that seek to always negate and dissipate this information.

Is there anything else, David?

David: No, not for the moment, thank you.

Jane: My question is to do with the arc of energy from birth to death and I just wondered whether that arc was there before the Fall?

Joseph: The arc was still there but it was of a different nature. If you set out – and I use the analogy of a holiday and a journey – if you set out on that journey, and you do not get lost in the jungle and lose your memory, then you *know* you are on a journey and you *know* that you will one day return home. The point is you take that journey voluntarily for the right reasons, and there was much excitement before the time of the Fall in the individualisations of God, God's children, who (similar to you going on an expensive, luxurious holiday) knew that they were going to set out into physicality; knew that they were part of a place that had been prepared; knew that that place had many opportunities presented by God-consciousness to enjoy; and knew that they could experience each other and their God in a new way by passing through this physical plane. But because it is a physical plane (because, ultimately, it is and has always been a 'construct') it cannot have a permanence. You cannot permanently be here, and this is part of the problem with the actions of the Fall, in that souls wish to make this their permanent home when it is only a 'port of call'.

So, *yes*, in answer to your question, there was always the arc. The arc would take souls into physicality, into the paradise that this level, this Field, once was, but would then extricate them from that physicality back into the higher vibrations where they could make choices about the next step in their journey – because the soul must always move and change and evolve and take in new experiences. That was a far easier thing before the Fall when you were angelic beings in nature. You are angelic beings now but you were angelic beings *in nature* then, in that you came here not blindfolded but knowing full well that this was an experience – nothing more – an *experience*, an *opportunity*.

And you must recall that you have soul-groups, you have families, you have *love* waiting for you on the higher vibrations, the higher planes. Therefore, as souls, you would not choose to permanently separate yourselves from that love, from those associations, from the joy of being with people that you are integrated with and who are moving on (as you are moving on) in harmony with you. So it was always decided – *decided* – by yourselves and by God that this physicality was not permanent and your visit to it would not be permanent. **It was decided!** So in that respect death was a 'return', was known to be a return and was requested by you as souls: 'I will go; I will experience the physicality of the plane; I will enjoy its many opportunities but then I will return home because that is what I wish.' That volition to return home, to first enjoy this level at the level of experience that it was originally created and then... [*interruption in the communication*].

Michael: Sorry. Come back, Joseph.

Joseph: I am sorry, we are coming near to the end of the communication but I was wishing to express that there had been a time before this when souls voluntarily came here and voluntarily went home. And so the arc of physicality, the arc of vibration, was built into the physical body on purpose – not as a punishment, not as people see it now: believing that they come here and inevitably have to face death, so no matter what they put their energy into is of no matter because one day they will die. That is not how it *was* – and it is not how it *is*! It is just that people have forgotten. They are blindfolded. They come here with no memory whatsoever of who they are; no memory whatsoever of their spiritual home; no memory whatsoever of the purpose of their visit, and so they are attracted more and more into this level of physicality because to them, with their lack of spiritual memory, this is all there is. So of course they want it; they want it as pleasure and they want it as pain because it is all they know and they fear anything else.

What we are attempting to do is re-awaken that spiritual memory so that future generations are born with that spiritual memory *in place* because it has been placed there during their previous journey so that, as they reincarnate, they are already predisposed to accept that they need to move on. It may take a couple of generations but you have to feed the soul *now* so that it comes back with at least some of that knowledge to take the blindfold off. Do you see what I am saying?

Jane: Yes. Presumably, before the Fall, they didn't age during the second half of the arc because the Field wasn't negative then?

Joseph: The physical body, in those times, was relinquished and was absorbed at a higher level back into the illusion, which operated at a higher level, so the decay that you witness at present as the arc returns to its start-point was not of that kind – it was a dispersion rather than a decay. The bodies that souls had before the Fall were far more robust than the bodies you have now and were things of elevated vibrational intent rather than some of the perversions that are built into those bodies now. The physical bodies dispersed into the *Light* of the illusion rather than being pulled at by the *depths* of the illusion as they are today, resonating at the same level as the depths of the illusion. So much of your world is corruption and decay and, once the soul has exited the physical body today, the physical body is prey to corruption and decay so it is absorbed back into the corruption and the decay of the Field, whereas in ancient times, before the Fall, the physical body was embraced back into the Light of the Field. It was not a degenerative event; it was a re-ordering of physical matter into Light from which more physical matter could be drawn. Do you see that?

Jane: Yes.

Joseph: Is there anything that either of you wish to ask before we conclude today's meeting?

David: An individual's arc of life has a predetermined departure date but is that still the case in something like a violent death, or perhaps an abortion or a suicide – or is it that the soul opted out of that arc at some point?

Joseph: It is an excellent question and it is one that is tied up with the whole concept of predestiny and choice, and to what extent a soul is allowed to have an influence over the predestined time for it to exit the physical realm. There is information I will communicate at a future date that deals with suicide, because suicide is one of those topics that fascinates spiritual seekers. You have within your midst, from your own group, one of your *guides* who committed suicide [*reference to*

Silver Star] and I will, at that time, bring him in to intersperse his own recollections of the act and what happened to him next.

With regard to lives that are seemingly cut short, often that point is the point that has been predestined or organised by the Lords of Karma for that soul. It is only from the point of view of Earth that it seems to be short or inappropriate because the people surrounding that soul expect it to exist on Earth for a reasonable amount of time, and so feel deprived or cheated when that soul goes to the spirit side at what is considered, from an earthly point of view, to be an early stage of its physical existence.

In the case of abortions, you have to consider that there are the karmic implications surrounding the parents and the doctors so there is a mix with those souls with regard to the soul that has incarnated momentarily and then is withdrawn to the spirit levels. There is *always* a purpose in that soul coming; there is never a soul's incarnation on a physical level that does not have a purpose – and that purpose is always to further the evolution and the enlightenment of souls. So a soul may come into the body of a baby to have ramifications on the mother, the father, the doctors and the potential grandparents.

The soul may also have a need to visit this Earth momentarily for a specific purpose of its own; to dip into the level of physicality for a reason tied up with that particular soul's evolution. It may only need to touch the Earth plane briefly or it may be pulled momentarily into the Earth existence to deal with something that we have touched upon in past communications [*reference to a question at a public trance demonstration*] because a part of that soul feels that it needs to return to sort something out and to put closure into a situation. That soul may be highly elevated on a spiritual level but there is still an element of it that desires, pulls and tries to come back to the Earth plane. And so the soul may fleetingly touch this realm through a few months of existence. It really doesn't dwell here at all but is drawn in *partially* just so that it can release itself from that aspect of itself that pulls – perhaps for the last time – so that it can be freed into the spirit realms without ever needing to incarnate on the Earth plane again.

Every life has a purpose and an effect: there is a purpose for the life and there is an effect on others. In the grand machine of enlightenment nothing is wasted, everything is as it should be and every opportunity is used to give as many souls as possible the opportunity to grow through observation, through experience and through enlightenment.

It is a vast subject, I know, but I hope that that partially answers the question. As I say, we will return to suicide because it is something that people need to understand and definitively we need to look at this to say: 'These are the consequences; these are the non-consequences; this is a myth; this is not a myth' – and to sort that out so that people are clear as to what happens in suicidal cases.

Your final question, please!

Jane: It is just a question about the separate consciousness of the body but I think it is probably too big a subject so perhaps it should wait for another day...

Joseph: There is an overall control to the physical body. The physical body is fed by the individualisation pool of energy. If you regard the physical body as a machine, then that machine has to know how to operate – otherwise you would spend all your waking moments operating the machine and not enjoying the experience. So the physical body is tailored to the soul and linked to the soul but has to have a degree of sentience or intelligence, otherwise your physical experience would be intolerable; you would have to control, as a soul, every single aspect of your body's functions and needs, micro-second to micro-second.

So the body has an intelligence, and built into the body is part of that arc of vibration so the cells know when to regenerate, how to regenerate and then react to the soul's gradual withdrawal of energy from that physical body and start to shut themselves down. Were *you* to do that you would have no experience here whatsoever except for the maintenance and running of the physical body.

When I talk of the intelligence of the physical body, I do not mean that the physical body has a personality, but I do mean that the physical body has a purpose and an intent. And that intent is to keep you protected; that intent is to anchor you within its field so that you can experience from one viewpoint (rather than from many), and it has an intelligence so that it reacts to the wishes of the soul. You, the soul, are within the personality and you project the personality, so do not feel that the physical body has a personality – it does not. Yes, it has an intelligence, but it is a 'communal' intelligence that originates from a 'field' that has been set up, which you can liken to a factory (although that is a very bad analogy) ...a *'headquarters'* from which souls can order a physical body. That central pool runs the physical body, gives it its intelligence and then, when the soul is separated from the physical body, that intelligence returns back to headquarters to be made into a bright, shiny, new physical body! Do you see?

Jane: Yes, it's amazing!

Joseph: The whole experience, Children, is amazing! Life is amazing, and this is what we wish to convey to people – the sheer wonder and joy of life – and I communicate with you in order to bring back joy to people, because in joy we can reach them; in joy they can lift the vibration of the physical Field; and in joy we can remind them who they are ...*and get them out of here!*

I ask you now to be quiet just for a moment as I attempt to extricate myself from Michael's mental processes.

Chapter Two
The Currents of the Soul – and the Astral Realms

Joseph: Michael is resisting me because he feels that the phrase I have given him is illogical, but the title of the second chapter is: 'Currents of the Soul' and it is with some amusement that I gave this title to Michael because it requires from him absolute faith that what is coming through is going to make some sense. Well, of course it is ...*Joseph* would not come here without bringing you something of meaning!

In the first chapter we touched on what happens to the soul and what happens to the body following physical death. You have a phrase: 'you cannot take it with you'. This is completely wrong, however, because you take *so much* with you! The soul exists within a slipstream of energy that contains within it the history of that soul (to a greater extent the history of the life that has just been lived but also, to a lesser extent, the history of the *lives* that that soul has lived in incarnations since its first individualisation from God and enclosure within physical matter). The soul cannot help but take with it to the next realm and the next phase in its existence this slipstream of energy; this 'history-book', if you like; this stage-presentation of the life that the soul has lived. This energy slipstream or 'current of the soul' represents a graphic presentation of everything – *everything* – that the soul has done during its recent incarnation...

...Everything!

33

You think on Earth that your thoughts are secret, that your actions are secret but everything is recorded by this band, this slipstream, this current of energy, from the time you incarnate to the time you pass into the spirit world. Every action, *every action* that the body has taken, every action that the *mind* has taken and, of course, the most important, every action that the *spirit* has taken... every *decision* and every *thought* is contained within this energy field. Consider that... *every thought* that you have ever taken, from the thought that says to you, 'My foot is asleep' to the thought that says to you, 'I hate this person' to the thought that says 'I will get even with this person' to the thought that says 'I love you' to the thought that says, 'I am in pain and I have had enough'... every thought is recorded. Every vision that you have had, every face you have looked at, everything you have touched, everything you have sensed is contained within this record. We will discuss the consequences of this band of energy later, but for now I want you to be aware that it exists and that, when you arrive at your next destination, this band of energy has a vibrational quality that links you to vibrations of a similar quality.

This is a momentous thing for you to understand: **the band of energy that surrounds your soul at the point of physical death draws to you – and draws you to – other, similar bands of energy.** This is not a judgement, it is a magnetic attraction, so if your thoughts *on the whole* have been uplifting, have been spiritual, have been enlightened, have been giving, then the quality of your band of energy or current of the soul is Light, and is (in metaphysical terms) something that will take flight, that will raise you up and you will be destined, via that band of energy, to link with similar bands of energy at an elevated level.

If your thoughts have been mundane, if they have been thoughts of simply existing where you have had no particular viewpoint on life (except that it is something you are passing through that you have never thought about), if you are neither positive nor negative in your approach, then this equilibrium of thought will automatically connect you to a field of energy containing souls whose current of vibration is similar to yours.

Here is a sobering thought and something that I want you to open your eyes to – to consider *completely* the ramifications of what I am saying: if your thoughts and your actions whilst you were on Earth have been dark (and by dark I am not necessarily talking about depression – I mean dark with regard to others); if you have observed others from a violent viewpoint, or from a selfish viewpoint, or from a corrupt viewpoint, or from a depraved viewpoint; if you have desired the flesh in unspeakable ways; if you have desired control over people; if you have lusted after violence; if you have wanted to manipulate people in a big way in order to bend them to your will, then all these things are contained within the history programme of your life, that current of your soul, and automatically that current of your soul, that energy-burst, will seek out and will connect to similar signatures… and you will find yourself with people who are *just like you*.

How frightening is that: to find yourself with people who are just like you!

And when you find yourself with these people, if you have been a spiritual person you will rejoice and be extremely happy. If you have been a neutral person you will find that your life, initially, on the spirit side of life continues in much the same vein. If you have been of low thought and of low intent then the people that are around you will be just like you. If you seek perversion and violence, is it not true that you want to do this to other people but would not like this done to you? But by the *law of attraction* you would find yourself with people who are as violent, as depraved, as angry and as manipulative as you are.

This is not God's judgement, I hasten to add; it is simply a mechanism. The original purpose of the burst of energy or current of the soul was to allow that soul (once it had returned home in full consciousness of who it was) to replay its actions whilst incarnated in a physical body and to make decisions regarding its own perception of itself and where it wanted to go next, based on what it had just done whilst in physicality. Not a judgement but a tool or aid to spiritual progression that became polluted and clouded by the actions of mankind – not as you know mankind, but of mankind many millennia ago.

My preamble talking about the currents of the soul is leading you into one of the places that is often mentioned in spiritual books, in churches, in circles and in meetings of those who purport to know about the spiritual realms; it is leading you to the doorway of the Astral Realm. In a future chapter we shall consider how souls are collected but today I wanted to bring you to the astral level.

The Lower Astral

Much is spoken glibly about the astral or the 'Lower Astral' as you call it – 'I am being affected by souls from the Lower Astral' or 'My thoughts are being invaded by thoughts from the Lower Astral.' Souls gather together in clusters of similar vibration and, in the case of the Lower Astral, you can apply the image of Marley's ghost, dragging behind it the chains and the chests of heaviness from its past life, to the vibrational quality of the soul's current of energy, in that that current of energy (because of the soul's perception of life and reaction to life whilst in a physical body) has weighed it down. The soul is surrounded by its own misadventures, and those misadventures drag it like a chain around its neck into a realm that is composed of similar vibrations. It is a field (as everything is a field) of reality but it is a field of *low* reality, and within that field of low reality are contained the souls of those who have not striven to elevate their vibrations above the base during their incarnation or incarnations.

There is no place on a higher level, for example, for a murderer who loves the violence that he or she has done – that is not a judgement but is a statement of fact. There is no place because the vibration of that person is too low to exist within a lighter, less dense realm *at this point* (and another thing we will touch upon is reaction to souls and how souls are helped out of their vibrational pockets but, for now, I want to take you on a journey through the Lower Astral).

The quality of light in the Lower Astral is very poor because the spirit atoms do not vibrate at a sufficient rate to show that purity of light, that luminescence that exists on the higher levels. This is because the atoms are coated with the heaviness of thought of the area that they exist in, so the Lower Astral is grey to black because the Lower Astral segregates itself into layers, as do the other spirit levels.

So the concept of the Lower Astral contains within it a number of levels and at the lowest you would say that souls exist in a *soup of blackness* where there is so little light that they cannot see. Then there are various levels or grades above that where, for example, perhaps the souls on a level are not as violent as those below them, and they can see and there is a greyness about them. They live in very impoverished conditions, or very impoverished projections of reality; you would describe them as 'slums' and this is because their creative process or ability to think higher thoughts has not been stimulated, so all they are capable of creating around themselves is the depravity that they are used to (depravity in the sense of lack) and so the houses and dwellings are poor. Then, above that level, you will find that there is a little more light and the people are in less crowded conditions – the lower you get on the Lower Astral, the less personal space there is between souls because the almost-physical attraction of their soul-currents binds them one to another. The magnetic charge is so great, with the violence attracting violence and the depravity attracting depravity, that they are stuck together like glue.

Of course, this set of conditions is not permanent and for each soul in the Lower Astral there is salvation. **Full stop!** ...Not the 'hope' of salvation but *salvation* (eventual or current, in the next hour or in the next millennium, but there *is* salvation) and I shall talk about how salvation occurs and the mechanisms that allow it to occur in future parts of the book.

The Lower Astral, quite rightly it is said, has an effect on the physical world, on the earth-field. It does so because its charge or vibrational signature is very similar to the vibrational signature of the Earth *at this time*. The two are only a hair's breadth apart and your dominant vibration on Earth – being one of violence, greed and depravity – sets up (because you are souls *now* with that current of the soul around you collecting, minute by minute, a record of what you have done) a resonance that is very similar to the currents of the souls that exist in the Lower Astral. Through magnetic attraction one attracts the other and you could say that souls from the Lower Astral are attracted to the Earth, but equally you could say that souls from the Earth are attracted to *the attractions* of the Lower Astral.

So much of the violence you encounter at the moment on Earth is stimulated, enhanced and magnified by the violence that exists in the Lower Astral. The solution is quite simple. **The solution is to raise your vibrations,** which is, of course, why we come back to you to show you a way out of this cycle of lower thinking and base vibrations.

Should you pray for the souls who are existing in the Lower Astral? You can, of course, but in doing so you hardly help them because your Light does not penetrate the density of those levels of existence – because those levels of existence cling on to their vibrational quality. *They do not wish to change*, so all the Light in the world directed into the Lower Astral will not, of itself, raise those souls. The souls have to *wish* to raise themselves, have to wish to change, have to wish to change their magnetic attractive-frequency... but more on this later.

You have paintings in your churches that depict Hell. You have discourses in your holy books about Hell. You have preachers who tell you that you will go to Hell if you do this and that, or if you think this and that (...you would be surprised at how many preachers are in the

Lower Astral), but what I wish to tell you is that those images of Hell are an echo of a race memory. You *know* within yourselves (because you know all things) that you have the power to create your environment when you leave the Earth plane. You have within yourselves a pointer or compass that tells you *vibrationally* whether your actions are elevating or heavy. You know within you to be true, as you read this book, that violence begets violence, anger begets anger, and that you, if you *choose* these things, place yourselves for a time in a low and unnourished place with regard to the higher vibrations that emanate from the Godhead.

I wish to take away the mystique regarding the Lower Astral. As with all elevations of the spirit – all spirit worlds, all spirit existences – it is a temporary construct but it is a construct that is visited and is dwelled in by those who have chosen during their lives to ally themselves always with the base, the material and the physical. The lesson, therefore, is plain: **if you wish to elevate yourselves, consider carefully what you do and how you live** – not for me, not for *Joseph*... but for yourselves.

It is difficult for us to consider that souls suffer in this way. It is even more difficult (as we shall learn in future chapters) to elevate those souls. We have no wish for any single soul to be in a miserable state but, through free will, you are allowed to make your own choices. Perhaps reading this you do not believe in God or an afterlife but I would ask you, for insurance' sake, to at least try to elevate your vibrations because – whether you believe in me or not, whether you believe in the scenario I have put forwards or not – *it exists*.

It exists!

To return (with reluctance) to the Lower Astral, at its basest it is a very violent place, and it is a violent place of *an unending horror*. If someone takes your life on the Earth plane that is a single act but if someone 'takes your life' in the Lower Astral it is a self-perpetuating, repeating act because they cannot kill you and you cannot kill them, but the violence is there and the essence of the act is there to be drawn upon repeatedly. The unenlightened souls at the lowest levels seek to do harm to each other but the harm they do is like an unending nightmare because it does not involve physicality and yet it goes on... and on... and on.

There is a lesson in this and you might think that this is a terrible state for God to leave souls in but God always allows souls to choose for themselves and, even on the darkest level, there dawns a day when a soul in the Lower Astral feels: 'Enough! All I have to do to stop this – is to stop it.' So simple: 'All I have to do to stop this – is to stop it, is to withdraw my desire to be a part of it out of the vibration and my vibration lifts' – and then we can step in and help them.

I also have to say that even though souls may seem to exist in the Lower Astral (with regards to earthly time) for a great deal of earthly time, it is but the blink of an eye in the scheme and evolution of the universe. So those souls, once they have been lifted into a higher vibration and into a higher current of the soul, only regard the Lower Astral as a dream that they half remember and which then disappears in the beautiful light of day – because the current of the soul or that burst of energy around the soul *changes* as the soul progresses in understanding and in appreciation of the transmission of God-love.

So the current of the soul that the soul takes with it upon physical death is not locked into a certain vibration *forever* but continues to evolve and to change in order to bring that soul new experiences. You see, the soul, at its essence, is unchanging, so experience has to change around it to *enlighten* it. Enlightenment is not a journey – it is a realisation. **Enlightenment is the realisation that what that soul amounts to it has always had but has forgotten.** So the soul does not change but its perception changes, and its perception changes by relating to the energy that it is clothed in, by taking experiences from that personal field of energy and by elevating that field of energy through personal enlightenment.

[*Speaking to David and Jane*] I did say that this book would be a vast undertaking and it is. There are so many aspects we have to touch upon… but we will get there and we will put everything in order. I hope that you have been entertained too by what has been said today, because the information is also for you to keep close to your hearts and say, 'Now I understand, even if others don't, now I understand.'

I did invite questions and I invite them now, if you would like to take advantage of this short period we have before the Earth plane encroaches to such an extent that we cannot continue…

David: How should we organise questions? Should we ask questions about the first chapter today and then, when you deliver the third chapter, ask questions about the second chapter? Would that be a good idea?

Joseph: What will happen with your questions is that they may stimulate in me some aspect that I had not considered at this time and the answers to the questions should be looked upon as inserts to the chapters or pointers in bringing the whole together. Many of the topics you ask me about will be covered in greater depth in future chapters, but also you will give me and yourselves bookmarks so that eventually you will have a number of chapters we have brought through together but also a number of questions and answers that can be inserted at the appropriate points within those chapters – perhaps at the end of them as a rounding off of a topic… or certain responses from myself can be inserted as part of those chapters to expand them.

It is good to start with a question about the questions! Are there questions proper? We will restrict them to three.

Jane: Do people in the Lower Astral know where they are – do they know they have gone to the Lower Astral?

Joseph: Perception in the Lower Astral is quite cloudy because it is driven by the baser desires so, if perception were a car, then the soul in the Lower Astral would be driving from the back seat. The spiritual aspects of the soul are shrouded in the heaviness that I talked about with regard to the spiritual atoms. That heaviness surrounds the soul and the souls in the Lower Astral at basest level are aware, as in a murky dream, of their existence in this dark place. As they are elevated to higher levels of astral existence their surroundings become more realistic to them – or, rather, their perception becomes sharper until there reaches that time of their waking moment into the Light.

God is not cruel and purposely the effects of the Lower Astral are presented to the soul as a dream because there would be too much for that soul to cope with were there a heightened reality at that level. So they are aware *murkily*, but increasingly aware as they are drawn out of the darkest levels, and this murkiness is caused by the current of energy that surrounds the soul. Their personal field is murky, is soupy, is foggy but then that vibration changes – and it must change, *has to change* for every soul – and they become more aware of sharper and more clearly defined realities.

Jane: In the Lower Astral do they ever form friendships and help each other – maybe in the higher levels there?

Joseph: At the lowest levels the phrase that comes to mind is *everyone for his or her self*, because it is that isolated thinking that has placed them there in the first place. You use the word 'friendship'- I would use the word 'attraction'. You talk of a 'den of thieves', so you would expect someone who had been manipulative of people in a very base way to be linked, on an atomic level via the current of their soul, to other people who are like that. This is an astounding thing for souls to go through because it is like looking into a mirror. Remember that souls, at their deepest level of being, *know* that what they are doing is detrimental to their existence and the existence of other souls. They do it *to* people but they do not expect that to be reflected *back* to them in everyone they see. But that is a kindness too because, in seeing themselves reflected back, there comes a time when they wake up to how they have been, how they have acted, and want to change.

So 'friendship' is perhaps not the right term. 'Attraction' is the term and they will find themselves with others. Remember they are not yet at a level where they show much in the way of compassion or love for others, or consideration for others. They have to grow into that and so, as always, God uses the circumstances to teach them by allowing them to see themselves in others; by allowing them to see themselves and say, 'This is not who I wish to be' and then by allowing them to move on by changing their core thoughts and elevating themselves above the darkness.

They are never alone but, again, this is something we will go into in depth at a later stage and will be quite an extensive section of this book. Remember we have only just begun and I have dealt with the Lower Astral before dealing with *'arrival'*. Now arrival, I suggest, should be my next chapter, that touches on what is waiting for a soul upon death and how the transition is made from the point of death on a physical level to the vibration at which that soul has earned the right to exist – be that the lowest astral level or one of the high spiritual planes.

So, unless I change my mind… it is very difficult, you see, to become linear with you. It is very difficult to link to you at points during your time perception because, for me, the book is already here and I am drawing on certain aspects of it that I hope to present to you in a time-frame that makes sense to you. But I also have to link up with you at points in your lives that, to you, seem to follow on from the last time we have spoken. But you sit here on a number of occasions *all at once*, so I have to remind myself where your perception is with regards to me giving you the communication that is taking place continuously until we have finished the book. It becomes easier to speak to you of these things as Michael becomes more comfortable (and of more use to us) with the notion of trance, because I can transmit more of an image of my realm to you than I could when you started the first book. The downside of that is that you are operating more on my terms of communication than on yours, and I have to remember that to make everything fit in in the correct order for you. There is something to think about!

I will invite one more question. I could talk all day and would be happy to talk all day but I do not feel that Michael would appreciate this or be of any use to himself for several days. However, the corridor of availability is expanding as you can see and (with what I have just said to you) there are points in the future where we *do* sit for considerably longer than we do at present and I can see these because they are all taking place *simultaneously* with me – but not with you. But for today and at this point, if I have got the calculations right, which I have (I am only joking with you), I will invite one more question.

David: It seems as though most people just don't even consider death – probably because they fear it, I suppose. Would it be possible at some point in this book to give them some meditations towards preparing themselves for death?

Joseph: The ironic thing is that daily they prepare themselves for death – they are just not aware of what they are putting into the equation.

The problem with giving a meditation on death is that you could conceivably release some of those souls from their physical bonds. With me communicating with you [*reference to David and Jane*] you have knowledge that you have gained during your lives, which means that you are not shocked when I say something to you because your souls increasingly remember that what I am saying resonates truly within you. We have to prepare people through the written word initially and so I would prefer to shock them 'at a distance' rather than reaching into their souls (I mean that on a dynamic level, not on a level of knowledge) because that is a dangerous thing to do with those who are not able, in many cases, to meditate on a light level.

By the end of the book there should be enough knowledge to 'take the reader away' so that we can work on their intuition whilst they are reading the book. We said in the first book that the book was aimed to shock but this book will shock at a deeper level. Some of the concepts we will talk about are frightening and they should be in the public knowledge; some of them are uplifting and take souls to places beyond physical description in terms of beauty and love and ecstasy. We have to tread a careful path but the book will give people (Please God!) a better grounding on the subject of death and the afterlife than has been given before in many books. That is the intention – to provide a manual, if you like (and it is amusing): 'The A to Z of Death and What Comes Next'. It is a manual they can look at that will prepare them, perhaps not so much for the next life as for this life, which is what you are saying, David.

David: Yes, it's just the stream of personal history that they can tag behind them, which they don't even examine, in many cases, whilst they are incarnate.

Joseph: That is our purpose in communicating: to make them aware (to make those who are *ready* aware) and to leave behind this communication so that there will always be availability to the level of soul-consciousness that is ready for this information. We cannot place this book in front of a soul that is not ready, just as I have said today that we cannot influence souls on the lowest levels of the astral (in fact, on *any* level of the astral) until they are ready to be influenced and ready to be helped. The truth that this book contains will always slide off the minds and the hearts of those that are not ready for it, but will speak to the hearts and the minds of those who *are* ready for it and in doing so, through capillary action, will draw up the next level of souls.

That is all we can hope to do but there are many, many souls at this point who *are* ready for the information we are bringing through. Many, many souls – millions of souls! The Earth is not the ignorant Field it appears to be at this time. There are those who are turning their back on the violence, the hatred, the manipulation and the materialism but they have no *food* for their souls. They know they need something more but they don't know what it is or where it comes from. We are providing food for those souls. We cannot reach the lowest levels but we can reach those who are ready and, in elevating them, we elevate the souls beneath them and they become ready, which is why it is so important that the information we bring through is perpetuated and we are working to perpetuate it.

I have done my best now to make sure that Michael's day is one of half waking and half sleeping. I will now withdraw from his aura, although it becomes very comfortable to speak to you in this manner but I do not think he would thank me for suggesting that I inhabit his body for increasing amounts of time... and I would not do that.

Chapter Three
Transition through the Buffer Zone to the Arrival Point

Joseph: [*addressing those present in the circle*] I come, first of all, in laughter and good humour to raise the vibrations this morning, because during the week you have had times that have pulled down your vibrations, and it is necessary to raise them up. But also the message that I am bringing is one of lightness. It may seem very involved at times but the essential message is that there is a way, there is a Light and there is a means of changing things – both internally as individuals and externally within the Field that you are a part of during your lives on Earth. So let us be uplifted as we begin today's session!

We have lifted you onto a plateau, spiritually. You are encased within a bubble of vibration, which we have extended around you and which raises your *speed of being* for a little while. So I will warn you in advance that this afternoon you may feel drowsy or disorientated but this will be because we have to (unfortunately) return you to the vibration you are used to at the present time. We cannot interfere and bring you to our side but we would love to do that. How wonderful if we could extricate each soul and bring each soul to our side and allow them to live in the superior atmosphere, the superior field, and have great joy… but we are not allowed to. You have to live out your span on Earth; you have to reach the end of the adventure that is unfolding for you at this time, just as we have to reach the end of our adventure before we can move on to even more rarefied fields and realities.

But we have other things to talk about; we have to concentrate on the third chapter of the third book – and I am raising an eyebrow (and Michael is also aware of the Persian Gentleman[1] being with me) because we are saying very definitely *this is the third chapter* ...but we hope it is and that I haven't missed anything out and that this will follow on in the sequence it is supposed to. Having spoken about death and having spoken about the Lower Astral and how people become stuck because of their own perception of death and life, we have to talk about the process of getting to one of the higher levels...

No one is left alone in death.

There is always someone who comes for them and who knows in advance because they are given information from higher authority (and by that I don't mean the Godhead, I mean spirits who are more elevated than they are and more involved in the business of life and death and karma). They are given information from higher authority to say: 'This person is about to pass over – would you like to meet them?' Now that is important: *would you like to meet them* – because there is always the option (even with loved ones) of saying, 'No, I would prefer someone else to go and meet them' – always free will. We never order. We cannot order. So they receive a message in advance and they know that they will be collected at a certain time and they will be transported to an in-between area or vibration, because a newly-passed soul cannot raise its vibration instantly (there would be too much of a shock which would result in confusion, and the last thing we want to do is to impress new images on a mind that is already confused because it is not mentally ready for the transition) so there is an in-between stage. What happens to the soul depends on the soul's perception of life after death and perception of life, so sometimes a relative will call for a soul and will appear to a soul at the moment of death.

I want to take away that fear of the moment of death, because on the physical level you see people who appear to be suffering and then draw a last breath; you may see people who are in great pain before they cross over and, from the physical perspective, it appears that a great, painful end has come to that person. Actually, the opposite is true because the release of the spirit is a peaceful affair and it is only the body that you are looking at that seems to be in such turmoil, such pain and such trauma. There is a moment of stepping away from the physical body and it is as simple as taking the next breath for the spirit that is passing... one moment they are perhaps in a bed, they are in pain, they are confused... and the next moment there is peace. The next moment they are still very much alive (in fact, more so) but there is peace. They can breathe again. They are without pain. They are without the stresses of the physical body and death has taken place. It is as simple as that! It is not the occasion or occurrence that many people think it is.

Your death, Reader, will not be the frightening experience that your cultures say it is going to be – no matter how you pass over. If you pass over in great pain, through an accident or through illness, there will be the moment of pain on a physical level and then suddenly you are free of it; suddenly you are standing tall again; suddenly you can breathe again; suddenly you are relaxed again; suddenly you feel better than you have felt for a long, long time... I digress.

If you are sufficiently aware *spiritually* to accept that there is life after physical death, then normally someone who you have known (a close relative, a close friend, or perhaps someone that you know as a brother or sister on a spiritual level but have never met on Earth but who you will recognise at the moment of death) will be waiting for you. That is what happens to you if you are aware of the process of things, if you are willing to accept that your family is waiting for you, if you are willing to accept that your friends are still alive.

For many people, however, there is an inbuilt need within the soul to continue a journey or *to go somewhere* as it were, and, for those people, illusions are set up to take them across from the vibrational barrier that buffers at one end with the Earth and at the other end with the higher levels of consciousness. A 'journey' needs to be set up; an illusion needs to be set up and so (and I have mentioned this in a previous communication) *people get what they expect*. They will, for example, step out of their physical body and find themselves confronted by a boat, or an aeroplane, or a train, or a carriage or any other of many vehicles waiting for them, and they will find themselves with other people who have passed and made the transition at that moment.

There will be, in charge of this vehicle, an organiser or organisers from higher levels of consciousness, and these people will instruct those who are newly passed into the spirit realms to board the vehicle and to remain calm. Your culture leans towards figures of authority; in times of panic there are those who say, 'Remain calm!' and there is built into your physical consciousness the will to obey people in such positions and to say, 'Well, yes, this person knows what they are talking about.' So, with newly-passed souls, in many cases, it is necessary for them to be told what to do: to be told not to panic; to be told that everything is alright; to be told that they must go here, and do this, and do that, and think this, and think that... in order to get them *away* from the physicality that they have just left. This collecting of newly-passed souls occupies their minds for long enough for them to be moved away from the attraction that may still be there with their physical body, so it is a smoke-screen; it is a busy-ness of the mind that gives them something to do.

Also it is important that they move onwards across the buffer – the zone that exists between the Earth and the first of the spiritual realms. So they will find themselves on a boat or in a plane with people who are in the same *predicament* (as they see it) and the vehicle will then appear to move across a landscape. That landscape may be a sky, or a desert, or a river, or an ocean – but there is the impression they are moving somewhere on a vehicle being organised by people that they instinctively *know* know better than them because of the Light that they give out from their auras: 'Here are people in authority who know what they are doing. I am in a strange landscape in a strange place. I don't know what is happening but I will follow them.'

Then the vehicle moves across this landscape (which I must impress on you is an illusion – just as everything else is) and appears to reach a destination. That destination is sometimes an airport, or a shore, or a railway station, or some other terminus and, when the vehicle reaches that destination, the people are instructed by the higher spirits that they must disembark.

We will return to the buffer zone, because souls obviously are moving into that zone or in-between state all the time in their hundreds – sometimes in their thousands – and many souls still believe that they are the limitation of the flesh: they talk a certain language, they respect a certain culture and so it is organised that that soul is met by people who appear to talk the same language, who appear to understand the same culture and be a part of that culture, so that they are comfortable or as comfortable as they possibly can be having made the transition.

The area between the Earth plane and the first 'sphere' (I suppose I should call it) is a 'buffer' in more ways than one. It has a quietening effect on the souls after they have passed; it has a deadening effect on them with regard to the life they have just lived; it has the effect of filtering out many of the things that the souls will have externalised before they passed. If it did not do this then there would be more of a pull from the Earth to continue with the episodes that are going on in a soul's life at the time that it makes the transition. In other words, it would still be worried about the payments for the house or the problems with a marriage or raising enough money – because all these things it has been immersed in for its lifetime and, yes, it will have to address the ramifications of the major dramas and the major karmic facets that have been around itself as it makes the transition but *not at that point*.

We have to move the soul on from the Earth plane and this is another reason why there appears to be a journey, but the effect of the in-between zone or buffer or *area of limbo* is a deadening of that externalisation of circumstance that relates only to the physical Field. So, as the soul makes its supposed journey and as it travels across to that far shore, or that airport, or whatever the terminus happens to be, then the effects of the Earth plane are deadened and lessened and loosened so that, as it sits there in its vehicle of choice (a boat, plane, train or whatever it is), it becomes more aware of its spiritual heritage and more forgetful of its earthly life *for a time*.

The buffer zone also has a filtering effect on any entities that may surround the soul at the point of transition. There are, as you will know, degrees of sentient entities that are linked to the Earth plane and the Lower Astral planes only. These entities may have been feeding on the soul and leeching energy from the soul at the point of its transition. They may also have been *influencing* the soul during its time on Earth – trying to create mental situations that will allow it to draw more power so, obviously, these entities are still attached to the soul at the point of transition. Sometimes the soul will be so attached to these entities that it will be persuaded at the point of death to remain with them for a time, but the intention is always to draw the soul away from such things and towards a higher vibration. As the journey takes place and as the vibration gradually increases within the buffer zone, then those entities (like parasites, ticks or mites) cannot hold onto a vibration that is faster than the one they are exhibiting and the one that they have been created in and are maintained in, and so they fall away from the soul. Now this is not something that usually can be seen (except by experienced eyes and except in extreme cases where a person is overrun by such beings); it would not be prudent for the souls who have made the transition to see that they have certain thought-forms attached to them so this cleansing takes place *invisibly* as far as they are concerned.

This does not apply to those who are spiritually aware. For those who are spiritually aware, their friend or their family member or someone from their group soul turns up and says, 'Come this way' and the soul is sufficiently enlightened to get rid of its own entities (if there are any) and to say, 'Of course I will come this way. Thank goodness I am going back home!' So that transition is a more rapid affair than the one for the majority of people where they need to be gradually raised in vibration and cleansed from the effects of the Earth plane as they move towards the first spiritual sphere.

Also, we have to deal with trauma on many occasions because, although the point of death that I have talked about is peaceful, people sometimes do not believe this. Their physical-mental-faculty is so enmeshed with the Earth plane and so accepting of what has been happening to them at the point of death that they continue the 'game'. They continue to feel that they are hurt – even though they are whole; even though they can breathe easily; even though they can be comfortable in the moment that it takes to change a thought – they believe in the circumstances that were surrounding them before death and so are shocked. They believe, for example, if they died in a fire, that they are still on fire; they believe if they died of cancer or a terminal illness that that illness continues. There are those who do not instantly release the pain (just as there are those who do not instantly release the entities and those who do not instantly accept that they have passed over) so we have to deal with pain. Some souls scream, some souls are in a panic state and to these souls we send specialists, who calm them down and move them onto the vehicle so that they can be transported across the zone. In some cases we have to put them in a kind of sleep – if we cannot reason with them and if we cannot accelerate their vibrational rate to the point where they suddenly realise that they are fine, then we have to put them in a kind of unconsciousness. It is a bliss – it is not like an unconsciousness that you have at night where you may have troubled dreams (or even good dreams) but you are aware of being still attached to the Earth plane. It is a bliss and they need to be withdrawn until they can awaken in a higher state of consciousness.

So there are many considerations that have to be addressed in order to get a soul across to the start-point of their spiritual journey. It is a complex and diverse operation and you can see why so many souls need to be involved in order to accomplish this process, which is happening *all the time* (as is the reverse of this process – people are incarnating at the same time, but that is an area I will address at a different time; we are concentrating on the passage *away* from the Earth at this time). So you have those who move across easily, you have those that need direction and you have those that are put to sleep for a time in order to get them across.

And what lies at the other end of the buffer zone?

What lies at the other end of the buffer zone is *segregation* – not segregation that is imposed on the souls by anyone from the spirit worlds or by God – but **segregation that is imposed on the soul by its actions whilst in an earthly body and by its beliefs whilst in an earthly body.**

So there is a collection point and there is a delivery point (both of these things being an illusion but everything is an illusion, everything is a construct) and we have to go with a certain sequence of events in order to placate and comfort and direct the majority (unfortunately) of souls. There is a collection point, there is a cleansing process through the effects of the buffer zone and then there is a delivery, there is a destination – but it is only an *initial* destination. For many it will be a shore, for many it will be an airport, for many it will be a train station or a bus station or the far bank of a river, and there they will find that they disembark from the vehicle that has come to collect them.

What happens next will be the subject of the next chapter – assuming that in my *old head* I can get things in a linear sequence. There is so much to pack into this volume and it must flow in a logical sequence because I am taking the readers on a journey from a point where they do not know about death to a point where they know about death, where they are going to and what to expect *in relative terms* – because what to expect is tuned to the needs and expectations of each individual soul.

At this point is there anything that you would like to ask regarding either what has been said today or what has been said in chapters previous to this one?

David: Joseph, would you like to comment on rescue workers who are incarnated on Earth that help in that transition – is it because they are of a similar vibration to the soul that is about to pass over that they can help to lead them into that buffer zone?

Joseph: Are you referring to incarnate souls or the spirits who come to ease the transition from the spiritual side of life?

David: Incarnate souls – such as myself and Michael, who have been involved in rescue work at night when we are asleep.

Joseph: In answering your question we have to enter the individual zones that souls put around themselves (not the greater or group-zone that I have been speaking about today) because many souls trap themselves within some of the circumstances we have been speaking about: the expectation that life continues as it is even after physical death; or there are souls who find themselves linked to traumatic events to such an extent that those events replay around them; or there are souls who do not deserve (...deserve is the wrong word) – do not *need* to go to the Lower Astral but trap themselves in an individual Lower Astral or astral plane of their own making for a time. You must remember that each of you is a god, each of you is part of God and each of you is (to a lesser or a greater extent, dependent on your experience) capable of creating around you your own reality. So there are those souls who, unconsciously and on the point of transition,

55

continue to create reality to such an extent that higher souls cannot reach them because they are using a similar energy to that inherent in the Field on Earth to extend their experience of physical life.

In such circumstances it is felt that someone who is on the Earth is better able to reach those souls than someone of a higher vibration. It is very difficult for souls of a higher vibration to penetrate these individual realities and make themselves seen and interact with the souls who have created these bubbles of continuous individual-reality. Someone who is in an earthly body can penetrate more easily (particularly in sleep-state) one of these bubbles, because the vibration of the Field that they are in and the vibration of the bubble that the trapped soul has placed itself in *are very similar*. So the trapped soul can see this person entering their dream, entering their reality and talking to them, and then higher beings and more illuminated souls can transmit information to the rescue soul (who is still incarnate on Earth) to persuade the soul that has trapped itself in a bubble of continued individual-reality to drop its barriers and to let go of the continuance of the illusion that it has placed itself in. Then, when the barrier is down, the soul is received into the buffer zone and the process that happens for most souls can happen to it.

It is a question of vibration, and a soul that is still in a physical body can more easily reach a soul who may have made the transition but is still within a reality-bubble that is close in vibration to the vibration of the physical Field. Do you understand this?

David: Oh, yes. I thought it might be of interest to the readers.

Joseph: I am hopeful [*laughing*] that everything will be of interest to the readers!

I must not diversify too much but you can say that the books are rescue vehicles or 'rescue souls' because the books are preparing people for transitions – both at the point of death and also on a daily basis.

That is the point of the books: to give this information in a way that is not lecturing and in a way that is interesting to get people to let down those barriers so that our job is made easier at the point of transition, but also easier during their lives in Earth in that, as guides, we can reach them more easily through their intuition and effect the change that must come about within the physical Field. The physical Field is a trap – so much of a trap on so many levels: on an emotional level, on a material level... even on a spiritual level, because so many of your religions are spiritual traps ('spiritual' is the wrong word – they purport to be spiritual but are traps). They trap people in bubbles of perceived reality that are nothing to do with the greater reality. We have to tear these barriers down and it is hoped that the books will do this.

Who would ask a question?

Jane: If we create our own individual realities, in the case of a religious fanatic (and there have been many examples throughout history) who persecuted people and committed terrible atrocities in their belief that it was in the name of God and that they would be rewarded in Heaven, what is to stop that person living in a 'heaven' of their own creation and being perfectly happy there when they pass over?

Joseph: Many do *but only for a time* because within the layers of consciousness that make up that soul there is the God-point, and the God-point will always manifest itself eventually. This may take a great deal of time; it may take thousands of years but eventually the conscience (you call it *conscience* but it is really *Divine Consciousness*) must manifest itself. In an ideal world (and we are working towards an ideal world) this is something that is the property of each soul. In an ideal world you would not need guides; in an ideal world you would not need the advice of others but you have not reached that point yet and so we have to send people in to suggest and to say, 'I have found this way and you can too.'

I understand what you are saying and it expands on what I was saying about traps. One of the greatest traps is to say, 'I am in Heaven and I have my reward' but eventually that view of Heaven and that reward become boring because there is nothing else; there is nothing outside that limited view of what Heaven or the reward will be like. There is no influence from another soul saying, 'Yes, I agree with you, you are in Heaven.' How can there be? Outside that bubble there are souls who are saying, 'For goodness sake, come to your senses because we need you to move on!' So the sweetest 'heaven' and the sweetest reward (as created by an individual soul) has to eventually dim and, as a soul lives within its own reality, if that reality is based on the lower molecules of the Earth Field then there has to come a time when that energy runs out and the soul finds itself in the limbo that I have been taking about. At that point it can either decide to retreat within itself or it can listen to the souls who come to talk to it and try to move it on.

We will talk about realities as we progress through the spheres but we are talking today about those *temporary realities* that souls place around themselves, and extensions of those 'realities'. (You understand now why this book is going to be so complex and so big because there are roots off that all need to be examined.) So, yes, there are people who think that they are in bliss. They will also create visions of great souls around them who they think are real but those souls are created from the psyche or from the perceptions of the soul that has placed itself in a temporary heaven; they do not really exist but they have sentience for a while because the soul has given them permission to have sentience – but eventually it will see through its mistaken thinking. Such thinking has built into it a 'timescale', whether that timescale is a year or a thousand years (not a million years – that is too long), and a decay rate, and within the most entrenched soul there is the *need* (not the will, but the need) to return to God. Everything that the soul puts around it is (either correctly or mistakenly) an expression of that need to return to God and that need has to eventually become stronger than the requirement to be in an illusion of Heaven and at that point we can get in. Remember, too, that the soul is expecting things from Heaven: is expecting bliss, is expecting comfort, and is expecting fulfilment and no construct of an *imagined heaven* can maintain the levels of comfort and expectation that the soul needs on a God-level. So the 'heaven' begins to fragment and to break down until the soul realises that it has, in effect, been placing itself in a play, in a film, in an illusion. At that point we can get in and there is work to do to re-educate that soul, to free that soul (always with love) from the confines that it has placed itself in… and move it onwards.

Is your question answered?

Jane: But if that soul has to go via the Lower Astral in order for it to progress, wouldn't it be reluctant to do that?

Joseph: I do not understand.

Jane: If it was somebody who had been very cruel and had mistreated people (so they should have naturally gone to the Lower Astral if they hadn't have created a temporary individual heaven for a while), when their illusion of that false heaven is shattered, am I right in supposing that they would have to go through the Lower Astral first?

Joseph: We are talking about vibrational resonances. The soul will always attract to itself more of the same and the soul will always have to raise its vibration through experience before it can experience, if you like, true Heaven – although true Heaven is a moving point. Built into each soul (and it may seem a strange word to use) is 'dissatisfaction' – dissatisfaction with the physical, dissatisfaction with concepts, dissatisfaction with religious beliefs because, only in becoming dissatisfied with one set of circumstances can it move on to another.

There is, at each point in a soul's progression, help and advice to move that soul onwards. If you are asking: will a soul break down its view of Heaven to find that it is perhaps in a far darker place – the answer is 'yes' because there are consequences to actions and consequences that the soul has brought to itself (no one else has placed them on that soul). So, yes, sometimes the heaven breaks down to reveal (in physical terms) a *hell* but that, too, is temporary and there is help at that point to move the soul onwards. But that realisation that it is not in Heaven inevitably has to come, otherwise that soul is stuck and that soul cannot progress; it cannot go back to the Earth through volition; it cannot move onwards through volition. It has placed itself in amber and there has to be a process of breaking down that perceived reality, then the process of acclimatising the soul to where it *really* is and then the process of educating the soul so that it can move on. Do you see?

Jane: Yes, thank you.

---

[1] The Persian Gentleman is our name for another guide from Joseph's soul group who sometimes communicates with us.

Chapter Four
Destinations and the Intermediate Sphere of Cleansing

Joseph: The title of this chapter is 'destinations' and concerns what happens when a soul reaches its embarkation point on the spirit side of life.

You may have a hundred souls reaching that point at the same time (and that is a small generalisation… you may have a *thousand* souls or *ten thousand* souls reaching that destination at the same time) but out of the hundred souls we are examining no two souls might go to the same spiritual destination because where a soul starts off from depends on that soul's vibrationary rate. **Vibrationary rate is the key to existence on any level,** as you can only exist within a spiritual vehicle within the sphere that vibrates at the same rate as your soul. So you are placed instantly when you arrive in the spirit world, when you have been segregated…

…Let me backtrack… I am not quite getting the link I require yet with Michael…

Yes…

I wish to talk about segregation and about the fact that a soul can only co-exist with an area of reality that corresponds with its vibrational rate, and the vibrational rate of each soul is determined by the experience of that soul and where that soul is with regard to spiritual evolution. This brings into the equation your traditional views of 'good' and 'evil' but we have to take out those terms and say 'experience' or 'lack of experience' and 'evolution' or 'lack of evolution'.

We have to bring you back to Earth with a bump at this point and say: **what you do on Earth determines where you will first go to on arrival in the spiritual spheres**, because your rate of vibration as a soul is affected by the choices that you make whilst in a physical body; is affected by the thoughts that you harbour whilst you are in a physical vehicle; by your intentions whilst you are in a physical vehicle, and the experiences that are brought to you by your karma and the way that you tackle those experiences alters your vibrationary rate and determines your destination upon arrival in the spirit realms.

We have covered the Lower Astral but there are other destinations that souls go to who are not ready for the higher spheres. If you think about it logically there will be souls who will have put themselves in the Lower Astral by their choices, but also souls who have not earned the right to exist in one of the more etheric spheres but, at the same time, have not placed themselves in the dire circumstances of the Lower Astral. So there are many souls who find themselves in a sort of 'between-place', and the between-place can be a mixture of their own thoughts plus a sense of reality that is given to that place by the number of souls that inhabit it. In other words, not *as above, so below*; rather *as below, so above*. It is a reflection of your physical Field – the Field I have spoken about in the first book exists in a more etheric form on a higher level of consciousness.

And so you have souls who shape their initial experience of the spiritual realms through a mixture of what they believe to be true and a mixture of what everyone else existing on that level of vibration believes to be true. So you have a very disjointed 'jigsaw puzzle' of a sphere. You have people, for example, who have been restricted by religion that create for themselves within that sphere great edifices –

churches, cathedrals and squares where people can worship, and yet these things are strangely unsatisfying to the souls that have created them. You will have one area where there are churches, where there are priests, where there are holy men roaming the streets, where there are images of Jesus... and yet all these things are constructs; they are a combination of thought-forms and projections from the souls living within that sphere.

There are areas where the housing is quite poor (and, yes, these souls choose for a time to live in houses), and the houses are a mixture of projections from the Field and beliefs from the individual souls who live in them. Souls who believed that they had lack whilst on Earth, who believed that they could never achieve anything, who believed always that they were going to fail, take with them into the spiritual realms those beliefs, and for a time they find themselves living in places that reflect those beliefs: *the house is not a grand one; it requires repairing every so often; the garden is untidy; the skyline is grey* – because those are the expectations of the souls who live in those areas.

So you may find in your terms (because I cannot explain something so complex *completely* in physical terms) the area where the fanatically religious souls have constructed their churches and their places of worship linked, like a jigsaw-puzzle piece, to an area where people live in poor housing.

Then you find areas where people *have a go* at one another. Not as they would in the Lower Astral... but you have people living together who are uneasy with each other. The problem is that these people are very similar and, because they are similar, they pull themselves into an area of existence and they look at each other (not recognising *the self* in the other) and take against the other. So you have areas where little thunderstorms break out, where the atmosphere changes according to the thoughts of the people living in that particular area. You have discord that manifests itself as the things they say to each other and the things they think about each other, but there is also discord *in the atmosphere.* You have storms, you have static electricity between people and, what is worse, because they are in a spiritual realm now they can see, they can hear, they can feel each other's thoughts – so any animosity from one soul to another is in the air around them and can be read, can be felt, can be seen… which aggravates the situation more.

You might say, '*Joseph,* isn't that what happens in the Lower Astral?' and it *is,* but this sphere I am talking about is not as severe as the Lower Astral. It is a destination for souls who have not yet worked out of their system the animosity that they felt for others, the disregard for others, the bitterness towards others, the suspicion about others they had whilst they were on Earth but has not quite placed them in the darkness of the Lower Astral through their actions whilst on Earth.

You have another sphere or 'area of life' where people do not accomplish anything. There are souls here who accomplished nothing whilst on Earth. These souls don't want to work; don't want to better themselves; don't want to reach out to other people – they wish to remain in bed. So, quite literally, you have areas where people maintain that illusion of wanting to do nothing and place themselves in surroundings where they will find themselves, for example, in a room with a bed in it and *there they stay.* They will have, if they wish, a television (because the television is a construct from their mind) and they will stay in that room for as long as they wish and will not progress. Should they go out of the door they will find other people in that sphere who, similarly, do not wish to progress and will maintain that level of non-activity for as long as they are comfortable with it.

There are hundreds and thousands of scenarios where souls group together with similar intentions or lack of intentions when they leave the Earth plane.

What we have not brought into this equation is the fact that these thoughts – these thoughts of religious fanaticism, or of not wanting to do anything with existence, or of animosity to others – can also exist in souls who are more spiritually exalted. If a soul is more spiritually exalted and sees within itself those areas where it has been mistaken or has hung onto something that it no longer requires then that soul can place itself in another area of that sphere where work can be done *voluntarily*, where a soul can say, 'I can see more than this; I wish to move on. I have integrated Light into my soul and into my being during my life on Earth. However, there are areas that I wish to drop, that I wish to let go of. Perhaps I was rude to people on a grand scale, or perhaps I allowed my religion to colour my spiritual beliefs, or perhaps I wasn't as industrious with the talents I had been given as I should have been. I now see those aspects of myself and I see that, in order to reside in a higher sphere, I need to let go of some of those beliefs.'

And so those souls find themselves in a very pleasant place; in a place that would perhaps reflect a university campus on Earth, with pleasant buildings and opportunities to go and listen to lectures, because that is what those souls do. In order to divest themselves of aspects of their earthly personality they no longer require or desire they can sit and listen to experts from higher spheres, who suggest to them how they can disentangle themselves from the aspects of their personality that they no longer need. Within that sphere of various influences and scenarios you also find a sphere souls can visit to learn how to peel away the skins of the personality they no longer need, so that that higher vibration they are already aware of can be attained and they can move on to a more etheric level of existence.

Now in all of this, in approaching this Sphere of Cleansing, I have not mentioned families... Of course every soul, except in a few extreme circumstances, wishes to be reunited with members of its family (family from the earthly personality point of view) when it returns to the spirit realms. So, interspersed with the experience of a soul finding itself in one of these realms (the realm of the religious fanatic, the realm of the person who does not wish to rise to any challenge, the realm of the person who has not yet worked out how to approach people properly, etc.) are periods when that soul is reunited with members of its family, according to the wish of the soul to do so and according to the wish of the family members to do so because, should a family member *not wish* to be reunited with a soul that has passed recently from Earth, there is no way that those vibrations will fit together.

Simple volition is essential in reuniting family members, and you also have to remember that those family members are each travelling at different rates through the spheres and, furthermore, that those family members (that once were) are now operating from the point of view of other, more etheric spiritual identities and the *suit of clothes* that they had during the lifetime in which they related to the souls who may wish to see them is only part of who they now are.

Within this complexity there has to be a time and a sphere where the souls who have recently departed can meet their *family members that were* as *who they used to be* and, because everything that happens to a soul (whether on Earth or in the higher spheres) happens through the vibration of God's love, it is permitted for these different souls to come together and reunite in love. This takes place at certain times and there are reassurances given to the souls who have left the Earth recently that they will be able to visit and revisit their family members at times during their progress towards higher spheres. Again, it is complex because, in the example of the person who is perhaps fanatically religious, those thoughts that go to create that illusion within that sphere may be so strong that they exclude family members. It is not always a given that souls get together with family members but it *is* a given that they are allowed to if *both* the souls involved agree.

So there is comfort for the souls in the spheres as they work out of their systems (and that is the intention) those aspects of the physical personality that prevent them from progressing to higher spheres.

If you consider what I have said, we are talking about *degrees of awareness*.

There is the degree of awareness of those souls who realise that they are greater than the earthly personality and need to divest themselves of certain aspects of that personality before they can move on – they are aware of that and they exist within this sphere.

There are also the other pockets of souls who may not be aware of that, but the purpose of the sphere is not to imprison them but to enlighten them and, by placing them (they have placed themselves in actuality) with similar souls, immerse them in circumstances that will eventually reveal to them that they need to move on from those circumstances. Eventually (be it in a year or in a thousand years) the souls in the realm of religious fanaticism realise that they are *going nowhere*. They also realise this because they are visited by souls from other spheres who try to instil them with a sense of enthusiasm for the journey ahead and who try to say to them: 'This way is alright for you now... but tomorrow it won't be. Try and open up and see things in a different way.'

There are the souls who are in the part of the sphere where they are antagonistic towards each other, and the purpose of that area of creation is to *eventually* say to those souls through the heart, through the soul, 'This isn't the way to act. I am tired of picking on someone else. I am tired of picking on myself. What is next?'

There is the sphere where people find themselves living in fairly poor surroundings, where, eventually, those souls say to themselves, 'How do I get out of here?'

...And in each case there is help. In each case, at the moment of the soul's turning away from the illusion they have propelled themselves into upon physical death, someone appears with information, with love, with illustrations of what comes next... and helps that soul *out* of that intermediate sphere.

The key to moving on from that initial sphere is *work*: work on the self, work on the image of the soul – work, realisation and alignment with higher vibrations in all cases. So the soul that is in the church praying for a thousand years will one day ask: 'What is outside of this church? Who am I praying to? Why are there no replies from above?' and at that point they will find themselves ready for the next stage of their journey and out of that sphere. The same thing happens with other areas of the sphere, with people gradually coming to the realisation that *there is more than this*.

You must not, in considering this sphere, consider God as being harsh or judgemental. God has not placed the souls within that particular sphere; they have placed *themselves* within that sphere because there are certain aspects of their lives that need to be lifted up, certain aspects of their personality that need to be worked through, and so they have prevented themselves from going any higher until they have worked those aspects out of their personality. The analogy of the Pearly Gates is a good one because the Pearly Gates will only open when the atmosphere within the Pearly Gates matches the atmosphere of the soul approaching those gates.

There is another aspect we must deal with at a later date and that aspect concerns soul-memory. The souls I have been talking about this morning are souls who do not gain instant access to their soul-memory – not in full. Some of them may do *partially*, as in the souls who wish to move on but realise that they have something to work out and, therefore, visit the areas of learning that allow them to work these things out. The souls we have been talking about today go to that particular sphere because they have become so enmeshed in the earth-personality (either through the life that they have just lived or through a combination of that life and many other lives in the past in their soul-history) that they cannot access their spiritual side instantly. In other words they still believe they are *John Smith*. They believe that they are *John Smith* who has passed over and is in a new situation but, all the while, within the suit of clothes that is *John Smith* there is the greater personality saying, 'Here I am!' But that greater personality cannot be heard at that point in the soul's development because there is too much materialism – not materialism in the sense of a house, or a car, or physical goods, but materialism in that there is a residue from the Earth as an experience of that Earth life they have bought into, that they are locked into to such an extent that it takes a number of days or years to disintegrate those vibrations, revealing the true personality within.

Unfortunately the sphere I am describing today applies to a great number of souls upon passing, and it applies to a great number of souls for the reasons I have outlined in the books thus far – the desire to return to the Earth, to the pull of the Earth for whatever reason, and a reluctance to relinquish the things of the Earth upon physical passing into the spiritual realms. The sphere I have described today, with its many areas, is a sphere that we hope to eliminate; and we hope eventually to eliminate that sphere by making people aware of their spiritual heritage whilst they are on Earth and in a book that describes what happens to you next. I will, at times, have to refer to what is happening to you now because I say to you, the reader, **you have access to your soul-memories now, if you want them.** Here I do not mean the tendency to believe that you have been great people in the past and to say, 'I was a king... I was a queen... I was *this*... I was *that*.' That is not the nature of the soul-memories I am speaking about.

Soul-memory surpasses the individual personality or personalities you have inhabited in order to grow. In looking beyond this Earth and in meditating for regular periods and letting go (as I and other communicators have said) you find that you can gain access to who you are – not your soul but *you*, expressing yourself through your soul. The memories I am talking about are memories of connection with God – not memories of who you are as a *John Smith* or as a North American Indian but memories of your connection to God through your previous existences in the spirit realms. When you begin to open up your soul-memories your perspective of the earthly life *changes* so that you approach materialism, you approach other people, you approach your daily life, you approach your families in a different way and you prepare yourself (through locking into and through connecting to that inner knowledge daily) for what lies ahead once you leave this place. If you connect with your soul-memories you will (in most cases) avoid that intermediate sphere that would otherwise require you to work out of your system certain aspects of your earthly personality.

It is an express-train method of projecting yourself into the spirit realms!

There is a great need on Earth for men and women to connect to their soul-memories and they do not know how to do it. This is beyond clairvoyant messages; beyond the sale of trinkets; beyond the casting of spells; beyond the hyperbole of many *so-called* channelled communications. This cuts through to your essence and it is your essence that holds your memories of what you are, of where you came from and of where you *wish* to be.

I can provide meditations that will enable you to connect with your true self and intend to do so as part of a future communication, but I have to bring you 'back to Earth' to say **what you do *now* – today – affects where you go to** and, if you are a soul that is seeking progression and seeking to be back in the bliss of God-consciousness (And which soul isn't?), then it would be a good idea for you to connect during your earthly life with your true self and bypass much of the periods of cleansing that souls have to go through when they leave this place because of the way they have thought, acted and projected whilst they were on Earth.

As I have said, this book is a *vast* subject and may even overspill into two books – I don't know yet; it depends on how you present it and how much information you want to put into it. At this stage may I invite any questions on what I have said today to clarify any aspects that may be troubling you or you may want illumination on?

70

Jane: Could I ask a question about the vibrational rate that determines where people are segregated to – is somebody's vibrational rate constant through their lives or does it fluctuate? Say, hypothetically, you had a good person and then in the last month of their life they were really crabby and unpleasant to people... would their vibrational rate have 'gone down'?

Joseph [*laughing*]: It is great to bring humour into our gathering and there is always this sense of urgency that sometimes prevents me from enjoying the humour we can share.

The vibrational rate of a soul changes from instant to instant but in all but the extreme cases it is *refining* itself instant to instant. I must also clarify that there is no *good* and there is no *bad* – there is only experience which results in stasis or lack of progress and experience which results in progress. Yet even that is too basic an explanation because the experiences that produce people you would label as 'bad' – those experiences are worthwhile in the greater view and bigger picture of the soul because they, too, lead to the soul progressing.

There are earthly traits and, as the physical projection of the soul begins to lose its cohesion as the soul moves towards the point where it will move on to the spirit realms, the earthly Field crowds in more and more. It is more difficult for the elderly to fend off the vibrations of the Field. Think about that! Michael himself has said that many old people surprise him because they seem to have learnt so little. They should not surprise him because what is happening is that, as that soul wishes to move back to the spiritual realms, the physical vehicle becomes weaker and it is more difficult for the physical vehicle and the physical mind (unless you have a very strong soul indeed) to fend off the dominant vibrations of the Field. Therefore, the aggressions of the Field, the upsets of the Field, the negative aspects of the Field (and remember that the Field is mostly negative) crowd in. So it is natural for that soul to on occasion be upset, on occasion be angry and on occasion have little patience with others. But that does not slow down the vibrational rate of the soul it has earned during its life on Earth, it simply means that that soul needs to go into contemplation, meditation and peaceful circumstances on the spiritual side and (as an analogy) *take a shower in Light*.

We have not yet touched on the review of a soul's life – that is another chapter and has to fit into the jigsaw puzzle of the book we are putting together but the answer is: do not look at the peripheral things – look at the heart of the person and see the Light that shines from the person and know that that Light is what the soul will take with it to the higher realms and not the pettiness that we *all* suffer from at times. Does that answer your question?

Jane: Yes.

Joseph: Another question!

David: Are some of the souls in this particular sphere actually aware that they are in this sphere and that God exists, or do they just see it as a continuation of the Earth plane?

Joseph: That is a good point and it is a point that splits itself into a few facets. So dominant are the thoughts and projections of the Earth that for a while certain of the souls in this sphere know that they are somewhere else on one level but blot out their being somewhere else on a conscious level. So they make it a *continuation*, even though the circumstances around them – the things that they see, the things that they sense and their abilities as a soul outside of a physical vehicle – show them that something has happened. For a time they refuse to accept that on a conscious level.

You also have souls who, having passed in a hospital bed, still find themselves in a hospital bed – for one of the areas of this sphere concerns illness and the belief in illness. The belief in illness is also a barrier to spiritual evolution for certain souls because they have invested time, energy and belief in their illness. Just as religious beliefs or an inability to want to progress can hold souls back so can a belief and an investment in the vibrations of illness. So many souls find themselves *still ill*, as it were, because they are comforted at the deepest level by what they are familiar with, and so they hang onto the illness as something that they can count on. That seems so sad, doesn't it? Nevertheless it is a truth. They are tended to by spirits who walk amongst them as *doctors* and *nurses*, up to the point where the soul that is suffering has proven to itself that it is no longer ill. At that point the nurse or the doctor will say, 'Now, here is some other form of healing for you. Now I can lead you out of this place to a better place. Now we can talk and real progress can be made.'

But in every aspect of that sphere there is help for those souls and there are those who walk amongst them who are elevated spirits, who see that a minimum of harm, in the way that they are thinking or viewing their surroundings, comes to them (absolutely no harm can come to them *physically*, of course). Very often these people go unrecognised until the point where the soul can elevate itself and think, 'I need to get out of these circumstances.'

I can sum it up in saying that all the souls come to a point where they say: 'I need to get out of here.' What they are really saying is: 'I need to get out of *here*' [*pointing to within*] because the *here* is within them (As the *here* for you is within you. It appears to be very real and to be *around* you, but in reality it is *here*.). And so, when they say, 'I need to get out of here' we give them the means to do so.

In answer to your question – yes, there are souls who feel that it is a continuation, but there are also souls who know that they have gone somewhere but retreat into aspects of the Earth plane that they are comfortable with so that they can (to their mind) survive and cope with the change in their circumstances. Does that make sense?

David: It does, yes, thank you.

Joseph: Another question!

Mark: Joseph, I was uplifted to hear about your meditations to help people prepare to connect with the essence of who they are as a soul because many people (myself included), not being able to access that kind of knowledge currently, will approach it from the aspect of trying to drop and release what we believe we are not. In other words, we realise who we are *not* but it is more difficult to realise who we *are*. Does that work in a way to create the space for the true essence of the self to come in by letting go of the things that we realise we are not?

Joseph: There should be no fight in your relinquishing of the things that you are not. Unfortunately, your view of what you are not and what you are is influenced so much by religion. You are told by many of the religions that *this is the way to act and this is the way not to act*, and your conventional views through religion of how you should act and how you should not act have nothing to do (or little to do) with how you should act and how you should not act as a spirit.

You have tools that you can use during your earthly life: you have the positive ray – the positive energy – and you have the negative ray – the negative energy. You are in control of those but you are told as souls that you are either one or the other and that you should extinguish one and embrace the other, and in doing this... in *attempting* to do this (because in truth you *cannot* do this) you cause problems for yourselves.

The way to eliminate those aspects of yourself that you see as hindering your spiritual evolution is to *love* them. You cannot change by attempting to expel an aspect of yourself; you cannot take out a section of your soul with a pair of scissors and free it from yourself, saying, 'That is no longer part of me.' That is impossible and that is where souls go wrong in attempting to evolve. What you should do is look at yourself and say, 'There are positive aspects of me but I am not the positive aspects; there are negative aspects in me but I am not the

74

negative aspects. These things are my tools, these things are my opportunities to grow, and when I look at myself and I wish to change I should not alienate that aspect of myself and *perpetuate* that aspect of myself that I want to change by abhorring it. Instead I must say that that area needs to change; it is part of me and I embrace it. In my quiet times and my meditations I bathe in love those aspects of myself that I wish to transmute.' In embracing yourself as a total soul with positive and negative at its command, you come to a point of peace and understanding.

In looking at your negative aspects (or so-called negative aspects) in this way, by embracing them in love and in Light, rather than trying to expel them or fearing them or trying to put a wall up between you and this aspect of yourself that seems to cause so much trouble, you begin to understand what the negative aspect of yourself is for. Through that aspect of yourself you understand an aspect of evolution; you begin to understand why you act in that way and, in understanding why you act in that way, you learn how to act in a different way. But that change has to come through embracing what you are, and 'embracing what you are' does not mean that you repeat an action or thought that you feel is wrong for you but it means that, when that thought or that action occurs to you, you do not fear it. You take it into yourself, you bathe it in the Light of your soul that is connected to God-Light and, in doing that, you begin to understand yourself.

You see that so much damage is done by religion trying to separate what it sees as good from what it sees as bad. You cannot separate yourself; you cannot tear yourself apart. Wasn't it Jesus who said that a house divided against itself cannot stand? This is what he meant – you have to embrace your total perception; you have to embrace all aspects of yourself and not fear them. In not fearing them, those aspects of yourself that need to fall away so that you can progress *will* fall away, because when they are bathed in Light they have no power – except the power of good, except the power of God, except the power to do good… to you and to the souls around you. Am I making sense?

Mark: So, if I was to embrace the concept of just loving myself completely would that help the process?

Joseph: Yes, that is exactly what I am saying and remember that the 'yourself' we are talking about is not the yourself that needs to eat; that thinks it needs a particular amount of money; that needs the warmth; that needs the house; that needs the companionship – the yourself I am talking about is the *true self*. So you are not aggrandising the ego by loving yourself; you are feeding yourself with Light and this is what all souls need around the Earth – to be fed by Light. Instead they feed from each other, instead they feed from the Field and you have the present situation of violence, and negativity, and illness, and sickness.

Days should be bright things; souls should enjoy their days on Earth. There should be upliftment, there should be a knowledge of God, a knowledge of love and a knowledge that each soul is on a journey and that journey will not bring any harm to it, that there is nothing to worry about, nothing to be downcast about and that everything is in its right place. Souls do not have access to these types of days because they do not understand how to become whole or to acknowledge their wholeness (of course they are whole but earthly society seeks to strip off bits of the soul and this cannot happen). The soul has to acknowledge itself as complete and examine its aspects within a field of love and then the aspects that the soul needs to drop melt away. Do you see that?

Mark: Yes, that was most helpful.

Joseph: Has that answered your question?

Mark: Very clearly, thank you.

Joseph: Is there another question?

David: In the sphere that we are speaking about, are there souls that spend a lot of time trying to correct their previous life because they realise that they have missed a turning that they should have taken? In other words, are they trying to relive their life in a way they see as being the way they should have lived it, rather than the way they *did* live it?

Joseph: There is the ability for each soul to project and to create, and within the sphere there are areas where a soul has such a volition to alter what has happened that it can create (in front of it and around it) people who are not really there and circumstances that it revisits. This will tie into what we will eventually talk about, which is a chapter in itself that we will call 'The Life Review', but, yes, there are certain souls who, through upset and regret, place themselves in areas of the sphere where they relive certain experiences. That question allies itself more clearly with the life review section and so I will address it, if I may, at that point.

David: Thank you.

Joseph: I have used poor Michael's body to a great extent this morning but I do it with his volition. If he did not want me to do this I could not do it, but I must vacate and return to my dream, to my sphere of influence and I look forward – with a blessing for you all – to speaking with you again quite soon.

Chapter Five
The Healing Sphere

Joseph: It is with joy that we open this meeting today and *joy* will be one of the themes I want to talk about. We bring joy first of all because joy disperses the attentions and problems of the physical world. One of the problems we have with spirits that make the transition who are not spiritually aware and who have not rediscovered their nature is that they are so very, very sad and world weary. There's a term: 'world weary' – it describes the attitude of many, many souls when they make the transition and arrive on the 'spiritual shores', as it were. There is no reason for them to be downcast; there is no reason for them to be world weary but, once again, they are so used to operating in a certain way that it becomes second nature to them and it takes some time and great, gentle persuasion, in many cases, to alleviate the mental suffering of many, many souls.

For that reason there are 'stations' within which souls can be healed, treated and prepared for the life and existence that is ahead of them. For many souls it is enough to make the transition in a series of events that looks to them as though they are going on a journey. At the beginning of that journey they are world weary and careworn and, by the end of the journey (because they have been 'processed' i.e. been approached by spirits who can reassure them and give them a glimpse of their own soul-memories), when they reach their embarkation point on the spirit side of life, they are restored enough to be able to move on.

79

There are many for whom this is not the case. For example, there are those spirits who pass through trauma; those spirits who have been murdered (not in all cases, but in many); those spirits who have passed through fire, through explosion, through great pain or through the slow erosion of the physical body from illness so that their mindset, when they make their transition, is a continuation of the pain, suffering or lack of energy they have experienced up to or just before that transition point.

So, what do we do with these spirits?

We enter their consciousness and touch them on a very superficial, light level to talk to them. We mingle our vibrations with theirs so that we can reach a level of consciousness where they are *aware* and we inform them that they are going somewhere in order to be healed. We may give them an image of a hospital; we may give them an image of a facility where they can convalesce; we may give them an image of a quiet room by a stream and trees or a beautiful landscape that is *theirs* where they can be quiet, where they can realise *in their own time* that there is now nothing to fear, that they are perfectly alright and that they can take part in and be a part of a new and energised spiritual community.

Our first step is for specialists amongst us to reach in, through the layers of physical consciousness that are causing the trauma and through the pain that that consciousness is experiencing, to the spiritual consciousness within and to break through that pain to say, 'We are taking you somewhere where you will and can be healed.' Through that contact we reassure the spirit that they will indeed feel better and that their suffering is not an eternal thing that will go on, and on, and on, as many of them believe it to be – particularly those that have been suffering with terminal illnesses and are used to pain and to their energies having drained away day after day as they became weaker.

Then we 'transport' or shift in consciousness to a place of healing the spirits we wish to heal (although 'heal' is a misnomer because there is nothing wrong with them). We seek to connect them with their spiritual awareness and we seek to strip away the pollution of the Earth plane in mental terms. So we gather around them and, in thought, we then transport them and ourselves to one of the points where spirits can be healed in this way.

In God-essence (as all other places are) this is a place of Light-energy but, because we need a frame of reference (both for the spirits who are being healed and for ourselves), very often these places will appear like institutions that the spirits have been used to on Earth. For example, we have hospitals but those hospitals are not the dark and often sinister, careworn places you have on Earth. Our hospitals are sometimes open-plan. If we need another wing, another bedroom or another bed we call these things into mind from the matrix of energy around us... and suddenly, they are there. Our hospitals are pleasant because there is no frightful surgery; there is no wondering as to whether a patient will live or die; there are no harmful synthetic (or indeed any) drugs that are administered to patients that give them harmful side-effects; there is no upset in the atmosphere. Our hospitals are situated in landscapes of our choice: we can have pleasant trees, valleys, rivers and oceans and, very often, when the patients are becoming used to their spiritual abilities, they can choose the landscape they wish to look out on. What a delight for someone to convalesce and choose the landscape; to say: 'This morning I will have an alpine landscape; this afternoon I will have an oceanic landscape and it is *my choice* – I am creating this and am being allowed to create this.'

So, we have hospitals and we have spirits who staff those hospitals, who use a portion of their existence-time to nourish, comfort and encourage souls who need to be lifted from the conditions of the Earth plane. We have pleasant rooms where people can come and talk to us and there is no pressure. We do not say, 'You have an hour from this point and you must tell me all about your life and what is worrying you.' When those patients feel they want to talk – *if* they feel they want to talk – then the room appears around them and we sit in one chair and they sit in another chair and we listen... and we *love*.

Of course, many times we are faced with anger because spirits leave the Earth plane *bitterly*. Sometimes they are angry because they have passed; sometimes they are angry because of their lives and need someone to blame; sometimes they are angry because they feel that it is our fault that they are still suffering. When they are ready to communicate (even if that communication is only anger) we bring them to a room and we sit in front of them, and they learn an extremely important lesson about existence in the spiritual realms: *they cannot hurt anybody*. They cannot hit us; they can shout and can let off steam but, because of the vibration they find themselves placed in the vibrations they exude cannot harm, cannot affect the atmosphere and (I suppose you could say) are streamed and funnelled out of them, are taken away from them and are 'earthed' (although it is not the Earth that does the earthing – it is the goodness of God that transmutes those angry thoughts).

Their anger exists for as long as they want it to. If they wish to be angry for a day, that is fine; if they wish to be angry for a thousand years, that is also fine but their anger eventually teaches them (because it cannot be directed towards anyone or to any situation) that they need to think in a different way in order to feel better. On the day that they let go of that anger there is a beautiful and subtle change in the lights around them in their aura or energy-field that signals to us and to them that a change has taken place and that they are ready to listen to advice, perhaps; ready to become calm and ready to move on in consciousness to recognise the worlds that they are now a part of.

In other wards (although wards on our level only exist where people wish to group together – otherwise souls are given privacy when they want it) you find victims of trauma who lie in beds and refuse to move. They feel that they are in a coma; they may have passed whilst in a coma or have been in a situation on Earth where illness paralysed them, robbing them of movement, and they continue with that belief. So those spirits are within themselves and very often there is a dialogue going on *within* arguing themselves in and out of spiritual consciousness. In the moments that they decide to look outwards we can help. In the moments when they are talking to themselves and existing in their inner worlds of pain, we can do nothing except surround them with love and with Light until their vibration starts to lift.

There are other special facilities for children who pass as children. The children who come over fall into two categories: there are those who realise (although they still appear to be children) that they are greater than their physical appearance, and there are those who pass as children who still regard themselves as children. As with every other visual manifestation on our levels of consciousness, this appearance is an illusion and children need to be accelerated in terms of spiritual-mind maturity to the point where they remember their individual existence beyond the frame of childhood that they have brought with them from the physical world.

So there is a healing that needs to take place with children, too, and, of course, they are allowed access to those relatives that have passed on before them, but they are then brought to beautiful, innocent landscapes and a beautiful, innocent series of facilities where they are advised, little by little, by the spirits who tend to them. By being educated in this way as to their spiritual identity and being made to remember, little by little, they mature visually and they mature as individualised expressions of God-consciousness far more quickly than children on Earth do. They are surrounded with love and they are taught (although not as you would teach children on Earth) – they are *educated* in spiritual ways until they reach the point where they *remember*, and once they remember they are then free and ready to journey onwards through the spiritual realms.

In the case of children who come across and already realise, in part, that they are mature spirits we surround them with members of their soul-group and with their advisors and guides, who are people that they recognise, and the rehabilitation change – from the physical and visual form of a child to the reinstatement of the form that they are familiar and happy with but relinquished for a time when they came to Earth – is much more rapid. Then they leave behind the facility and move on to live for a time with their soul-group or with their soul-families (more of which in later communications).

So, there is a level that exists purely to rehabilitate souls, and that level is of a high vibration compared to the vibrations of the Earth plane and the vibrations of the souls entering that level but is not of the accelerated levels of vibration that spirits can dwell in once they have left behind the shackles of the Earth. It is, as with all levels spiritually, not a level of judgement or condemnation but a level of progress. For those who work in it, it is an extremely demanding level because they are having to associate with the vibrations of the Earth plane once again in trying to re-establish spiritual awareness within the souls that need to move away from the conditions they have brought with them *mentally* from the Earth. And so the spirits who work in this level can only do so for relatively short amounts of time before returning to their own vibrationary harmony and to their own sphere to re-energise themselves and to divest themselves of the vibrations that they will have picked up and absorbed, to a certain extent, from the very souls they are trying to help.

These spirits are very noble workers for the cause and it is a dedicated and unique job that many look at and say, 'That is not for me!' Also, these spirits have to have the ability to reach into the minds of the spirits who need help and to *harmonise* for a little while (which is dangerous) with those vibrations they are holding to be true for as long as they can maintain that connection, and then, at the end of that connection, to just leave the consciousness of that spirit, as they come away from it, with a view of something better. So they enter the vibrationary field of the soul who is suffering, which means that automatically they identify with the vibrations of suffering of that soul. Then they very quickly come out of that connection, leaving the soul with something more, with a slightly higher vibration, with something of themselves and with something of their own love so that the soul *gradually* lifts itself out of its vision of pain into a more receptive state so it can be brought to spiritual consciousness and can break out of the clinging vibrations of the Earth.

Around those spirits who actually touch the auric fields of the spirits that need to be lifted there are spirits who constantly place energies into the facilities, into the landscapes, into the buildings and into those souls who work with the souls who need to be made aware of their new existence – in order to maintain a level of vibration that is not polluted by the masked minds of the spirits in the facilities who need to awaken.

It is a great operation but a very necessary one because there is danger in souls being associated so strongly with the Earth. If we cannot lift the consciousness of the spirit sufficiently so that they let go of those vibrations, those vibrations – even vibrations of pain – pull on them constantly, those vibrations reconnect them to the Earth plane and those vibrations form a need within the souls of those spirits to be constantly fed by similar vibrations. If all we can do is raise the consciousness of certain souls to an awareness of being in an in-between station, their wish upon awakening is not to go forwards... but to go back to the Earth. Such is the pull of the Field and, therefore, you will see the necessity and the vital importance of this sphere that exists to cleanse spirits of their connection with the Earth on an emotional and on a pain level. So, yes, I am indeed saying that with certain souls, the pull of the Earth – *even in pain* – is so great that they wish to return to that level of consciousness and to that state of affairs rather than to move onwards. The physical plane of the Earth pulls at them, pulls at their consciousness and convinces them that that is all there is.

This only happens with a percentage of souls we treat but, nevertheless, it does happen and I hope this illustrates why souls come back to Earth in such great numbers. Is it not true to say that sometimes there is comfort in pain because the pain is what you are used to? The pain is not what you desire (not on a conscious level) but what you are familiar with and certain souls feel: 'Well, I have this pain, but perhaps over there there is a greater pain so I will stick with this one.' So a percentage of souls that come back to the Earth plane do so because they are unable (or we are unable on their behalf) to raise their vibration sufficiently to sever that trauma-connection with the Earth plane that draws them back.

This is not an automatic thing; they are not drawn back in their state of unconsciousness or unawareness of spiritual levels. What happens is that we eventually reach in and elevate them to the point where they are conscious within the facility or sphere of recuperation but then they refuse to move onwards, saying: 'I know this place is beautiful but there is somewhere calling to me and I need to revisit it.' We explain patiently and in love that, were they to do so, they would be energising similar vibrations to those that we have just severed for them and they would likely have a life that would be difficult. Nevertheless, the pull of the Earth plane is such that they eventually say, 'Well, I understand that but I may have twenty or thirty years where I can experience the Earth again and *I miss certain things*.' Divorced from that pain for a time they forget how painful it was and they are willing to trade and accept the pain that may come at, say, the end of their life, in exchange for years spent again on the Earth plane in similar conditions to those that they left.

This sounds illogical, I know; it does sound a bad choice – and it is – but *not to them* because they are, in effect, confused and polluted by the Earth plane. Every spirit (including myself) who visits the Earth plane to teach from higher levels has to be cleansed before they can go back to those levels. Sometimes it is a rapid affair (in our case, it is simply like passing through an energy chamber that cleanses us of pollution, and it is a quick process) but for those novices who visit the Earth plane sometimes it takes considerably longer as the Earth plane pulls at them. The Earth plane is a very seductive place to those who have been encased in physical matter and we work hard to release as many souls as we can into the spiritual realms and to ensure that they do not want to return... *but many do.*

So... there is a realm, an area, a 'sphere' (and 'sphere' is an apt word, because everything is circular in its nature in God-reality) or a department, if you like (I am searching for words that will make sense to your readers) that is concerned solely with moving spirits on, with disconnecting them from the trauma they have experienced on the Earth plane and with cleansing them to the extent that they can then begin their lives in the spiritual spheres and *hopefully* not return to Earth.

There are areas within this facility where, if you were to visit it at this very moment, you would see people in wheelchairs sitting in pleasant surroundings; you would see people with sticks walking up and down the pathways; you would see, in certain circumstances, people with oxygen masks who truly believe that they need these things (as the people believe they need the wheelchairs or the walking-sticks). These souls are spirits we have managed to reach and to raise their awareness but the awareness in many cases is a gradual one. They cling onto the vestiges of their illness, trauma or pain and have to follow mentally, according to their rules (not to our rules, not to God's), a series of events that takes them from being (as they see it) diseased or ill to being (as they see it) healthy.

They do this in stages. When they first awaken they lie in their beds for a while and they feel as though they have had a great fight take place within and outside of themselves. They feel that they need a few days or a few weeks to recuperate and we give them the illusion of what they are used to. We give them liquid to drink (which is, in fact, energy that is imbued with Light and is absorbed into the spirit to further that process of distancing itself from the pain of the Earth plane) and we give them food in certain circumstances because they expect to eat. The food is not real (but then, the food on your level is not 'real') – it is simply an illusion that enables us to donate energy, Light and love to those spirits until they feel better. Built into each spirit is a sequence of events concerning illness: 'I cannot instantly be well; I cannot instantly get rid of my pain; it is gradual… my body is healing' – when in effect they do not have a body. The body that manifests around them is simply an impression that they are putting into the field of energy they find themselves in as a recognition point for themselves and for others.

There are also, it might surprise you, spirits who walk these grounds with babies in their arms, because mothers either come to this sphere in pain because they have died in childbirth or because they have been nursing the hurt of losing a child for many years before they crossed to the spiritual realms and there is a conditioning or need built into them to be reunited with their babies. Of course, in most cases, the children have moved on to appear as adults to us or to appear as the elevated spirits that they really are but such is their love that they prepare themselves to appear *for a time* to their mothers as the babies they once were to allow those mothers to heal, to allow those mothers to let go of the pain and then (once they have let go of the pain) they can see their offspring as either the child they expect them to be or the elevated spirit that they really are.

And, finally, part of this sphere is an area where *non-knowers* can find themselves (and by 'non-knowers' I refer to those who do not believe in a Divinity or Divine Creation). They find themselves still existing, of course, and they cannot move either way… They cannot move back to the Earth because *as far as they are concerned* there is no Earth any more – because they are 'dead', and they cannot move forwards because *as far as they are concerned* there is no forwards – because they are 'dead'.

They are placed in a very secure wing, and by 'secure' I mean a place where the energies are of a particular persuasion to enable them to eventually realise that they still exist and that they are *somewhere*. We sit around them and, from a visual perspective, they are placed in beds so that we can recognise their form, and we attempt to elevate them. We attempt to surround them with vibrations that demonstrate to them that they are still conscious, that they are still mobile, that they still have will and that they still exist. This can be a very difficult thing to do because over the years they have conditioned their mind to say, 'There is nothing! I will be nothing!' They cannot be nothing, of course, but they can exist in a mental state of nothing until they choose something else. So, in effect, we are taking them out of the void. We are saying, 'Isn't it time you rejoined society?' and we do this by loving them and by sending energies to them until one day (relatively speaking) they open their 'eyes' and say: 'Oh, then I do still exist... then there *is* something!'

There are then teams who work with them to counsel them. Always with each of these spirits we *counsel* them once they have let go of their trauma, because it is not enough for them to simply let go of their trauma – they need to realise that they are on a journey, they need to be made aware of where they are, what their potential is, where they can go and the options open to them.

We have, of course, to also work with those who are in mental pain, and very often this is more difficult than working with those who have been in physical pain. It is relatively simple with physical pain to advise the spirits, but mental pain is a difficult one to dislodge because they are involved in a mental process, because they are operating mentally and the soul is feeding the mental abilities. In circumstances such as these we have to talk to and again get into and touch the soul of the person; we have to become their friend; we have to harmonise with their exact problem and draw them out of that problem through many, many conversations, through much reasoning, through much love directed towards them, through much spiritual logic, and we have to gently persuade them to let go of those mental barriers that are causing them pain. It is a very exacting job, it is a very difficult job and this happens with a percentage of souls who pass over.

When I say 'we' I am not talking about myself (I am involved in other activities) but I speak for every spirit that has elevated itself because *we are one*. So, in effect, when I am talking about the doctors, nurses and staff of the facilities I have just mentioned, a part of me is in them and a part of them is in me… just as a part of me is in you and a part of you is in each other. There is no separation. There is only *We*. There is only *I*. There is only *One*. There is only *God*.

I hope I have explained to a sufficient extent the function of the area of spiritual life that we have covered today, but before I leave you (and again, that is a relative statement)… before that percentage of my consciousness that is not you, (or not linked to you) goes back to reside in my area of existence, I would like to invite any questions.

David: Joseph, what effect does grieving have on a soul – pulling it back to the Earth plane? You gave the example of a mother who has lost a child – her grieving must have an effect on the soul that was the child by pulling it back? Also, we celebrate the war-dead every year and that must have a pull on those that died on the battlefield… and, recently, a big celebrity has died [*reference to Michael Jackson*] and millions of people have turned their attention towards him and that must have a pull on him. How do you deal with that?

Joseph: You have insects on this level and you have lions and tigers on this level (who are also influenced by the Field, but that is another story), and if you were to be chased by a lion then you would be quite traumatised as opposed to being chased by a fly.

Where you are in the spirit realms determines whether the thoughts of the people on Earth affect you like a lion or a fly or a microbe because, as you elevate your soul, the things of the Earth fall into perspective and their effect on you as people think of you, as relatives think of you and as people pull on you becomes in perspective to the place that you are in now versus the Earth lives that you have lived. In other words, you are far more able to cope with the signals than you would be if you were on one of the lower levels of spiritual reality where the pull is felt more like the tiger-bite than the insect-sting.

Grief is necessary. It is right that you should mourn the loss of those you love but (as you rightly say) to perpetuate that grief, to bring it out and dust it down and parade it through the streets is, again, unfortunately, an effect of the Field, because don't you look at those who have fallen and say: 'They died so young!' – not seeing that they had a number of years in which they were able to influence themselves and others for the good? The Field loves a parade! The Field loves regurgitating and re-invigorating grief because it serves the Field's purposes as it reminds people of their mortality (as they see it) and stirs up negative emotions in people which add to the Field's strength. It is claimed, is it not, that these parades exist to say *we must not forget and we must see war as the evil that it really is*, but that is an illusion from the Field because what is actually happening is that the Field is drawing from that grief. If you truly did not want war *there would be no war*! So it is no use bleating and banging your drums and holding your banners and saying, 'How terrible, we must not forget!' You must *not* forget but you must also change the future now by working and saying: 'No more war! We believe in peace, therefore there is no more war.' You have to be careful of the Field because the Field works behind the scenes to perpetuate itself through those seemingly innocent activities that, on the surface, say, 'Isn't this terrible!' …but are really saying, 'Please grieve again so that I can feed from your energetic fields and I can keep you just where I want you.'

Is it right to grieve? Yes, it is, because you are in an earthly body and you miss the physical representation of the people who have moved on, but remember that you also meet them at night, that you are never separated from them and, in your soul-memory and in your times of being out of this consciousness, you know that they are perfectly alright – in fact, that they are better off than you.

Are people in the spiritual realms affected by the pull of the Earth? Yes, they are – dependent on where they are on the ladder of spiritual evolution, and for some it is difficult. For some it is as though they are being chased by a thousand or a million lions but also remember at the point that they recognise that the earthly personality is not who they really are it becomes easier for them to separate from the pull on the earthly personality rather than the pull on who they really are.

In the case of a celebrity, let us say for argument's sake that immediately they come to the spirit side of life that celebrity part is put to one side as the spirit remembers who it is (i.e. a greatly elevated soul in this particular, hypothetical case) and that soul moves on to a highly elevated level realising that the celebrity part was just a 'suit of clothes' that it was wearing. Now, the people of Earth who are grieving and who want that celebrity back simply want a 'suit of clothes' back so they direct their vibrations towards the 'suit of clothes' (that recognisable, physical part of that personality that is no longer being worn by the celebrity) so the celebrity is free of that pull and the 'suit of clothes' is perpetuated on a lower level of reality by the pulling of the people on Earth.

Do you see that, because I need to disentangle myself from Michael at this point as the energies are falling and I do not want to go into 'overdrive' on this occasion.

Chapter Six
Anger in the Spiritual Realms

Joseph: I wish to talk about anger today and the management and dissipation of anger in the spiritual realms, because many souls who make the transition from life to greater life carry with them a great deal of resentment and anger: anger that arises from jealousy or a sense of not having achieved what they felt they should have achieved whilst on Earth; anger that is directed towards others, seeing them as the source of what has gone wrong in the soul's life before they passed. Many different aspects of anger are contained within many souls.

Most souls have not thought in such a way during their lives as to drag themselves into the Lower Astral but, nevertheless, they still have anger within them that needs to be let go of.

Again, you have to 'grade' souls: there are those who come across with anger and instantly (or 'instantly' as you would measure time) realise that that anger is of no use to them; realise that *they* are the source of that anger and are instantly able to let go of it – to let it dissipate from their souls – and, therefore, move to their correct position in spiritual hierarchy, depending on how they have lived the rest of their lives and how the molecules of their spiritual bodies have elevated themselves because of challenges in life and the way in which they have met those challenges.

There are other souls who need to migrate to a higher sphere but are prevented *initially* from doing so because of the amount of anger they are holding to themselves. These souls do not find themselves in the Lower Astral; they find themselves in a half-way point, a non-sphere or 'sphere-between-spheres', which is extremely pleasant. It is comparable to the place they left before they came to the spiritual realms. It is a place of houses, trees, parklands, amusement areas and blue skies, and (compared to the life they have been living on Earth) is a lovely, refined place. Perhaps they will find themselves in a house that is very like the house they had on Earth but *perfected* – it no longer has the defects with work needing to be done to it. They find themselves in a community with other houses, other people and other races, and they find that if they attempt to walk away from the sphere and try to escape the area of the community *they are turned around*. It is as though they take a road out only to find that that road actually leads *back* into the community.

There is no escape except through evolution of the spirit ...and the evolution of the spirit they need is the release of anger, the release of aggression and the release of violence (though this is not the degree of violence you find in the Lower Astral). They are advised by higher spirits who work amongst them and are always with them (not in the personal sense that they are always next to them, but in the sense that they can be called upon at any time). They take their part in the community, they are allowed to live in their house and they are allowed to live (to all intents and purposes) what is a continuation of the life they had on Earth.

However, because they have not exorcised the anger from their souls, there will inevitably be times during which they are angry – and during those times that anger *manifests around them*. It manifests as a redness in the atmosphere; it manifests as a jaggedness in the atmosphere; it manifests as 'spikes', 'blades', 'arrows' and shards of energy that consume their immediate environment ...and their perfect house is suddenly in ruins! Their perfect house is destroyed by their anger!

Their furniture is knocked over; their roof collapses; their floors collapse; their trees are pushed over and they find themselves sitting there in a ruin. Then an advisor explains to them that this is the effect of their anger on their environment (in reality, on their *soul* because that anger is containing their soul and not allowing their soul to expand). When they have calmed down (not because of the action of the higher spirits around them but because of their own actions) their house re-integrates, their furniture is righted, their garden is perfect again… they have roofs, floors and a house once again.

In another example, it is inevitable within this community that one spirit will direct anger against another. When that happens the same red energy and discord erupt but they find they cannot direct anger against another because, again, it is turned back on them and they feel constricted. From their point of view, as they become angry towards another, they feel their world is being disintegrated. They are not harming themselves in terms of physical pain but are restricting themselves by taking away the essence or sweetness from their life. For the time they are being angry towards another it is as though their life is robbed of its finer qualities, its joy and its flavour. They find themselves in isolation, as though everyone around them has been pushed away and they are within a band of restriction or tight energy that they have created. The only people who can reach within that band of tight energy on a mind-level are the helpers, who are sprinkled throughout the community, and they advise the angry soul to relax and to let go of the anger. The moment they do so that constricting band disappears and their life (this very good life in a sphere that is a beautiful place when not agitated by anger) is brought back to them.

So, little by little, they are taught and shown the effects of their anger and (rather like the road that leads out only to turn round and come back) everything in this sphere reacts to bring any *less than loving* actions back to them. Their anger is always directed back to them so that they harm their own environment, so that they cut themselves off from others and so that they learn that **they can do no harm to anyone other than themselves.**

Eventually (sometimes within a short amount of time; sometimes within a great deal of time) they realise that anger is not a good idea – not good for the evolution of their soul. You would be surprised at how long it sometimes takes a soul to realise this and, when their house is in ruins, when they have cut themselves off from other people, they initially say, 'See – *that* is why I am angry! I am angry because everything is against me – the environment is against me and the people around here are against me!' They continue to project it onto someone else, which in turn brings more of the destruction and upset to themselves ...but at some stage they break the cycle. At that point they are ready to move on and they see the sphere for what it is. It is as though they are looking at a training camp or a school and they see that they no longer need to be in that house and they no longer need to be in that community. Those houses and that community are very close in form to the Earth and they no longer need that aspect of perception and are ready to move on to the higher spheres.

There is also help given to those who cause their own illness through anger and who perpetuate that illness in belief when they reach the spiritual realms. I have to relate this to an earlier chapter about hospitals on the spiritual side of life [*reference to Chapter 5*] and cross-reference to this chapter the fact that first of all we have to manage the soul's perception of itself as being ill. Then, once the soul has released its view of illness as being reality, if that soul is also angry the soul has to take itself into the sphere I have just described. There they can work out that anger and see how anger has affected them and caused the imbalance in their physical system that resulted in illness whilst they were on Earth and their belief in illness since they left the Earth plane.

The evolution of souls can be quite a slow business (like the drip of water onto a stone in the case of some souls) to get them to reach a point where they can evolve to the stage where their vibrations are in harmony with the sphere around them.

Anger is such a major factor in the psyche or makeup of many souls who leave the Earth plane. It is a fear response; it is a response to feeling inadequate; it is a responsibility response in which anger is directed towards others and to objects and situations to avoid that soul (at soul-level) having to take personal responsibility for its own evolution and wellbeing. The advisors who work in the area where spirits are slowly trying to rid themselves of anger, and who also work in our hospitals, have to tread very carefully in awakening the souls to the spiritual reality within of each soul being responsible for the place it is in and its perception of its surroundings because, if they are *not* very careful, the soul's anger is directed towards those who are attempting to help and (because you cannot harm anyone in the spiritual realms) that anger is then pushed back towards the soul. It is a cycle of anger.

We can conclude this examination of the problems we have with angry souls by asking souls on Earth to examine their angers. We understand perfectly that you are under extreme pressure: you are under the pressure of the Field; you are under the dictates of society; you are (in many cases) an angry person surrounded by angry people, but you need to understand that anger holds you back – both in the physical world on Earth and in the spiritual realms. You need to understand the nature of anger *before* you come here, which will save you (and us) so much work and so much pain – allowing you to live in an enlightened sphere that much more quickly.

Anger is a fear response; anger is a responsibility response; anger is a response when you feel that the universe, in your view, is not delivering to you what it should, but anger is not the way to obtain that which you need. The way to obtain that which you need is to accept that *you already have it and don't need it.*

Please examine your angers as you read this book. Where do they come from? If they come from other people seemingly agitating you, *don't allow them to agitate you.* Let go of your need to be justified and to be accepted *fairly* by the other person – that will not happen if they

97

are angry towards you because their anger is a need for them to be justified by you. It is a treadmill; it is a wheel within a wheel; it is a situation that can never be halted until someone stops being angry.

Stop being angry!

I will try and answer questions, although both Michael and I have expended a great deal of energy – is there anything, dear friends, that you would like to ask?

David: Joseph, besides the sphere that deals with anger is there another sphere that deals with fear or some other aspect inhibiting spiritual progression?

Joseph: You would be surprised, David, at how many aspects of the human soul that go wrong can be attributed to anger, and once anger is let go of – fear (in most cases) is also let go of.

It is quite a complex set-up because each area (I should not call the anger sphere a 'sphere' – really it is an *area* within a greater sphere) is set up to help take out of the soul (with the soul's volition) one aspect of that soul that needs to be refined and dispensed with. Within those areas we have specialists: we have spirits who counsel, illustrate, advise and listen to different aspects of the human psyche and who deal with anger, with bitterness, with fear and with a sense of loss.

If I might just go off at a tangent briefly to talk about loss: many souls on Earth (because they do not believe in a life after death) believe that their relatives who have pre-deceased them have gone forever and when they get to the spiritual realms they cannot see their relatives, even though those people are standing right next to them... and they have to be counselled out of that belief.

Anger is a belief and a perception; fear is a belief and a perception; loss is a belief and a perception and there are many, many souls who have not placed themselves in the Lower Astral but, nevertheless, have aspects of their personalities they need to refine before they can move on to a higher sphere.

It is a malleable area and you have to understand that the spirit goes through a number of experiences, and at one moment can find itself in the community where it learns about anger but in another moment can find itself facing a fear situation and ridding itself of fear, or a bitterness situation and relieving itself of bitterness. All this can take place whilst they are in a house that is very similar to the house they lived in on Earth but which changes according to the needs of that soul to divest itself of certain aspects of its personality that it has solidified, as it were, whilst on Earth. So a person living in that area will have many experiences within its home and within its community and also many experiences with people who talk to it, who counsel it and who work with it.

Once the soul has moved on, this situation (which might have seemed to take place over a number of months or years) will be viewed as a flash or a half-memory. It will seem to have taken place extremely quickly once the soul has moved on beyond it.

We could, in fact, with this book, turn it into a volume that would be impossible to open because it would be too thick – but, yes, there are other 'applications' that a soul needs to move into in order to rid itself of certain beliefs. Then, of course, there is the ferocity – or not – of its beliefs. Some souls (as I have said) let go of anger and fear instantly, whilst other souls are so ingrained with those beliefs that it takes quite a long process in order to take them out of it. Is that a sufficient answer, David?

David: Yes, thank you.

Tony: Can I ask something on the same lines, Joseph, as a therapist working with patients? If there is an area in the spirit realms where anger is dealt with, does that mean that when souls reincarnate back to the Earth they come in 'clean' of all anger so that they start their present lifetime freed of that negative state of anger?

Joseph: Souls *choose* to come back to the Earth plane and the Field stores within itself certain harmonies that have reacted with the soul whilst the soul has been on Earth. As we have said in other communications, souls often come back because they feel that they have unfinished business; they feel they have to return to certain situations that are so pressing to them that they are blinded to the option of elevating themselves through the spiritual spheres.

Once a soul reincarnates that soul has, within its lifespan-energy, certain prerogatives, certain goals, certain challenges, and those challenges may be – as *you* have chosen to do – to approach people and make them aware of the very things we are talking about at the moment. However, once the soul is brought back into physicality the soul, drawing on its soul-memories, activates (to a lesser or greater extent depending on its spiritual awareness) the dominant vibrations from its former existences that have caused it to come back in the first place.

So every soul is clean but every soul is tainted. Every soul is clean because, if you divorce that soul from the Earth plane, it is a beautiful, perfect, evolved soul …but every soul is tainted because when it dips itself back into the 'bowl of dye' some of the dye taints it.

As a spiritual therapist (not the peripheral therapists who deal only with the surface problems) you are requested to use your spiritual perception and to listen to the guiding influences who are helping you and channelling information to you, and to listen to your own perception so that you form heart-mind pictures of what is *truly* wrong with the person – and you must trust those images. This is nothing to do with seeing them as who they were – it is to do with knowing instinctively where their problems lie: 'This person has a problem due to a relationship in the past – not in this life. That person has a problem due to a violent act that happened to that person – not in this life but in a past life.'

Then, in a way that person can understand (often without opening up what your perception is) you have to relate that incident to their *present* perception and clear it. In other words, you have to say to them: 'Do you feel very angry?' or 'Do you feel that people have been violent to you?' without mentioning the soul's history. Then, once they relate to what you are saying, you can rid them of the connection to the vibration because it is always *the connection, through volition, to the vibration* that causes the problem. In any illness and imbalance it is connection, through volition, to a belief in imbalance that the illness is caused. Once you disconnect that thread, the illness is cured. Does that make sense, Tony?

Tony: That is incredibly good, thank you.

Joseph: I wish I could go deeper and I will attempt to go into greater detail at a time when we have more energy. The soul is a beautiful, blameless thing but, unfortunately, it places itself in an illusion that it has been in before and aspects of what has happened to it before are within its soul-memory. At the moment that it takes up and chooses to select that soul-memory, the connection is made with a similar vibration and you have a recurrence of what has happened to that soul in the past – albeit in a different guise but exactly the same occurrence because the soul is always pulling towards itself that which it *remembers* on a soul-level and not necessarily on a conscious level. Does that also make sense?

Tony: Yes, absolutely. Thank you.

Jane: Joseph, could I ask what sparks the anger off in people in this sphere, because here on Earth a lot of our anger is from the irritation of the Field and other people, but if you were in a lovely situation in the spirit realms with a beautiful house and gardens there would be nothing to spark the anger off – or is it because of their memories of the past?

Joseph: That is an excellent question and one which we must re-address because the anger on this level and in the cleansing levels can be summed up in two words...

...And what are those two words?

...The Fall.

All anger, all violence, all disharmony, all power seeking comes from the Fall. The natural state of the soul is one of bliss and the natural state of the soul is one within which anger does not exist. The anger, disharmony and *abrasion* that you see around you (but also within this area of space) is caused by the Fall.

Energy-volition applied to energy tears down and builds up – that is its nature. But destruction or re-integration of matrixes of energy should not be violent and is not violent outside of this area (no matter what your scientists say – they do not understand at this moment). Destruction (which is a terrible word) is really the re-integration of patterns that are no longer required back into *Everything That Is*. That is how simple destruction is.

Destruction *after* the Fall is destruction plus the agitated vibrations of the Fall that give rise to the process being violent, and the Fall gave rise to disharmony between souls and to violence and anger between souls ...but that is a book we are going to write, isn't it? [*Reference to the book on the Fall*].

I must extricate myself from Michael.

I love you and I love the Earth and I *love* our time together.

Chapter Seven
The Life Review

Joseph: Today's chapter is of vital importance – it is of vital importance from the spiritual side of things, and it is of vital importance to you, the reader of this book, because today's chapter deals with *contemplation*.

There comes a time after the soul has moved into the higher spheres of existence when it needs to withdraw from its surroundings to contemplate its existence to that point – to contemplate what it has achieved and where it wants to go. There is a plane on the spiritual side of life where souls can go to, and, depending on the evolution of the soul, for certain souls this is a process of going inwards, whereas other souls need to be led and need to externalise their experience of life to this point.

For those who are evolved souls it is a matter of withdrawing into a vibration of peace so that their physical life can be reviewed and viewed again. For those who are not ready and who have not accomplished the ability to view their life dispassionately from within, it is necessary for the spirits around them to lead them into the process. Sometimes this needs to be done very gently because a spirit will say, 'I don't want to view my life. I want nothing to do with my past life!' – especially if that life has been traumatic and particularly challenging in a way that they do not want to view again. So we very gently have to say to them, 'That's alright – in your own time. We will come back to you at a future date when you tell us that you *want* to contemplate what you have done.'

There is, within each soul, the need to contemplate their lives and the need to understand what they have achieved. Many souls still operate for a time with a human view of their past life and this current life in a spiritual sphere, and say, 'Thank goodness! Thank God (literally) that I have escaped that life now, and I have no wish to review and revisit it, thank you very much!' But that is still something of the physical mind; it is a remnant of physicality that is saying this to them, and within their soul (not from us forcing them, but within their soul) there is a need and compunction to actually view what they have done, where they are and where they are going.

...And slowly but surely, as souls relax in the spheres (the pleasant spheres they find themselves in) there comes the demands of an inner voice. You can call it 'conscience' if you like, because that same inner voice operates on Earth – and it is the voice of the soul, the voice within the soul, or the God-within speaking to them, saying, 'In order for you to come back to Me, you need to see which point on the journey you are at. You need to look at the map and to see the points that are leading you back to your starting point, your origination, to your issuing forth from Me.'

So this voice begins within them, and for many of them it is like reconnecting with the voice of conscience which they had on Earth and stifled. There is a growing unrest with these souls. They find themselves in the most pleasant of surroundings; somewhere where they feel they can live forever (but are not allowed to) and this voice begins again – something they thought they had dispensed with, something that urges them to look at their lives and brings into their minds visions of things that perhaps they want to forget, visions of things that they thought they shouldn't do whilst they were on Earth... and here they are being presented with them again in an area where *no one is judging them*. And that is the most frightening thing, because we do not judge them; the people who are around them in the sphere they are existing in do not judge them... *they begin to judge themselves* ('judge' is the wrong word...). They begin to *stimulate* themselves and to say, 'Well, I must see what I have done.'

We, of course, can read this; we can look at the souls who are coming to the point when they must withdraw into contemplation to review their lives because it is painted on them as a light, as a vibration, and we see something of the earth-light in that vibration and something of their soul in that vibration. In other words, were you to see through our eyes a soul that is ready for contemplation, you would see a vibration that didn't 'fit in' with their surroundings and didn't 'fit in' with them. It is difficult to explain because you would have to view it to understand it and you cannot view such a thing with your earthly senses. Suffice to say that we know when a soul is ready and we are around that soul – not pressing, not coaxing, not cajoling but waiting for that soul to say, 'I cannot stand this any more. What do I do?'

At that point we talk to them again as we have talked to them in the past and say: 'It is time to review your life... If you want any peace then you need to contemplate your life.' Maybe they are not ready to do so and go away again for a period of time, but slowly and surely the voice within them (which is *their voice – God's voice*) becomes so loud, so overwhelming, that they can no longer enjoy their spiritual surroundings and are forced to do something about it *from within*.

At that point (often in tears, often terrified) they say, 'Please help me!' and at that point there is help from the angelic sphere and there is help from the guides of the spirit who wishes to do something about the clamour of this inner voice. We lead them (although it is an instant thing) out of the sphere they are existing in into a dream-world (I know they are all dream-worlds but there is a difference of feeling). It is as though they are surrounded by molecules, by atoms that calm them and distance them from the Earth life they have lived and from their present life in one of the spiritual spheres; it is as though they enter a dream-like state where nothing is quite real and where they feel a little anaesthetised.

In this dream-like state there is angelic help because there has to be a connection to the *highest* vibration and, if they cannot obtain that from within, it has to come at this stage from without (until, through successive incarnations and experiences, they have reached the point where they can review their life from within and do not need this angelic bridge). So there is an angelic connection to them and a guide connection to them and they are led to somewhere that makes sense to them. Usually it is one of the halls we have in the spirit realms; usually it is a big, imposing building ('imposing' is the wrong word, because it is welcoming – it is not like one of your courts on Earth, for example. It is a building that has... a *sense of occasion* to it... is what I want to say). They are accompanied by us and by their angelic influence into this building and there they are led into a chamber, and their perception of the chamber depends on their evolution as a soul: some see it as a simple room with a table and chairs and some see it as Infinity around them – it depends on how they view their existence and how they view themselves.

And, *with great love*, we – and a hierarchy of spirits they cannot see, and the angelic influence that is with them – access the record of the life they have just lived, as contained within their soul and accessible with permission within the field of energy that their soul exudes; a record of everything that that soul has done from the minute of its individualisation (which, again, is a misnomer) or its expulsion from the Godhead to the present day (we will talk about this at a later date). Everything is contained and everything is readable: every heartbeat; every thought; every intention; every fear; every dream; every pain; every smile; every act of kindness. *Everything!* Not only that, everything that that soul has experienced *outside of its field* is also contained within its soul: every sight; every number-plate; every window; every drop of rain... **everything is there to be viewed and reviewed.** Not as you would view a television set or a film but (because the soul-memory contains *every* holistic view of what has happened to that soul) everything can be reviewed with its original intentions, emotions, feelings and sensations. In other words, the life that was an illusion (but *so real* as an illusion) is available for viewing in fullness once again. The only difference between the soul viewing it as an illusion and *re-viewing* it as an illusion is that this time they are aware, whilst being in the review, that they are also *outside* of the review.

So, the process begins and the soul may feel that it is reviewing its life in the finest detail *for a few moments*, or may feel that it is reviewing its life in the finest detail *for years* – as though it is reliving the life but viewing it again. At any time, if it becomes too painful for the soul, we can stop (as it were) the 'recording', withdraw the soul, place the soul in a kind of peace and sleep or talk to that soul and then start the review again from that point onwards.

As the life unfolds *around* the soul, this time because the soul is a viewer (just as we are viewers when working with yourselves or working with the Earth plane) the soul can see the *effects spiritually* of what it has done and the decisions it has made – the effects upon *itself* in terms of colour-vibration, in terms of what it has attracted to and repelled from itself because of the choices it has made, but also in terms of *what it has done to others*. Remember, the soul is now reviewing its own life (it is not living that life with the blindness of being encased in physical matter) so it can see as a soul the pathways it has created for others, and those pathways are presented to it in greater detail. For example, if a soul has humiliated someone they will remember within their soul-memory having humiliated that someone but, when reviewing and contemplating their life, they are also allowed to see the results of that humiliation on the soul they have humiliated and the souls that that soul has touched – because what you see physically is only part of the pattern. If you upset someone there are ramifications and there are extensions of that upset into the ether and into the lives of other souls and, because you are the instigator of that pattern, you are connected to the whole pattern – not just to the point at which you humiliate someone. So now, looking at its own life from the viewpoint of a spiritual realm, the soul is allowed to see the full story.

Similarly, if the soul has done good, has sent positive vibrations to someone or has instigated a positive pathway – the effects of that positive pathway are shown in full. Maybe they only said a word or two to someone but that word is carried out to make that soul feel better… and the souls that that soul touches feel better.

All these pathways are shown to the soul as the review of the life unfolds, and you may say, 'Well, this seems such a complicated and vast procedure,' – and, yes, from your viewpoint it is, but it is a procedure that, from the soul's viewpoint, makes sense. I can only say to you that it makes sense; the complexities of it are taken care of by those behind the scenes and the soul viewing its own life feels that the process is quite natural, flowing and of use and benefit to them.

You can imagine that there is a great deal of upset with certain lives: there is a great deal of anger, there is a great deal of sadness and there is a great deal of embarrassment because here is the soul embarrassing itself by its own actions. Not so much embarrassment because it is surrounded by us (who are also helping the soul to view its life) but embarrassment that it could have caused so much upset and so much pain; could have been so brutal; could have been so blind; could have been so cold. Again at points we sometimes have to withdraw that soul from the review of its own life and administer to it, counsel it, talk it through the situations that it is seeing and explain to it that what it is seeing is not a critical analysis of its life but is an analysis of its life *to enable it to decide how best to evolve next*. The triumphs and the pitfalls of a life are there, after all, to enable a soul to progress and evolve. So we have to, in a way, encourage the soul to be dispassionate, to view its life as though it is watching a drama and to look out for the flaws and the successes in the drama.

As the life unfolds and comes to a conclusion, the soul is then given some time to contemplate its life, and again we add vibrations of love and peace and an almost anaesthetic or divorced quality from the rest of Creation for a time to that soul's aura so that the soul can contemplate what the life has been about. At this point there is also input from the Lords of Karma (on an intuitive level with souls who are not able to talk to them directly) to show the implications of the life, to show the patterns of the life and to indicate to that soul whether that life has been one of upliftment, or one of stasis, or one where damage has been done to others unnecessarily, or where damage has been done to that soul that has inhibited that soul's spiritual growth and understanding.

There is a plane of contemplation where the soul needs nothing other than to contemplate. It doesn't require surroundings; it doesn't require comfort through manifestations of chairs, and beds, and grassy meadows and that type of thing – it requires contemplation on its own life.

Then there comes a point where we can look at the soul's vibration and see that it has absorbed all it can from viewing that life and at that point it is returned to its original point in the spirit realms, but with the knowledge of what it has seen. The knowledge of having viewed that life and gone through that experience is contracted so that it now seems like a memory with a conclusion in terms of what must be done next presented to the soul. So the soul knows that it has gone through the experience of viewing its life but the *greater reality* is the conclusion of that within that soul. In other words, the soul knows it has gone through its life review, it has 'results' in its hands – it has a report (like a school report, but it is an internalised school report) and the review of the life is a distant memory but the report *looms large*.

Before I move on to what happens next, I must talk about the souls who do not *need* to go through this type of life review. These are souls, such as yourselves[1], who have attained a degree of spiritual knowledge

111

and have evolved to a certain point. Your review of your life will be a far more condensed affair, and you will be able to choose to review that life at an earlier point than the souls who have had to be prompted through their own conscience to do so. You will withdraw into a field of contemplation, and your friends and loved ones and your group-soul members will be connected to you, and the review of your life will be over quite quickly because you are bringing spiritual reason and understanding to the review of that life. You already know what it is about, you already know what you are looking for and you already realise that you are not that person that is in that life you are reviewing (you are the soul that adopted the persona for a time in order to evolve but you realise that you are not that person). You have your spiritual knowledge and memory back and the affair is a quick one. It is an easy one and it is nothing that should be worried about.

Let us return now to the souls who have undergone this extended version of life review. They have a report and we do not write upon that report: 'Must do better!' – we write on that report (or God, working through us, writes on the report): 'Here is the way to come back to Me. *Here is the way to come back to Me* through certain experiences you need to understand something about love.'

Every life review ends with that simple terminology in your terms: **You need to understand something more about God's love that is already within you.** If a soul has been violent, they need to understand more about love; if a soul has been cruel, they need to understand more about love; if a soul has been unable to reach out to others, they need to understand more about love; if a soul has been harsh to themselves, they need to understand more about love. From (in your terms) the greatest criminal or dictator to the person who says the odd sharp word, in both cases the soul *needs to understand more about love* and that is the only conclusion of a life report – but is the *degree* that changes and it is the means of understanding more about love that are infinitely different.

So, it is suggested to that soul that they can stay in the sphere they find themselves in for as long as they want. But, again, the inner voice – as the memory of the Earth life is gradually stripped away – that voice from within says to the soul (and it is the soul's own voice and God's own voice), 'It is time to do something!' A yearning begins; a yearning to be closer to God (not closer in distance but closer in feeling and in essence to God). A yearning slowly but surely emerges from that soul. They may stifle it for a hundred years, or a thousand years, or a million years but sooner or later they have to move on in some way. At the point where again we can see their vibration is ready to make that choice to move on, to do something about their life and to evolve further, then we are with them instantly. They find themselves talking to us and we suggest ways in which they can evolve, ways in which their past experience has held them back and areas in which they need to expand.

...And the key question at this point is: do we advise them to go back to the Earth? Here we will differ with many books you will read, with many doctrines you will hear of and with many beliefs you will hold, because – *no, we do not*. Let this be written large in your book:

NO, WE DO NOT!

At this point we pray that they will choose to move on through the spiritual spheres without returning to Earth.

Again at this point you have to understand that the soul has free will, and we advise the soul of every consequence of their choices at this point – *every consequence* (with a bias, of course, towards the soul moving away from physicality) – but the soul has free will. With far too many souls, because of their beliefs whilst they have been on Earth that they have not yet got rid of (also, in some cases, belief in reincarnation or belief that they *have to* come back), they say, 'I want to choose the rocky path.'

How amazing!

Here is a smooth path: it is a gentle slope; it takes you upwards; you can interact with other souls to express love more readily and to eliminate those areas from yourself that are holding you back; it goes through beautiful meadows; it goes up the mountain *gently* into the sunlight – into the God-Light.

Here you have the heavy path, the rocky path, the path of physical pain, the path of mental anguish.

Which do you choose?

...And so many souls say, 'I choose the rocky path' – not because it is noble but because it is *known.*

Do you see that? The gentle path up the mountain is unknown (or, at least, unknown to their consciousness – it is known to their God-consciousness but not to their consciousness at this present time) and, because the rocky path is known and has its attractions (remember that we are dealing with the lives of many souls, some of whom are *almost* ready to take the smooth path but many are not), when souls see their life review, many of them are so attracted to some of the things they have been used to that are no longer available (because they are no longer necessary on the spiritual planes) they want *more.*

They want more!

They want particular physical objects again; they want particular physical sensations again, and also in looking at their life many of them do not understand that the life review is showing them areas where they need to expand and where they need to express love more. Instead of seeing this, they see only *unfinished business* and things they wish they had completed. Because they have been locked into a material cycle, they see everything as having a beginning and an end

114

and if, according to them (not according to God or to us) they have left their life with certain things unconcluded, they want to go back to conclude them... despite the fact that those situations no longer exist, despite the fact that many of the people they are looking at in that life review have also moved on to spiritual planes and despite the fact that we (with love) tell them again and again that there are no beginnings and endings in the human sense – there is only a stream of consciousness and experience, and you cannot fit everything into a box and lock it up and say, 'That is concluded.'

So many choose to come back, and when they choose to come back, when the decision has been finally and absolutely made and we say to them, 'Are you sure?' and they say, 'Yes,' they begin to take on human characteristics again at that point. They say: 'Yes,' with an *anger*. 'Who are you to interfere?' ...They are already pulling themselves back towards the Earth plane through free will.

Then, reluctantly, they are taken to a waiting area – an area where their consciousness of who they are becomes masked again, becomes muddied, becomes misted... and with certain patterns programmed into their physical field they are drawn back into physical incarnation.

You must remember that we *use* that physical life. ...We use that physical life to teach the soul more about love so that eventually it can come out of the physical life. The life is not wasted; it is simply lengthening the time which it is taking for *all souls* to leave the physicality of the Earth so that the Earth can be renewed and restored to what it once was – a *playground* for souls. I do not mean that in the kiddie or toddler sense, I mean a playground as in a ground of reality – a field of reality – wherein souls can play to find out more about themselves and to react with each other.

So they are drawn back

But then you have for other souls a determination to move on, an opening of the eyes and a falling away of the scales with regard to the Earth life so that that soul knows finally and totally that it does not want to return (except, perhaps, to *help*) and that soul can then move on into further spiritual realms. We will cover those spiritual realms at a later date. The mechanics of how the other souls are drawn into incarnation are not really part of this book but we will cover them in another talk at another time.

There has been a great expenditure of energy this morning to put across what is an exact and complex procedure. I will try to answer questions but I may have to pull Michael back in so that we do not damage him. I cannot guarantee, but please ask what you want to ask.

Jane: Could I ask a question about entities and energy-feeders? Is it taken into account in the life review that somebody was more bad tempered and badly behaved because they had things stuck to them that they didn't know about?

Joseph: You must remember that, although an entity or energy-feeder (as you correctly called them) can change the *mood* of someone, ultimately they cannot change the *soul* of someone. So, there has to be a degree of ability to exhibit that kind of behaviour within a soul in the first place in order for that soul to react in that way. You cannot, for example, take a vessel that is filled with White Light and expect that White Light to suddenly exude blackness from within itself. So, however difficult this seems to accept, the feeders and entities are able to stimulate that part of the soul (or that part of the human being connected to the soul) that has traits that are either genetic or linked to that soul through past lives. This may sound harsh but you are all evolving (each of you – as am I) and the aspects of your creation in physical matter and your path in physical matter are still there – not just the aspects of what you appear to be in this life but the aspects of what you have been in the past.

So, in a way (and you will find this strange) the feeders and entities are giving you an opportunity to say, 'Yes, I have been influenced in this way and I no longer like this aspect of myself,' and to grow beyond that aspect of yourself. I am not saying they are friends (they are not) but I am saying that if you deal with them in that way, if you say: 'Thank you for this opportunity. I realise I have been bad tempered (or, 'I realise that I have been violent; I realise that I have been depressed'). Thank you for showing me that I still have that tendency and now you have given me an area to work on and to move away from,' the next time you are attacked by such a parasite, the time that it influences you for will be less, because you will say: 'I recognise you! You do not vibrate at the same vibration as I do and, therefore, you have no power over me!' You will be able to divorce yourself from the effects of that parasite, which will then have to leave you because it is not getting what it wants – which is more of the disruptive vibration that it feeds on.

You mentioned 'taking into account'. It is the soul that takes into account its life – no one else. We do not take into account anything; we simply wish (as part of the human stream, the spiritual stream of energy that is streaming back to God) to educate the souls who *wish* to be educated so that they can escape the loop of incarnation they have placed themselves into. There is no accounting – except from within, except from the individual soul. Accounting is a good word because they add up what they have achieved spiritually and they add up what they have restricted themselves with spiritually... and then have to make choices.

You must remember that even upon seeing the life review certain souls do not recognise and will not accept that some of the things they are seeing are down to themselves, even though they have been shown the consequences of those things. Isn't that appalling! They do not even recognise that some of the things they see around them unfolding again (with all the sights and sensations) are part of themselves and that they are responsible for them. Do you see?

Jane: Yes, thank you.

Joseph: Who else, please?

David: You have mentioned in an earlier chapter the area in the spirit world where people can just be sat on a bed doing nothing because they have done nothing with their life. When do they go through this life review? Do they just sit there until eventually something happens within their soul that says, 'I need to move on!' and at that point you can help them to go through that life review?

Joseph: That is exactly what happens!

There is a deceit on Earth. Say on Earth you kill someone and remove all your fingerprints from the room; then you drive away from the town and get on an aeroplane; then you change your appearance through plastic surgery and you live in a completely different house and you speak a different language and no one knows about it. The problem is: *you know about it*. On a conscious level that might not bother you but on a sub-conscious level you know there is a problem and, because you are a soul and you have a dialogue with your subconscious level, you are constantly telling yourself that this problem needs to be addressed and sorted out. You might have the most arrogant and most unfeeling conscious level but your soul will chip away at that – chip, chip, chip away at it – until one day the voice begins to emerge, and you may put yourself in a bed in the spirit world and look out of the window, read your books, drink your beer (figuratively speaking) and watch the television that you have created... but there is no escape.

Ultimately, Reader, **there is no escape from yourself** and you know what you have done; you know whether it advances you or retards you and that knowledge will surface. I say this to those who are smugly feeling that they have 'got away with things' – **you get away with nothing!** We do not hold you to account – *you* hold *you* to account,

118

and sooner or later (whether you lie in that bed for a thousand or a million years) the voice will emerge and you will not be able to live with yourself until something has been done about it.

I feel that that has answered what you have asked.

David: Thank you.

Jane: Could I ask a question, Joseph, concerning not wanting people to come back to Earth (and I am playing devil's advocate here): in view of the probability that mankind will destroy the Earth in three generations' time if we don't change our ways, if that catastrophe did happen – wouldn't that be a good thing from a spiritual evolution point of view because it would force people to progress in the spirit realms?

Joseph: Are you suggesting that souls come back to accelerate the apocalypse?

Jane: No, not at all. I mean if the apocalypse *did* happen wouldn't that have the advantage of there no longer being the option to come back to Earth so people would *have to* get on with it in the spirit realms?

Joseph: You are forgetting that the souls that are involved in the end of civilisation are placed (through their own volition, through the effects of the Fall and through that memory) in a 'no place' until such time as the planet can sustain them again and they are incarnated in physical matter to begin the process of evolution out of that physical matter a further time. It would result in a state of affairs where those souls were for a long time unreachable, until such time as they were able to reincarnate again and we could send amongst them points of Light to accelerate their spiritual knowledge and *this time round* hopefully to convince them that there is a better way than the society and the matrix of the new Field that they would inevitably form. Because of the effects of the Fall the Field that is formed when a new civilisation is born is subject to the memories of the souls that are reincarnating again. There is the point of danger – not just that civilisation at present could come to an end... but that the civilisation that is *subsequently* formed will repeat the same mistakes because it will be drawing on that energy that comes from that field of stasis rather than from the higher spiritual realms.

Doomed to repeat itself – unless we can change consciousness!

Doomed to repeat itself – individually and globally, nationally and internationally!

It has happened before more times than your myths tell you. This is why there is an urgency to our work – we are trying to liberate souls. We are trying to rectify the effects of the 'experiment' that went wrong and trapped souls within a Field that is negative. It sounds like a simple equation (and, from our viewpoint, it is) but from your viewpoint, encased within that negative Field, it is almost an impossible task. We have to liberate souls, not send them back to the Field that is imprisoning them. Do you see that?

Jane: Yes, but do they have to come back to a physical field? Couldn't they just progress in the spirit realms or are there still some people in limbo that haven't come out from the darkness from the Fall? Why have they got to go through a physical existence?

Joseph: Once – and *if* – civilisation exterminates itself and comes to an end then those souls that are still trapped within the thinking of the Fall – those souls that have not elevated themselves sufficiently to escape the cycle of existence on and around the Earth plane *have nowhere to go*. They are in a non-existence for a time. They are, in effect, asleep. They are still individualised and they still exist but they have nowhere to go. They do not accept the existence of spiritual realms above the one that they have just left and so we cannot (and are not allowed to) manipulate them because of free will. We can only allow them to exist in that stasis-state until an expression of existence that is suitable for them is prepared, until the Earth has replenished itself to such an extent that it can sustain them once again (or some other planet if the Earth's existence is itself coming to the point of cataclysm from which it cannot regenerate). They are then drawn – because they are closer to a physical existence than to a spiritual existence – back into physical existence. Also interwoven with that drawing back into physical existence there are the effects of the Fall that have not yet been acknowledged and worked out of their systems, so they have to go through a process... and the part of the process that we are trying to eliminate is the part that involves civilisation destroying itself and having to come back. Do you see?

Jane: Yes, I do – thank you.

Joseph: Is there something from you, Mark?

Mark: Yes. Are there people or beings that have influence on Earth that have an agenda to keep people reincarnating and preventing them moving up into the spiritual spheres?

Joseph: That is an excellent question and that is why we fear so much when the soul says, 'I want to go back!' because it is as though the soul finds itself between two poles. There is a magnetic pull from the Earth and there is a magnetic pull from God. The soul is at a point between those two poles and, yes, it is in the interest of the Earth plane (as it exists at the moment) to keep those souls deprived and depraved.

Now, most souls that reincarnate are not those who will do great wrong to others but they can, nevertheless, be influenced by the darkness of the Field to buy into the illusions of illness, the illusions of possession, the illusions of lack so that they are always questing for power. These things can pull the soul back but remember that the soul has volunteered to go back to the Earth plane – *volunteered* to go back into that Field, so the soul wants it at that point. This is why there is such a movement from the higher planes; this is why God allows souls to be influenced by guides and by intuition to move out of that darkness. It can take many, many lifetimes for the souls who are violent and who wish violence, wish cruelty and wish the negative aspects of life, to come to a point where they are *conscious* of a soul-life – so steeped are they in the effects of the Field.

The Field must change! We work to change the Field by changing the souls who are at present in the Field and who are going back into the Field so that they can take with them (as well as the desire to conclude situations that they feel they have not successfully concluded) something of Light that will come out during their life. It is almost like sneaking a virus into a computer so that the virus affects the 'software' – affects the Field. The virus that we seek to put into the Field is one of Light and we do not seek to corrupt the Field, we seek to cleanse the Field because the Field is a negative piece of software… but a negative piece of software that is also sentient because it is being contributed to by millions of souls every day.

It is in the interest of the Field that is drawing energy from those souls to maintain itself as it is – to maintain itself as a negative Field and so, yes, it draws on those souls. But what we try to do in the time that the souls who are not spiritually aware (to a great extent) are back here with us is to teach them and to bring into their lives some knowledge they can take back with them, which (combined with the patterns of karma that are woven into that soul's physical bubble) will bring Light – not only to that soul during its incarnation but Light into the Field.

You see the task we have – that you have – when you have millions of souls influenced by the negativity of the Field and just points of Light here and there. But fear not because for every point of Light, it takes thousands of souls to dim that Light. **The Light is the only reality.** The Light is more powerful than the darkness and it is the Light that we are working to bring into people's souls.

Michael is approaching again and is intermingling with my communication. I must say that this chapter is not complete in that we have to talk about souls who voluntarily go back to work for the Light but I will add that on at a future date. I do not wish to take advantage of the instrument to that extent today so that he will be completely depleted – especially when we have another opportunity to talk to people in a week's time and his energy is required for that [*reference to a public trance demonstration*].

So, God bless! My deepest joy and love to each of you and thank you for continuing to fight for the cause that is, ultimately, *the only cause*.

[1] Here, Joseph is referring to the four members of the circle.

Chapter Eight
The Nature of Appearance in the Spiritual Realms

Joseph: I would like to talk this morning about appearance, because one of the burning questions of your readership must be: how do people *appear* on the spirit side of life? Are they human in appearance? Do they have a body? Do they have a consciousness similar to earth-consciousness? How does one person recognise another person?

I have to tell you that *initially* the point of recognition of one spirit to another is exactly the same as it is on Earth. In other words, when you pass from this world into one of the other worlds, initially you will be *as you are now*: you will have a body with arms, legs, hands and feet, and a head with eyes, ears, nose, mouth and hair. You will be exactly as you are now but you must understand that the projection of yourself now on Earth is simply that – *a projection*. It appears to you (because you are surrounded by dense matter) to be solid, when really it is nothing of the sort – it is a projection from your soul. So, when you leave the earthly life to re-instate life on the spiritual levels you will also have a body but, because that body is a projection, you can alter it as you see fit. For example, if you leave this world without teeth or hair and covered in wrinkles, you can re-instate a vision of yourself at a younger point in your earthly life before these things happened to you. So, there are advantages to being 'dead' (I say this with great humour and a smile because, of course, you are *not* dead), and those advantages with regard to appearance mean that you can appear *as you wish to appear*.

125

As an aside, I must tell you that you appear as you wish to appear on Earth. You appear as an expression of your soul, your soul's energy and your reaction to life, at any point in your life. If you appear to be bowed, old, wrinkled and careworn it is because your soul accepts these things to be true and you project an image of how you are inside at your soul's source and core. So it is on the spiritual side but, freed from the cares of the Earth plane, from the heavy matter, from the stress, from the worry and from the fear, you will find it far easier to make a conscious projection from your soul out into the atmosphere around you. 'How do I do this?' you may ask. 'Do I constantly have to monitor my appearance?' No! Do you constantly monitor your appearance on Earth? You will appear as you wish to appear – a request from your soul to be, for example, thirty years of age with a full head of hair, a full set of teeth and to appear in a certain way. That projection is then accepted by your soul and projected outwards to be a point of recognition for you and a point of recognition for those around you.

You also have to understand that, because you are in a spiritual realm when you have passed from the earthly plane, you exhibit certain other aspects and impressions from your soul. The greatest of these is colour because you will project from your soul *colours* that you have put into your chakras and into your auric field. You will appear as a human being, but you will also have the *option* of showing 'your true colours' (but no option at all with regard to some of the higher spirits who will come to visit you because they can *see* your true colours). Your senses are advanced and enhanced in the spiritual worlds. You have more than just sight, sound, taste, smell and feeling – you have an increased spectrum visually; you have an increased spectrum audibly; you have an increased spectrum that you can feel and you can smell. Part of this increased spectrum (when you choose to view it and when you choose to exhibit it) is the colour you have placed into your soul through the life that you have just lived on Earth and through your lives before that one.

Now, to those in the spirit worlds who are used to these things (and this is a matter of instinct rather than of conscious appreciation) *your colours say everything about you* – the colours that you give out show others and yourself where you are on the spiritual evolutionary-ladder. The colours that you give out change: the background colours remain the same but, because the colours you can see in other people and yourself are layered, the surface colours change according to your attitude and your mood. The amazing thing, Ladies and Gentlemen, is that that is happening *now* on Earth but you cannot see it. If you are in an argument with someone on Earth your colours become discordant, angular, sharp and destructive. If you are in love with someone on Earth your colours blend with them, embrace them and mingle with the colours from their chakras and auric field. All that exists in the spiritual realms exists on Earth too – you are simply at a dense appreciation, at the moment, which does not allow you to see this.

Very quickly in the lower spiritual realms you learn that you have to guard and 'treat' your thoughts – not to hide or mask them but to work on them because your thoughts are instantly displayed in the colour-shield that you have around you. You cannot approach a person in one way and think towards them in another. There is no subterfuge – you *do* wear your colours 'on your sleeve' and those around you recognise what you are thinking, what you have thought and what you have done because of those colours.

So, do you all walk about as brightly coloured people instilling a riot of colours into the atmosphere? Well, yes, on one level you do but you can also *choose* to see people simply as human beings and filter out that aspect of colours if you do not wish to see them. You can liken it to the option in an earthly body of seeing what is straight ahead of you or turning to see what is behind you – they are two aspects of the same thing – it is your perception that changes *through choice*.

As well as colours, you also have sound around you and this, too, is an aspect of your personality that you and others can choose to tune into. Your soul is a vibration and (similar to hitting a tuning-fork and holding it against your ear) the rate of your vibration gives out a sound that can be appreciated by yourself and by others if you so wish. I say 'appreciated' – it depends on how you have progressed spiritually. If you are in harmony with others and if you have lived a harmonious life then the essence of that harmony is in your vibration and your vibration can sound like a beautiful melody. If, however, there are certain aspects of yourself that you need to work on, certain views that you are holding onto that really should be dispensed with and left behind, those attitudes, those fears, those biases and those egotistically-based aspects of yourself create little pockets of discord within the symphony of your tune. To those who are practised in the ability to listen to the harmonics of each soul those discords can be heard and identified (in conjunction with the colours that are in your aura and emanating from your chakras) to give a complete picture of who you are, where you have been and where you need to get to. Again, with this harmony and aspect of sound you will give off as a soul without a physical body there are clues to the complete story of who you are, where you have been and what you need to do to mount the steps to higher spiritual levels.

When you are in the spirit world in one of the initial realms (I do not want to say the 'lower realms' because the term 'lower realm', of course, refers to the Lower Astral we have talked about) and you are about to embark on your wonderful journey into the higher realms, you will see your guides, advisors and angels visiting these realms at times. Around and emanating from these spirits you will see immense amounts of brilliant colours and you will hear wonderful symphonies as these people visit you. This is not because they choose to flaunt the aspects of themselves that have elevated beyond the point that you are at – it is because in the realms where they live (which we will approach and examine in future chapters) they are used to showing themselves in this way, as colours and as sounds. And why should they not do so?

It is a higher expression of what they are than the physical they have left behind. They are at a more elevated – a more distant – point from the physical than a soul in one of the initial levels. Indeed, when they come to visit, they have to mask some of their vibration in order not to disturb the viewers on the initial levels and in order not to create disharmony with the vibrationary level that they are visiting. In other words, they have to come back through the passage of their spiritual evolution to a point at which their colours and sounds are dulled to a certain extent so that they can operate within the sphere they wish to visit. What you are seeing from the initial level, when you are seeing these great beings of colour, is only a pale perception of their true majesty and true brilliance.

At times you will also witness spirits visiting or travelling through these levels who appear to be very difficult to see. You will see them as a blurring of the surroundings and you will know that someone is there, but you will not be able to see great colour or hear great sound from them. Rather, there will be 'something' that you will find difficult to latch onto with your advanced perceptions. This is because you will be witnessing spirits who come from *even higher realms* and their expression of being and of self in those higher realms is so far above yours at that point that it is impossible, even with your enhanced senses, to pick them up. You will sense that there is something there but your senses will need to advance beyond that point before you can truly see what they represent and what they have achieved ...and the way that your senses will advance is through your spiritual evolution (which, again, we will talk about in future chapters).

As spirits grow away from the Earth and advance through the spiritual spheres or levels, there is less of a need for them to express themselves as human beings. The human form was only a shell that allowed consciousness to permeate the earth level in order to grow, and it is natural and right that initially the human spirit that has moved on from the Earth plane would wish to identify with itself in the form that it is used to and comfortable with. But as the human spirit progresses beyond that need it may choose to express itself simply as a vibration that identifies it as being present within the sphere that it inhabits. This is difficult, I know, for you to link onto, but what I am saying is that **there is absolutely no need for the human form as the spirit progresses.**

The spirit may choose to express itself as a ball of colour, because the circle and sphere is, of course, a reflection of the nature of God and, as the spirit grows more God-like in its perceptions and abilities, is it not natural to want to be an expression of its Creator? You say that you are made in *God's image* – and you are, but not physically. You are made in God's image vibrationally, conceptually and perceptionally; you are made in God's image in your ability. God's image (if we are trying to give an image to God, which is difficult) is, of course, *the dot within the circle*. Many of these spirits choose to express and imprint on their surroundings an image of themselves which is Light, which is a circle and which is colour. Then, at times, they will revisit their past lives and their past forms and are perfectly capable of changing from that ball of colour into an image of a man or a woman, clothed as they would have been in one of their past incarnations but with clothing made out of Light rather than fabric.

You must understand that there are also other expressions of life that the soul can go through and so why should they simply be confined to a human form? But, for the most part, in the spheres we are examining, you would see people as human beings or as balls of Light or as a consciousness. There is a point where the spirit is a consciousness and chooses not to manifest in a material or physical form at all (although those are just concepts because we are dealing with spiritual realms) and will simply be there as a 'presence', because that is the essence of the soul: to exist as a presence. At times don't those of you who are psychically aware sense your relatives from the past who have gone on to the spiritual realms and don't you sense them as a presence? And sensing that presence don't you say: 'It feels as though my father has been here,' or, 'It feels as though my sister is here,' – because, contained within that presence, is all that they are. *All that they are!* And, yes, they may be standing next to you as a spiritual being that you cannot see, but their expression comes from their soul, and you recognise, soul to soul, who they are by that vibrational signature you can sense *even now* in a physical body.

What of past lives?

What of past lives? If you are able to manifest yourself in the initial levels as who you have just been, is it not also possible for you to manifest yourself as who you have been *before* that? Yes, it is, because those imprints of who you were are within your soul's memory and experience so it is possible with training and time to also manifest yourself as who you were …but not initially (unless you are of a higher spiritual consciousness that manifests itself quickly when you come into the spirit realms). You will have access to who you were once you have examined what you have done as *who you have just been* (you must refer to the chapter on Life Review). Once the current life review has been made accessible to you then it has served its purpose – you are the spirit that is the sum of that life and all the other lives you have lived (plus, of course, you are the essence of the child of God that is none of those lives), understanding that those lives have only been a tool that you have used in order to learn, evolve and become more God-like. So, you can manifest yourself as who you were in your last incarnation and then you can manifest yourself as who you were in other lives. Surprisingly, you may feel more comfortable with an expression of who you were in a past life than with your current incarnation.

However, there is also the element of perception from other people that determines how you appear at any time. For example, you may be walking around one of the spirit realms as who you were in a past life and then you bump into someone that knew you in your most recent life on Earth. Because they are a spirit with spirit-perception and you are a spirit with spirit-perception, they will recognise your spiritual and soul vibration, which will manifest itself to them as who you were in that most recent life – unless of course [*laughing*] you knew that person in one of the previous lives and then they can see you *either* as who you were in the most recent life or who you were in one of the past lives when you and they were together …and the same applies to how you view them. You see how complex and wonderful a thing appearance is!

I have to say to you that you have to consider this in your earthly life: *appearance is deceptive*. When you view someone in front of you on Earth – your 'friend', your 'enemy', your 'relative', your 'loved one' – you are only seeing one aspect of them. The soul of that person has gone through many incarnations, many experiences, and you do not really know who you are addressing. With the people around you, were you to see who you were really addressing you would be shocked, humbled and amazed and you would change your attitude towards many people. You would approach each person and say, 'I do not know who this person is; I cannot judge them; I cannot be angry with them; I cannot feel superior to them because I do not know who they really are and what they have achieved to this point in their lives.' Appearances are deceptive – please remember that and it will help with your transformation of the physical world. *Appearances are deceptive!*

Appearances in the spirit worlds can be changed. **The only appearance that you cannot change is the appearance of *who you really are*.** …That appearance can be read by those who are more advanced than you and, as you evolve along the spiritual path, you, too, will be able to read the souls of the people around you. Why would you need to read the souls around you? Because that is the way it is – God is open; God is honest; God has no secrets. Isn't that an amazing concept?

God has no secrets!

They are all there to discover but they have to be discovered through the evolutionary spiritual path that leads back to Him. God does not hide – God is in plain sight ...and so your brothers and sisters are in plain sight. Deception, subterfuge and the hiding away of secrets is only an aspect of the Earth plane that you have become used to.

So, to sum up, you can be who you have been; you will have physical form (but it is not actually *physical* – it is a projection and you will be aware of it as being a projection); you can change your appearance as you would change a 'suit of clothes' to suit you at any time in your spiritual existence and your appearance will eventually change – and continue to change. You are taught by your physical form that your appearance is constantly changing. If you look at yourself as a baby, as a young person and as an older person you can scarcely believe that those aspects are of the same person and the same spirit ...but they are. Unfortunately, those aspects are corrupted by the effects the Field and the effects of the Fall so you are seeing only the physical change but it is still a representation of what will happen to you in the spiritual realms. You will continue to change and, in terms of earthly time, you will look back from one year to the next in the spiritual realms and hardly recognise yourself as you will have changed so much in the amount of Light that you give out, in the amount of sound that you give out and in the amount of *love* that you give out.

I think I have spoken enough. It is a very deep subject, but before we conclude this session are there any questions on the subject I have raised this morning?

Mark: Joseph, on the Earth plane when we first meet someone and have a gut feeling and instinct about that person which is contrary to their appearance, is that the true guidance that we are tuning into?

Joseph: Yes. The human spirit is masked and layered and when you meet someone it is always, initially, *soul to soul* – it has to be because that is what you are. Those of you who are spiritually gifted and enlightened, who have some measure of spiritual instinct that has not been totally masked by the Field, are aware of a burst of energy when you meet another person. Contained within that burst of energy (which is, if you like, a psychic or spiritual handshake) are all the details and dominant trends of that person at that point in time. Therefore, it is always wise to go with the instinct that you get regarding that person – not to condemn them, not to judge them, but to decide instantly (based on that information) whether that person is harmonious to your path or whether that person would present a blockage and diversion on your path that you may not need.

The problem with the spiritual instincts is that when they are intermingled with the physical, the physical mind begins to feel guilty. 'I should not be thinking in this way. I should not look at this person who is sweet, light and nice and decide that they are otherwise.' But you are not 'thinking' in that way; you are receiving facts through your heart-centre *soul to soul*; you are reading that person and that information is of value to you as a travelling and evolving soul because, if you live your life making connections and avoiding connections *dependent* on what information you initially receive soul to soul with the people you meet, you will save yourself and them a great deal of trouble. You will save yourself a great deal of trouble because you will avoid circumstances from those who are less spiritually evolved than you that would pull at you and seek to create a smoke-screen around your spiritual work and draw you back into the Field. Also, you should not feel guilty by avoiding certain people because *they* will find *you* an irritant at that point in their spiritual evolution and you would not be able to connect to them... In other words, you would not be able to elevate them to your level given all your strength and all your time because they are not yet ready for that. You have to allow those who are not as spiritually evolved to be guided by their guides working through the Field and through God working within them to teach them lessons through the experiences of the Field.

Therefore, always use the soul to soul contact (that initial burst that tells you so much and by-passes the physical mind) to determine whether or not you should make associations with certain souls. Each of you reading this, if you do that and if that information is coming from your spirit, you will save yourself a lot of upset, a lot of displeasure, a lot of side-tracking and you will evolve that much more quickly. You will allow those souls you have decided to by-pass (whilst giving them love and wishing them well) to evolve quickly, too, because they will not be distracted by someone they will feel animosity towards because they cannot connect to your vibration.

Is that a sufficient answer?

Mark: It is very clear, thank you.

Jane: This is a bit of a trivial question – if people give off a colour and a sound in the spiritual realms, do they also give off a perfume?

Joseph: There *is* a spiritual perfume and there is an olfactory resonance to the spiritual levels. You sense this sometimes in your circles when you say, 'There is a smell of something in here,' or, 'There is a sweet perfume they have brought in.' Sometimes it is because a spirit is trying to connect to a smell that was relevant in their life as an identification to someone in that circle, but sometimes it is because the sweet perfume is emanating from a guide or an elevated spirit. You are only sensing a degree of it within your circle (or within your home if you pick it up psychically) because you are using, to a certain extent, a combination of your spiritual senses and your physical senses.

But, yes, there is a perfume to every object if you wish to tune into it. You will also find that your sense of touch is different on the spiritual levels and that you can blend with objects and not just to touch them on the surface as you do usually on Earth (although on Earth you can also psychometrise objects and read their history). Is that a sufficient answer?

Chapter Nine
Endeavour in the Entry Levels of the Higher Realms

Joseph: Good morning and a greeting from the higher side of life – or, should I say, the more enlightened side of life (and by 'enlightened' I mean the side of life that has more Light apparent in its workings, in its dealings and in the way it conducts itself). Over the past few weeks we have watched the situations on Earth with great interest because, here and there, there are pockets of resistance to the Field – pockets or bubbles of Light that are trying to expand. But, for every ten bubbles of Light that exist *only* one or two come to the surface. That is because the Field dampens down anything that threatens it and also because, with many people who are working for the Light, there is an enemy within, so they fall at the first or second or third hurdle because they do not have the conviction that overcomes all the workings of the physical mind. We watch and we pray, and we add Light to the bubbles of Light – praying that one or two of them will make it and will pour enough higher energy and sufficient Light atoms into the Field for there to be a difference ...and for there to be a breeding ground for *more* bubbles or pockets of Light.

But that is not why I am here today. I just wanted to make it clear that the work continues on our level *all the time* to ensure that somewhere, somehow, Light gets into the matrix of thought that is the Field of human consciousness and the Field of human endeavour.

What I want to talk about today is 'endeavour' and its purpose in the higher realms, and I hope that the people on Earth will pay *particular attention* to this aspect of spiritual evolution.

There has to be purpose.

How often do you hear people say, 'I have no purpose'? There are some souls who come over to us and say, 'Well, if I had known that there was life after death, I would have had a purpose, but I did not perceive any purpose in my life and so I took it away,' ...only to discover that they cannot take their life away because it is not theirs to take away; it does not extinguish if the physical vehicle is separated from the spiritual body.

We look on the Earth with disdain at the present time because so few people seem to have a purpose... and that is not the fault of God or the fault of the people around these souls – it is *their* fault because they do not *strive* towards a purpose. They say, 'I don't want to do this and I don't want to do that. I do not have a goal – I simply want to sit here to vegetate and remain the same as I have always been.' They have no purpose and they have *created* that lack of purpose.

That is so sad, because when a soul comes back home to the spiritual side of life one of the first things that prompts it is a lusting or need for purpose, but also a recognition that *there is a purpose* to that soul's existence. The purpose is to expand its existence, expand its experience and expand its understanding (not mental but spiritual understanding) so that it can become aware of other planes of existence; so that it can become aware of itself as what it is but can also become aware of finer levels of reality; finer levels of *illusion*, in actual fact, that have as much cohesion to them as the Field of human consciousness does to it on a physical level.

The soul that is reborn into the spiritual realms (please note that I am not using the term 'dies into') is immediately struck by a longing, once the detritus of the physical world has been sloughed away, once the auric field has been quietened and once it has been made aware of its surroundings. It is the same longing that *all people* have on Earth but do not recognise. It is the longing to become *more*, the longing to understand *more*, the longing to experience *more* and the longing to grow. There is often an analogy of God sending forth his children as 'seeds' and that is a wonderful, perfect analogy because seeds need to grow. Unfortunately, on Earth at the moment the soil is not fertile; the soil only gives the illusion of growth. It gives the illusion of growth through the growth of the physical body; it gives the illusion of growth through the materiality that is sought for the physical body and the physical mind – but these things are of the Earth. It is the spirituality and the spiritual aspects of the 'seed' that need to be nurtured ...and they are not being nurtured on Earth at the moment.

So, there is a shock when a soul comes over and suddenly realises what it has known *as a soul* throughout its journey across the Earth plane – that it needs, wishes and has a longing to become *more* than it is at this particular point in its existence.

The need leads to all kinds of trouble for souls who are on the Earth. It leads to dissatisfaction in relationships because there is always a feeling, deep down, that *there should be something more*; it leads to dissatisfaction with employment and dissatisfaction with materiality. It is felt that there should always be something more ...but the 'something more' can only come from within and from spiritual growth.

So the soul, having been freed from the confines of the Earth plane, finds itself in a situation where it has to ask someone, 'How do I grow? I am happy – this place I find myself in is a place of Light. It is a place of beautiful trees, beautiful buildings and beautiful people. It is a place where I am freed from the problems and restrictions of my earthly life and physical body. It is all these things to me and yet I am being 'called' somewhere else – I still have a longing. How can I have a longing in such a beautiful place?'

Then the spirit is made aware, through meditation and contact with the God-within, and also through counsel with those who are 'in the know', as it were. It is explained to the soul that what it is experiencing is its need to be aware as God is aware, its need to see things as God sees things, and that that yearning to return home is a *jewel* (and by 'home' I mean a return to a point of God-consciousness where everything is viewed from that viewpoint of God-consciousness). It is not something designed to give discomfort to the soul – it is a *telephone call from God* that says: **'There is more for you! Come back to Me! Come home to Me! Grow! Experience! Learn! Travel! Change!'**

So, the first thing that happens to the soul is that it is made aware that this longing is not something to disquiet it as the distorted longing on Earth has done. It is something to be embraced, it is something to be cherished and it is something that gives the soul identity because the soul is aware from that point onwards that it is a part of God (whereas so many souls on Earth are blind to that fact – blind physically, blind mentally and almost blind at a soul-level, too). The soul discovers – through meditation, through contemplation, through counselling from other spirits – that it is on a journey back to God and that it is still *becoming*. Also the Heaven (if it has been steeped in religious entrapment) that it expected as the *end* of the journey exists ...but is the *beginning* of the journey! It cannot simply sit down and say, 'Now I am peaceful. Now I am away from the toils of the Earth plane. Now I can take it easy. Now I have arrived!' It has arrived at the *start point*; it has arrived at a plane from which it must move if it is to satisfy the yearning and longing to be more than it is.

At this point let us assume that we are dealing with a soul who has freed itself from the need to come back to Earth... but here I must put in a couple of paragraphs to explain something to the dear people who will be reading this book: the longing that pulls people God-wards and encourages them to progress in that direction can sometimes become *distorted*. When souls arrive it is explained to them that they should meditate, that they should understand themselves and the longing they feel... but many souls *mistakenly* feel that that yearning is a longing to return to the conditions of the Earth plane. They are counselled, they are loved and they are taken into meditation by evolved spirits but still they decide that that longing is a longing for the Earth plane – for the perceived pleasures, the physicality and the experiences of the Earth plane.

I point this out to you, the reader, so you can contemplate this situation in your meditations and in your lifetime – so that, when you come over to our start-point, you will have the knowledge **that the longing you feel from that point onwards is *not* a longing for the Earth plane.** It is a longing to become *more*, to expand... not to restrict yourself through free will and subtract yourself from experience, creation and joy by putting yourself back into a physical body. **I cannot emphasise that too heavily, too highly or too much!** Contemplate what I am saying and I will be with you during your meditations so that you understand the concept. If you are longing at this moment, what you are really longing for (whether you consider it to be love, materiality, status or freedom from pain) is, as a 'seed of God', to become more God-like and to *return to the One*.

We have to assume that the soul we are dealing with *hypothetically* today has realised that the longing it feels is not a longing for the Earth plane; it is a longing to become *more*. We emphasise to that soul in counsel and in meditation that *the journey* is important and that each point and each experience in the journey is like a rare fruit which needs to be experienced, tasted and embraced at leisure; slowly and not hurried (there is no need for hurry – it is not on the Earth plane any longer). We advise the soul to advance through the different levels of evolution *at its own pace* – not to rush but to experience the wonders that God has made manifest through His children on the various levels of cleansing and evolution that lie ahead for that soul.

Again, we have to sidetrack (and you will now realise why this book is such a complex and vast subject to put across to the people on Earth) because souls are, as we have said, at different stages of spiritual knowing and spiritual evolution. Many souls are reborn into the spirit realms who very quickly divest themselves of the entrapment of the Earth plane and quickly divest themselves of the personality that they have just used in order to gain more knowledge spiritually. They then find that they are *already* at a certain stage of spiritual evolution that can take them up and beyond the level they have initially returned to. At that point it is allowed (i.e. made possible by them and by those from their own sphere) for them to return to the sphere they harmonise with vibrationally and to advance from that point onwards as part of the group soul that they are contained within.

…We've had a side issue and now let's return to the soul who has not, through past lives, already taken itself to a higher sphere of existence – a soul that finds itself on one of the entry levels of higher consciousness on our side of life.

We say to the soul, 'You must advance slowly,' and the soul asks: 'How do I advance? I have reached this point and have the longing to become *more*, but how do I advance?' We then counsel the soul and say, 'On this level, as on all levels, nothing stands still.' On the Earth plane many people shy away from work and the experience of work and feel that they should be doing nothing. On this level you will find that you *want* to do something because doing something expands your vision of who you are, expands your experience and feeds your need to evolve, which eventually eliminates that longing from your soul.

So we ask the soul, **'What would you like to do?'**

'Would you like, for example, to counsel other souls who are returning from Earth? Would you like to, by simply sitting with them and telling them of your experience of passing over and what has happened to you – as an everyman… would you like to help them in that way? Would you like to open *them* up to the new experiences they find themselves in through having been reborn into the spiritual realms? That is something you can do and we will teach you how to do it.'

'Were you musical on Earth? Did you like music? Would you have liked, instead of listening to music, to be able to *play* music? There is that opportunity for you on this side – freed from a physical mind that says you cannot do it. Of course you can! Would you like to study the basics and advancements of musical form and see yourself playing where you are surrounded by colours and by visions that you have created through your music? You could become involved in that.'

'Would you like to become involved in spiritual science? Would you like to learn how this realm is put together and understand your potential and the potential of others in this realm... because we can teach you? We are not teaching you anything that you do not know already but we will teach you to *rediscover* that understanding within you.'

'Would you like to paint?'

'Would you like to sing?'

'Would you like to take care of those who still believe and feel that they are sick? Would you like to bring them back to full conscious health? We can train you and help you understand how to do that.'

'Would you like to work with animals in a wonderful and delightful way, in that you will be able to communicate with them? Would you like to work with those animals who have been damaged by their experience on Earth? Would you like to rectify some of the mistakes of mankind by being their representative in working with animals to bring them to full co-operation with spirits of the human form again? In other words, to work with them and say, "I am sorry. I am bringing love to you. I would like to be your companion. I would like to be your counsellor. I would like to learn from you." *Would you like to work with animals?'*

...There are so many things a soul can do so that it never again need experience a state of stagnation. There is, however, the *option* of experiencing stagnation, and we find souls who have broken the path of coming back to the Earth plane who then say, 'I do not want to do anything.' We assure them that they *will* but they insist that they won't and they encapsulate themselves in stillness (which is wonderful and is something, of course, that we have taught you to do on Earth). Eventually, however, they tire of that lack of perception, lack of creation and lack of experience ...and they need and want to *do* something. Their attitude to work is slowly dissolved and the soul discovers that there is joy in experience (and that is all work on the earthly plane is – *experience*, albeit experience that is corrupted at this time). What we say to the soul on the entry levels of the higher spiritual realms is, 'If you wish to grow and to evolve you need to *experience*.'

There is no other way! Yes, experience silence and experience the *no-thing* – these are essential states of being which need to be entered into regularly – but as part of a program that also incorporates things to do. Interact with others; interact with yourself; realise your potential, because in singing, in playing, in painting, in creating, in healing you are discovering that you are capable of *all these things* and in accepting that capability as a soul you expand your consciousness by freeing yourself from the *I can't*.

The entry levels of the higher spiritual realms are those levels where people have decided that they will move on and **the purpose of the entry levels is one of self-discovery and discovery of spiritual potential.** They do not include the healing sphere or the preparation level where people (against their better judgement and ours) choose to come back to Earth. I am trying to paint a picture of the purpose of the entry levels and of that journey which is not too abstract. I can fill in blanks as to how those levels appear to eyes, to ears, to taste and to senses but it is the *purpose* within those levels that I wish to get across to you.

I must obviously talk about where the longing eventually takes you but before I do that I feel I must fill in any blanks regarding the entry levels. Then, in other chapters, we will address (in physical or earthly terms) *where* a soul goes (as you know it actually 'goes' nowhere – it goes within, it expands from within) but next I want to talk about the changing landscape that occurs as you climb up the steps of spiritual evolution…

Chapter Ten
Landscapes in the Entry Levels of the Higher Realms

Joseph: I suppose I should end this particular segment [*reference to the communication session started in the previous chapter*] by saying something about the entry levels of the higher spiritual realms: they are like the Earth plane …and yet they are not. They are like a *super* Earth plane. They are like the Earth plane in sharp focus or, to use terminology that Michael has recently embraced, in 'high definition' [*reference to advances in television broadcasting*] – they are the Earth plane 'perfected'. Souls find themselves in landscapes that are very familiar to them and yet are brighter, cleaner and more polished. The skies are bluer; the clouds are whiter; the architecture more perfect; there is a symmetry to the trees (and by symmetry I do not mean they are equally balanced on each side – I mean that the God within them is more apparent, so more symmetry, perfection and harmony is perceived within their form) and there is nothing that jars about the landscape.

There are areas that relate to particular groups and to particular nations: there is desert landscape and ice landscape, for example, and, at points where souls are learning to live with each other more easily and are wishing to take on board other experiences, you will find that there is a blending and a blurring of those landscapes. So you could find yourself… not in a landscape that fits together like a jigsaw-puzzle with one piece being ice, another being desert and another being city… but somewhere where there is a delightful blending of those elements

147

for the souls that are becoming more universally accepting of all nations and all states of being on the Earth (remember they are still close to the Earth plane in perception). You find that there are landscapes that 'blend' together.

There are also architectures that blend together... it is not unusual to find someone who, for example, has lived in an igloo deciding that they will now live for a time in a more condensed town environment where there is also greenery, and so that igloo (because that is their perceived home) will be moved and placed next to buildings that on Earth you would say: 'Well, *that* doesn't fit with *that*.' Yes, it does! The mistake is not on our part but on yours – it is you who segregate and say: 'This part of the Earth is like this and that part is like that and they do not fit together because they are opposites.' Not on our levels! On our levels you can blend, mix and harmonise different aspects of earth-culture as perceived by souls who still retain that knowledge and believe that that is how the landscape should look.

The entry levels contain landscapes that are in super-detail but are not harsh – they are harmonious and more colourful than the colours you see on Earth, which are muddied by the Field. There are colours in the entry levels that are impossible to describe in earthly terms – they are not colours that you would perceive here because the molecules of the Field or the dampening effect of the Field make such colours impossible to see on Earth. So, mixed into the landscapes on the entry levels you have different colours that are more evocative of the God-energy that is within them.

Within the landscape you see animals that you would describe as 'wild animals', but these animals are linked to souls – these animals have decided they will co-habit with souls for a time. You see wild animals and domestic animals (as you would call them) co-habiting with spirits in harmony and without violence or fear on the part of either the human spirit or the animal spirit.

You see great landscapes that on Earth would perhaps frighten you or be too awesome to contemplate. There are towering cliffs, waterfalls, basins of cascading water and vast plains. There are mountains that, to you on Earth, would seem too immense to take in, with dimensions too great to understand. You see spirits who have come from Earth living in places that would *terrify* you on Earth – living at the edge of waterfalls, living on the edge of chasms, living high in mountains *without fear* (because there is nothing to fear) ...taking in the majesty of the landscape rather than concentrating on fear of harm to the human frame, which no longer applies.

There are communities and, initially, these communities can be towns or areas of tents, igloos or individual houses – reflecting many tastes on Earth. We must also talk about 'time' (as you perceive it on Earth) in relation to the entry levels of higher spiritual evolution ...which is another chapter.

I hope I have given some brief insight into the initial higher realms. I have to say that the realms are sentient and, because they are being created by the souls that inhabit them and held together by greater souls, they respond to the *wishes* of those living in them.

There is a *rapport* with everything within the sphere that the soul finds itself in: there is a rapport with the house, with the plant life, with the skies, with the clouds, with the grass, with the tables and chairs. There is, as part of that expansion of consciousness, an increasing realisation that **everything is alive, everything can be shaped by thought** (which is also alive) **and everything has to be respected.**

Everything that is created has to be respected and has to be *communicated with* – if you create a chair to sit on, when you decide that you no longer require that chair, you have to ask the chair *if it wishes* to go back into the Continuum. You have created it and given it form (it is, in effect, *your child*) so you have to then say, 'Child, do you wish to remain as a chair or is it OK for you to go back into the

Continuum to be recreated as something else?' This is something that you will no doubt feel must take such a great deal of time – to bring forth something then send it back, first asking whether it wants to be sent back – but, no, this is something that can be done very, very quickly. There is respect for *everything* that is created by the communities and by the individuals on those levels.

I have given a fair amount of information today and I think I need to retreat to look at the other aspects I need to talk about – but before I do, as always, would you like to ask me anything with regard to the topics we have covered today?

David: Joseph, were the entry levels originally built and designed by souls as a consequence of the Fall to help pull people out of the Earth plane or were they always there?

Joseph: They are gradations or 'chunks of experience' that seem appropriate to the souls who are travelling through them. In other words, each level is enough to take in at that soul's stage of experience and evolution. If you consider your own life on Earth, when you were a child it was enough to take in the world as a child and there seemed to be a division between being a child and being an adult. Then, there is a time where there is enough to take in as a young adult, enough to take in as a middle-aged person, enough to take in as an old person …in terms of the changing experiences.

They are there because they are the most effective way of transitioning the soul (through cleansing and inner reprogramming) from a position of being trapped within the effects of the Fall to a position of once more emerging into God-Light and into that soul's original identity. They have been there since the Fall.

Before the Fall it was possible to visit the God-level of consciousness quite easily, even whilst in a physical body (although the physical was not as it is now), because it was known that the

Earth plane was an 'experience' – a chosen experience in order to define oneself in different ways and to have spiritual adventures. When a soul returned to God-consciousness (returned in the sense that it let go of the adventure for a time) it did so in complete knowledge of that and so was able to re-establish itself in terms of experience and perception *instantly*.

Because of the effects of the Fall souls on Earth are not able to do that now, so there is a cleansing process going on that prepares the soul *in stages* to accept new information and to divest itself (like shedding a skin, then a further skin and then a further skin) of the vibrations that have done it harm since the Fall by becoming part of its consciousness and part of its belief in reality. So, the spirit levels beyond the Earth plane exist to gradually strip that soul (through its own volition) of the altered perceptions it has taken onboard and integrated since the time of the Fall. This can only be done *gently* – otherwise the soul retreats from the process and chooses to return to the Earth plane.

The passage that initially would have taken the blink of an eye can now take thousands of years (in your terms) but you are quite right in that those constructs or spheres are increasingly rarified examples of the adventure, and they become less earth-like and more God-like as the soul progresses from level to level. Contained within each level (and 'level' is only a term to describe a period of experience) is a set of experiences designed to cleanse the soul, to take it back gradually to what it was and to fulfil and satisfy in stages that longing I talked about at the beginning of today's communication [*reference to Chapter 9*]. That longing was not there before the Fall. That longing is a memory from the time of the Fall – a memory that: 'I should not be here. There should be more than this. I should be more than this. I am missing something.' The longing has to be satisfied and taken away in segments and chunks. The spiritual molecules that have affected the consciousness of each soul have to be separated from that soul *very slowly* and, because of free will, have to be separated from that soul *by the soul itself*.

So, the levels are designed to allow that to happen through the structured experiences that come to that soul to remind it of who it is and what it is part of, and that there is a different way of existence than the one it locked itself into so long ago.

Is that a sufficient answer?

David: Yes, thank you.

Mark: Joseph, does 'duality' exist in the initial levels you have been describing or is that gradually phased out – and by duality I mean polarity in perspective i.e. good and evil, dark and light?

Joseph: We have dealt to some extent with the Lower Astral and also with the effects of the Field of consciousness on Earth. **Duality is an effect of the Fall** (we are discussing many grave things this morning, which is good). Duality – that split of consciousness – is an effect of the Fall, and if you consider that you are each an angel, why should you have a split of consciousness; why should you have a masculine and a feminine side; why should you not be androgynous; why should you not be one; why should you not be whole? Because, on a subconscious level, the effects of the Fall were to *split* the soul – not physically, with regard to spiritual atoms – but in *perception*, and that links to the longing I have been talking about today.

That longing is a *symptom* of the Fall. The soul cannot forget who it is *at its core* but the soul has forgotten what or who it is on the outer levels, so there is a split in *desire*. The soul at its core wishes to be with God (and cannot be otherwise), but the soul at its 'extremities' (where it experiences the physical plane and the initial spiritual levels) pulls away from what the soul at its core wants. There is still that burst of energy integrated into each soul that occurred at the time of the Fall. I suppose the analogy would be radiation: the souls at that time were affected by a 'radiation of collective desire' that integrated not with their core but with the levels surrounding their core. There was a fusion of intent with the original intent, so from that point onwards you find there is a seeming duality.

That seeming duality must be addressed so that the soul on Earth can once again perceive in consciousness from its core. Have I not said that you use the positive and the negative to create because, when the positive and negative are in harmony, you can then create as the soul that you really are? The split only exists in consciousness but it is a deep consciousness. It is an *earthly* consciousness but it surrounds the soul's core. It makes the soul believe that there are two aspects to it – there are not two aspects to it. There is a core that is shaded, coloured and tinted by the memory of the Fall that was accepted at that time by the souls on Earth and since that time has tainted the soul's perception of who it is and what it is capable of. Am I making sense?

Mark: Yes, it has given me great understanding, thank you.

Joseph: The Fall is a complex subject and I must say to you with great humour – if you believe this book is complex, wait until we start in earnest on the Fall, because the book on the Fall with really rip asunder your view of how things are, of what you are, of how the universe works and how *all universes* work – how God's universe works. It is a complex subject and it is one we will go into in the future to the Nth degree.

It is sufficient to say that positive and negative are an effect of the Fall. We have talked about God using positive and negative and both being contained within God (and they are) but they are used to different purpose. It was that 'mistake' of the Fall that led to positive and negative having to be re-integrated in each soul as they travel through the different levels (and I don't mean mistake as in 'sin' with guilt attached to it but mistake as in 'missed path' or the path travelled that led to error).

I hope that makes sense. It is only a small glimmer of what actually took place but I am over-using Michael and, in conjunction with my colleagues, I want it to be something that is studied in depth once we have covered the path of spiritual evolution that the human soul takes through the spheres of consciousness and existence that follow this one in order to release itself from the effects of the Fall. Have I answered that? I feel that I have not...

Mark: You have given me a greater understanding, so from that point of view you have done a great job, thank you.

Joseph: Is there anything else before I withdraw?

Jane: The feeling that draws people back to the Earth – is it similar to our nostalgia, where we can mistakenly think that a time in the past was better than it really was? Is that what pulls people back?

Joseph: No. The molecules that are integrated with the covering of the soul as a result of the Fall have a 'velocity' to them. Every thought that you send out has a velocity to it – it will eventually lose its cohesion or keep its cohesion according to your *voracity* in producing that thought. At the time of the Fall millions of souls were thinking the same thing – having a purpose in mind that they believed *absolutely* to be true. They, therefore, integrated into themselves a belief that had a movement or a longevity to it, and that was the prevailing consciousness for quite some time and caused a great deal of damage that we are now attempting to put right – that *you* are now attempting to put right.

What I am saying is that, contained or integrated within your desire to evolve and go back to God *on this level* there is the duality that we have briefly talked about. There is the 'other side of the coin' as a result of the molecules that are attached to you because of what happened in the Fall. There is almost an unconscious volition to return to this state of play or state of being. It is as though the soul has two

154

minds (which, of course, you know it has) – a heart-mind and a head-mind. The heart-mind is saying, 'I want to go back to God' and the head-mind is saying, 'I believe that my God is the Earth plane because of what I did during the Fall. This is what I have created. I am a God too (which is correct) and I want the Earth plane.'

We are actually trying to teach souls to 'lose their mind' – to lose the physical mind that dominates them, and what we say gently in other passages: 'Try to use the heart-mind; try to see from the heart-mind' is such an *important thing* because the minute you use the heart-mind you are working from your soul-core and you are loosening the bonds of the physical mind that have held you here for so long. The more you use the heart-mind the more you make decisions based on your *original pattern* as an aspect of God and not on your decision to incorporate a skewed view of the Earth plane into your consciousness and to return to it.

Have I not said that people return to Earth to try and put things right? They return because they feel that there is 'unfinished business'. **The echo of the Fall is the ultimate unfinished business in the depths of the physical mind** – the unfinished business that says: 'Come back to me! Don't go that way – come this way!' We are trying to sever, lessen and loosen the tentacles of that original volition, that original desire, so that you can discover your *true desire*, which is to return to God and be who you once were and to experience once more as who you once were.

It is not nostalgia – it is instinct. It is like the salmon returning upstream to spawn, which then kills the salmon – that action kills the salmon. Many millions of souls are operating from a skewed spiritual instinct – they are pulled back (like the salmon fighting upstream) and return to the Earth to be reborn and then go through the same pattern again. It is spiritual instinct but you also have a core soul instinct, which is stronger and becomes dominant *if* you can divest yourself of the trap of the physical mind. Do you see that?

Jane: Yes.

Joseph: It is spiritual instinct – spiritual not in the sense of harmony but in the sense of an imprint, an original 'mistake' or original concept that you return to time and time again because you feel, through the dominance of the physical mind, that it is the right thing to do …when it isn't.

Chapter Eleven
Time in the Spiritual Realms

Joseph: First of all a *good morning* from my side of life, which you could describe as an *upbeat side of life* – it has a 'beat' to it that is above the vibration of the Earth plane. It is difficult for us to see the suffering within your level of consciousness at times when a far more attractive and agreeable way of life is only *a beat* away from you. However, you are immersed in the effects of the Field and the consciousness that is part of man – and yet separate from man – so all we can do is say that that upbeat vibration *does* exists and we can surround you with energies that will allow you to feel something of that upbeat vibration. Then, unfortunately, when we leave you, we have to 'un-create' and destroy the vibration we put around you and take it away so that you are immersed once again in the vibrations of the Earth plane. Such a sad state of affairs but we are not allowed to do otherwise. As you know, we can only change things through changing consciousness – but for the time that we are here we give you our love and we wish to elevate you somewhat into your true state of consciousness.

This morning I would like to talk about time – not time with regard to the earthly consciousness but time as it exists within the spiritual realms (or *doesn't exist* within the spiritual realms) and what can be done with 'time' – as you understand the concept – once you have passed beyond the level of the Earth plane.

Time is *perception*. As you understand on this level you can accelerate or decelerate time within your consciousness dependent on how you are experiencing a situation. A situation that brings you pain will seem to last forever; a situation that brings you joy and you are totally engrossed in seems to fly by so that you are forced to leave it sooner than you would wish to. You are operating on the Earth plane in the way that you operate in the spiritual levels of consciousness but you do not realise it. Once you pass through that door (mistakenly) marked 'death' you find yourself in an area where you can *adjust* the length and quality of your experiences. Also, you find that **you can do more than one thing at once** and that you can, as it were, have 'files of time' that you can refer to, expand upon, conclude or link to again *according to your wishes*. That must all sound very strange to you so let me try and give you examples of what I am talking about.

For example, it may be that on a certain 'morning' (it is not actually a morning but a *period of experience*) you decide that you would like to set up a meeting with a friend – so instantly you send out a request, which your friend instantly receives and (for the sake of this illustration) your friend says, 'Yes, I want to be with you and we will spend some *time* (i.e. some length of experience) together.' Then, instantly, you and your friend set up, through your creative abilities, a matrix within which you can enjoy each other's company. You may draw your friend to you within your matrix of where you have chosen to live (to all intents and purposes – he or she comes to your house) or you may go to their 'house', or you may decide that you wish to meet in a wood, or in a street, or in a *colour*, or in a past memory that is common to both of you... and you create those things *instantly*. You do not consciously have to *work at* creating them, you just think of them and there they are around you... and you are together having your meeting.

At a certain point during that meeting or *evolution of experience* (which is all time really is: the evolution of an experience) you receive a request *spiritually* (you would say 'psychically' from your point of view on Earth) that you attend another meeting that is important with regard to some work you are doing to heal someone or to contact someone on the Earth plane. Now, if you were on the Earth plane in this situation, you would have to put off one or other of the meetings – you could not do *both* things at the same time ...but in spiritual terms *you can*. So, you can say to the friend you are sitting with, 'I just need to put this meeting on hold whilst I attend to another situation,' and your friend will say, 'Go ahead, that is fine.' So you freeze yourself as a participant in that particular experience of the meeting and you freeze-frame that meeting. You then align part of your consciousness with the other meeting that requires your help with regard to healing or contacting someone on the Earth plane and your consciousness then moves into the experience of that second meeting.

The degree of yourself that you put into each meeting is up to you but for the sake of this illustration we are saying that you have 'freeze-framed' or withdrawn yourself in consciousness from the first meeting and you take part in the second meeting, do what you have to do with regard to healing or contacting the person on Earth through spiritual channels and then that meeting is concluded. You would expect, from your point of view, that time would have elapsed with regard to the first meeting, wouldn't you? ...But it hasn't. When you withdraw yourself from the second meeting, you re-enter your consciousness into the experience of your first meeting and resume it from *the exact point* at which you left it with no 'time' having unfolded.

From the point of view of the person you are meeting with, at the point that you freeze-framed the meeting, they have the choice either to participate *to a degree* in that meeting (even though it has been stopped) or to withdraw themselves and move onto something else – receiving the call from you instantly to resume that meeting at the moment that your second meeting ends. Then they come back into it and start to experience it again. Both things are happening at the same time because **there is no time – there is only progression of experience.**

What could also happen is that, at the time that you decided to enter your consciousness into the second meeting, you decided only to enter *a degree* of your consciousness into the second meeting, feeling that it only required eighty percent of your consciousness. If you decided to do that you would be attending that second meeting but would also be running the first meeting, and both meetings would involve *you being there*. You would be investing the degree of attention and consciousness into both meetings that each of the meetings required ...and you would be enjoying both experiences at the same time.

There is a certain protocol that takes place in contacting people on the Earth plane from the spiritual realms because, being outside of physical time, we have to contact you within a linear progression from your point of view. When we withdraw from you and stop communicating with you *openly* (as I shall do today), we have to freeze-frame our half of the meeting so that when we contact you again we are contacting you within the expansion of your own timeframe so that we do not come back to you earlier (from your point of view) or far later than we last contacted you. We have to work within the parameters of the consciousness of the Earth plane in order to contact you *linearly*. If we did not do so communication would be impossible. The same circumstances apply that I have just used in the illustration of attending two meetings at the same time. We have to freeze-frame our participation in the communication with you so that we can pick it up within your timeframe when we next contact you, otherwise communication could not take place.

This does not mean that you, within an earthly body, are any different than we are in a spiritual body, but the process and the experience is different. You, within the confines of the Field and mass human-consciousness, have solidified progression of experience into something that you call 'time' and you have applied that progression of experience to your physicality and applied a matrix of destruction or a timeline to yourselves so that your bodies decay according to your subconscious perception of what you feel should happen to them –

whereas all that you are doing *as a spirit in matter* is experiencing one of those 'meetings' that you experienced in the spiritual realms. You have placed yourself (for want of a better word) into a 'meeting' that will take place for the length of your physical life but, by doing that and by incarnating into matter, you have divorced yourself from the true meaning of time – which is progression of experience. **Time is evolution** – it is the acquisition and absorption of experience by the soul. Time in the spiritual realms is completely different to time on the Earth plane with regard to perception but not with regard to what it is at its *heart*.

You are able (using the modern idiom) to 'multi-task' quite easily in the spiritual realms, but you multi-task with your full participation in different aspects of your experience. You can have as many or as few experiences at the same time as you wish, and you can be as involved or as uninvolved in those experiences as you wish. In other words you can be casually involved in a conversation but also be aware that you are undertaking great spiritual tasks at the same time whilst also being aware that, on another level of your consciousness, you are absorbing knowledge whilst you attend a lecture or speak to highly evolved spirits about the evolution of your soul ...and all these things are happening with your conscious participation *at the same time.*

It begs the question then, doesn't it, as to whether you are experiencing all parts of your evolution on your journey back to God *at the same time* once you enter the spiritual realms. To a degree that is true but what prevents you from existing on more than a number of levels at the same time is your ability to absorb experience. In other words, because you are God, you have *all* the stages of your evolution contained within you but they can only unfold at a certain rate (as you measure time and as we measure time) dependent on your absorption and understanding of certain truths and experiences. What I am saying is that the spirit that exists in the spiritual realms *can* exist on a number of evolutionary steps at the same time but there is a ceiling and a floor beyond which that spirit cannot, at that point in its evolution, experience *consciously*. The steps will expand and the ceiling and the floor will get further apart as the spirit absorbs more experience and understands more about itself.

We, as guiding influences, exist on a number of levels at once in order to contact you. In order to contact you from our spheres of existence we have to revisit our earlier stages of spiritual and physical evolution to present ourselves to you in a form that you can pick up within the parameters of your physical existence. In other words, we can at one moment (as am I at *this moment*) exist within our ceiling and floor of existence in a place that we are comfortable and happy with; we can be discussing things between ourselves (as we are at this moment to make sure that we bring you the best representation of communication and the most information that we can) but at the same time as we are experiencing our level and our interconnections we are also experiencing a previous expression of ourselves in physicality so that you can make sense of the communication that we bring to you. In your terms it is rather like me at the moment existing and being fully aware of the year 2051 and yet at the same time communicating with you and being fully aware of myself as existing in the year 1886. Confusing, isn't it! And the reason that it is confusing is because your consciousness is trapped and limited by the walls of your physical experience. Once you make the transition to the spiritual realms then very quickly you will find that you can experiment with and enjoy multiple experiences at the same time.

This will not happen instantly to the souls who are not already highly evolved. It happens more quickly to those who have descended into physical matter from higher realms because they very quickly regain their memories and abilities as to *who they really are*. For those who are slowly evolving, for those who visit the entry levels and then decide to move on and this is (for argument's sake) their first time at having done so, they *initially* have an existence that appears to be linear. They exist within communities that they construct through thought (and sometimes, in the early stages, through the expression of physical work); they exist within communities that live in houses, in streets and in towns because this is what they are used to. But as they progress and leave those things behind, then that volition to live linearly dissolves and they find that they are freed from the limits of viewing things from an earthly time-clock and can experience so much more fullness of being and do various things at the same time.

I have to be careful that I do not look at one area and then say, 'Here is another lecture' – because in explaining, just then, about people physically putting things together there is another lecture and another chapter, but *Joseph* must not get side-tracked because this is about 'time'. I must pull myself in and I must not see another version of myself fully involved at a future date from your point of view (but from my point of view happening *now*) talking about people putting in physical work to create towns and houses on a spiritual level.

Another modern 'humourism' (if that is the right word) is: *Did you see what I did there?* ...because I have given you an illustration there. If I had wanted to, at that point, I could have invested my full consciousness into giving you a further chapter on a specific subject. But that chapter would have been given to you, from my point of view, *at the same time* as I am giving you this chapter but, from your point of view, it would have been received at some point in your future. The book that I am dictating to you now is already in existence in my mind with regard to how I give you the information. I know exactly how many points of reference are needed in order to bring the book through, but from my point of view it is akin (for part of my consciousness) to standing up one morning and deciding that I will deliver a book to you and not finishing talking until I have completed that book. I have segmented it, I have invested parts of myself into the book (as have other spirits) but we have to contact you in a linear fashion, from your point of view, otherwise we would overwhelm and confuse you and you would lose the plot and we would lose the thread.

So... does time exist on our level? 'Time' exists only with regard to the soul's volition to move forwards. In viewing the spiritual realms you have to take away the title 'time' and replace it with the word 'experience'. As a spirit evolves through absorbing more experiences it can expand through the spheres that lead it back to God, and there is a 'time' when that spirit will say: 'It is time for me to move onto a higher sphere' – but it is not, in fact, *'time'* but a point in absorption of experience that urges the soul to want to move on to different experiences.

At that point the soul then moves itself, with the aid of spirits around, into a different frame of reference – into circumstances that are created from within itself (always), but also from without itself via the consciousness of other spirits living in that sphere. That sphere or new set of circumstances offers opportunities for the spirit to grow again in experience. All the experiences that the spirit has had before that point (although 'before' is an earthly term... *previously* in terms of adding experience to its soul) are still there and can still be visited. This is how we can travel between the spheres we have earned the right to – so in full consciousness from sphere B we can revisit sphere A and we can revisit the Earth plane from sphere A because we have had experiences in those spheres and, therefore, they are a part of us. We travel easily in 'time' and also in structure through different realities because we have visited them before.

The other experiences ahead of us are still there waiting to be accessed through the experience that leads us to them via the higher spheres. There are certain points that we cannot visit in terms of a 'reality' around us but, as we progress higher, we can access the 'feeling' of those spheres, just as you can access the feeling of spiritual peace or healing power. We can only access the feeling of them because the vibrations of our souls differ from the vibrations of those spheres and we cannot visit them until we have absorbed enough experience to be able to progress to sphere C, and sphere D, and sphere E, and sphere F, etc. We are, in effect, placed within a certain 'restriction' of experience... although it is not a restriction because we are constantly adding to that experience so that we can expand the area of experience and visit other spheres, all in God's time, all in God's love and all in God's experience.

Nothing is ever lost; no experience is ever lost and I have been impressing Michael for a few days with very vivid past memories and he, as usual, has thought that he must be dying because he has been accessing his past in such vivid 'Technicolor', but I have been impressing him with those memories to say to him, as part of this chapter: 'Look! This is what it is like. All the things that you have experienced are still alive and you still have access to within spiritual time.' And you do – nothing is ever lost. People on Earth think: 'If only I had completed that experience! I wish I could revisit that point in my life' – and you can. You can't *effectively* whilst in a physical body but you can when you move onto the spiritual staircase. Part of your time can be spent (if you wish), not just reviewing what you have experienced in the past and in past lives, but actually re-entering those times in the full consciousness of who you were at that particular time whilst also standing back and reviewing that time as the spirit *that you now are*.

I would stress to the readers of this book that you have a wondrous experience ahead of you. You might think from what I have said to you (in trying to shoehorn spiritual concepts into physical concepts) that being able to access various levels of consciousness and experiences at the same time is very confusing. It isn't – it is wondrous! Imagine what you can accomplish! Imagine that you can, as an example, talk to me at the same time as reading a great spiritual book; at the same time as working on a great spiritual concept; at the same time as revisiting someone on Earth; at the same time as planning your spiritual future; at the same time as visiting your own past to review what you have done and experience certain things that you thought had gone for ever; at the same time doing various other things – all without confusing you and all bringing experiences to you.

165

On Earth you experience *linearly* and it appears to you that you can only have a certain number of experiences at the same time… you can be talking to someone, be aware of your physical body and be thinking of something else at the same time but that seems to be about it. There are no such restrictions on the spiritual levels – your only restrictions are having to tune into a certain set of scenarios so that you can learn. You are only restricted by your ability to learn, to observe and to absorb and then move on from those experiences. Having said that, I must not get onto my soapbox about the amount of time remaining for the Earth. I must not say that time is running out because this *particular* book is not about that and I would refer you to the other books if you wish to learn about that [*reference to* **Revelation** *and* **Illumination**].

I must also say, to lift the vibrations of the people on the Earth plane: **if you wish to spend forever with someone you *can* do** (*if* they also wish to spend forever with you) …but at the *same time* you can do other things. In the spirit worlds you can also choose to investigate an aspect of Creation – perhaps you would like to look into an aspect of animal life and study one animal. If you wish to do so, you can do so constantly for as long as you like, even if you move up to a higher sphere, because part of your consciousness can be involved in that particular project. If you wish to study music and teach yourself and be taught about music, you can involve yourself *in full consciousness* in that but also involve yourself in full consciousness in other things and that will not hinder your progression. There is *all the time in the world* because you are not in the world!

It is nearing the time when I have to withdraw myself from this phase of the delivery of this book but I want you to know that, when I do so, I am only withdrawing from your point of view. From my point of view I am involved in the next stage of communication; that communication already exists and I am already delivering it to you. But I have to work with the linearity of the Earth plane with regards to the Earth plane's perception of time, which itself was muddied, encapsulated and crystallised at the time of the Fall. Originally your experience of the Earth plane as spirits was very similar to our experience in the spiritual realms now with regard to the passage of time, which was known to be the accumulation of experience.

I would say to you reading this book: do not constantly look at the watch on your wrist but instead view each day as an accumulation of experience and, with regard to your spiritual progression, never, ever feel that time is running out. Time may be running out physically (and, unfortunately, it is) but it is not running out with regard to your ability to continue those pursuits that bring you pleasure and bring you enlightenment, and you can spend an infinite amount of time on those experiences without those experiences having to absorb and demand the whole of your consciousness.

Are there any questions on the subject that we have looked at today before I withdraw from this particular communication?

Jane: Can I ask a question, Joseph? If you are already preparing all the chapters and know everything you are going to say, how do you answer our questions... because I have only just thought of this one?

Joseph: It makes my task a great deal easier knowing the *trends* of the things that you are going to ask, but you have to remember that in my lecture on 'time' I have not talked about *free will* and the ability of each spirit to make decisions for itself. Remember that I am contacting you in a continuum, as far as I am concerned, but when I meet you through that continuum you have made certain decisions of your free will from the last time I linked to you. Half of the equation believes in physical time and half of the equation doesn't, so the preparation from *my side* is there and delivered and being brought to you but the preparation from your side is dependent upon what you think, feel and demand within the matrix of physical time that you have bought into. So your questions are independent of my delivery; my delivery is there and your questions are up to you. Do you see that?

Jane: Do you know in advance what questions we are going to ask?

Joseph: We know in advance what questions you are *likely* to ask but we are not allowed to interfere with your perception of how you connect to us. For example, you could decide that you will stop the communication mid-way; the communication would not be stopped from my point of view but you are free to interfere with it from your point of view. What would simply happen at the next point of communication (from your point of view) is that I would reconnect with you at exactly the same point that I withdrew myself from the previous connection (from my point of view). We are in synchronisation with regard to the communication coming through but we cannot be in perfect synchronisation for the rest of the time because you eat, sleep, make decisions and have experiences within the illusion of linearity of time on a physical level. We know from your souls that you are likely to ask certain types of question but, just as we enjoy the intercourse between souls on our levels, we enjoy involving you in questing for information and it brings out of your souls certain topics that you can then consider.

You also have to remember that, although we are existing within different spheres to you, we are not superior to you, so we would not demand that you, as puppets, supply us with questions that we can answer without you having to think about those or *choose* them. Yes, there are certain topics that you are bound to bring up (as would the whole of the human race if they were placed in front of us one at a time) but you have free will. We enjoy the connection and communication with you and we enjoy you examining your own souls from within by asking questions, learning and adding to experience that eventually will take you outside of linear time. Do you see that?

Jane: Yes. I don't quite understand the mechanics of it but I probably will when I get to your level – *if* I get to your level.

Joseph: The mechanics are extremely difficult to produce in earthly terms. We have to give you the communication in a form that will be written down so it is further divorced from being in a person's mind or in a person's soul. We are dealing with terms that will not penetrate, as feelings or as experiences, your physical realm, so we have to translate. I am not only a communicator but I am a translator of concepts that are known, and felt, and experienced, and lived, and breathed on a spiritual level into concepts that are an *approximation* of them on an earthly level. You cannot write down the spiritual physics of how communication takes place. This is something that will annoy your scientists and they will say: 'I want an equation,' but an equation is of itself of the earthly or physical realm. There *are* equations but they are equations that are trans-dimensional or multi-dimensional, which the physical mind cannot pick up, let alone translate into a form that can be read in a book. It is as though we are saying to you: 'Can you smell this colour?' ...And we *can*, but you can't, so we have to couch things in terms that the physical mind can accept but then the soul *knows*. Do you see that?

Jane: Yes.

Joseph: Is there another question, please?

David: Joseph, there have been points in the past where Michael, Jane and I have been together and the guide talking to us has said, 'Right at this very moment you are with us now.' For example, the Persian Gentleman has said, 'You are in my house now drinking coffee with me.' Is that an example of what you have been talking about this morning where we can have parallel perceptions?

Joseph: Yes, it is, and also it is an example of you existing within a certain ceiling and floor of experience. You could not, for example, visit with the Persian Gentleman and be aware of that aspect of your consciousness being there if you had not, previously to this incarnation, been on that level and accessed that level through absorption of experience. So, when we say to you, 'You are in the Persian Gentleman's house' – you *are* in the Persian Gentleman's house and you are also on Earth. You are multi-tasking from the point-of-view of the spirit that does not actually exist in either of those realms but chooses to bring forth those realities in order that it can experience. Does that answer?

David: It does, yes.

Joseph: Before I leave I know that *you* will gather again before Christmas but I also know that Michael has made the decision that there should not be another communication before Christmas because of the amount of work that needs to be done and I honour that. I am always ready to bring through more communication but it is a good idea to conserve your energies, particularly at this time of year. The Field becomes stronger as a portion of the Earth goes into winter because, as that happens, it delivers to people more of the energies that they *expect* from the Field – they expect to be depressed, they expect to be cold and miserable… and that strengthens the Field.

So, I wish to thank you for your endeavours during this year (as you see it) and, as I always do, I must leave on an upbeat note and I want to say to you – if you think this year has been difficult …you wait until you see the next one, when there is so much more for us to do and so much more information will be moving out into the Field.

Remember that as the book is whole and the book is with me, the *plan* is whole and the plan exists as an entity and as a force. It is so sad for us to have to leave you back in physicality where you cannot see where this is going but I emphasise that **it is going places;** that you next year *physically* are going places [*reference to public trance demonstrations in Ireland, Cheshire and Merseyside*] and mentally are going places. There will be far more demands on you because, as you work to put the information out, the Field will see your Light and there will be those who will try to side-track you to take you off the path. I give you a bulldozer so that you can all get on it and move forwards through the year despite what is ahead for you …but there are glorious things ahead in terms of communication, too.

God bless, and we will communicate again before Christmas, but not to bring through information for the final book in the 'trilogy' – or is the word 'quintology'?[1] – I don't know.

[1] A reference, with humour, to there perhaps being more communications books from Joseph in store for us than we are aware of at this time.

Chapter Twelve
The Nature of the Spheres

Joseph: It is a great pleasure to communicate again and I want to bring through a sense of *joy* this morning, as we begin what for you is a new year. In winter there is in a 'retreat', which is natural to the physical body – the physical body wishes to slow down and conserve energy, so at this time many people around the world are struggling with their *biology* and are trying to fit in a normal day's work and a normal day's input into society when really they should be giving into their instincts. The effect of going against those instincts is that people become depressed and descend even further down into the 'pit of despair' so it is difficult for spirit communication to take place at this time of year – as I explained at the last demonstration [*reference to a December public trance demonstration*].

However, if we bring joy into the proceedings and if we anticipate all the good things that are going to happen this year then we raise the vibrations, you raise the vibrations, and you allow communication to take place. My communication this morning begins on a high note because my message is one that appears to be doom laden. However, the reason that I am communicating *now* and the reason that the communication is being put into book form is because we hope and we pray and we hold onto that vision of things righting themselves and people *this time* coming round to God's way of thinking, to our way of thinking, to their spiritual way of thinking. So, whatever the outcome of your endeavours, there *is* great joy and there should be great joy in all that you do.

Back to the book!

I wish to explain a little today about the *nature* of the spirit realms. Everything, as I said in **Revelation** [*reference to Joseph's first book*], is based on the concept of a circle – everything is circular, everything is contained within God and everything is an expression between the point at the centre of the circle and the edge of the circle. All experience takes place within that sphere ...and so it is in the spirit realms.

You talk about spiritual spheres and spheres of existence but you do not understand the term. Each level of conscious appreciation *spiritually* is contained within a sphere and each sphere exists within the same dimensions as the next sphere. The difference is a difference in *vibration* and the spiritual spheres that lead away from the Earth plane towards escape into infinity also exist within the same dimensions as the Earth and its surrounding area. All the steps of evolution that allow you to escape the effects of the Fall take place within the same dimensions as the sphere with the dot at its centre – which is an expression of God.

Therefore, if anyone asks you: 'Where do you go to when you leave the Earth plane?' – **You go nowhere else.** You don't actually *go* anywhere; it is simply that your vibrations, as a result of your endeavours whilst inhabiting a physical body, elevate themselves to an extent that coincides with a level of 'reality' in one of the spiritual spheres. So, upon leaving the physical body, you gravitate *automatically* towards the sphere that resonates at the same frequency as the vibration that you display, having released yourself from physical matter.

If all spheres exist within the same framework and dimensions then travel between the spheres should be possible ...and, of course, it is, but it is only *totally* possible in one direction, and in the other is restricted according to the *evolution* of the individual soul. What I mean by that is it is possible for an elevated soul to retrace his or her steps down through the spheres of denser, more intense vibration so that he or she can manifest within other spheres of 'reality'. However, for the soul encased in matter and the soul that is leaving matter by physically dying to the Earth plane, that soul can only approach those spheres that exist *within the harmonics of its vibration*. By that I mean that a soul can only visit the sphere that harmonises with its soul-vibration and the spheres below that one. This goes some way to explaining why you can have spiritual messengers visit you from the higher spheres... From the highest messengers can come, but from the lowest the steps of spiritual evolution can only be climbed *up to a certain point* because, beyond that point, the spheres of existence are not yet open to that soul, until that soul, through various experiences, has raised its vibrations to be able to harmonise with those spheres.

I am also trying to explain the migration of souls and how souls have to experience a *cleansing* of each level of reality before they can move on to the next one. This is the underlying reason for the spiritual spheres – each sphere exists as a gradual 'cleansing station' for the soul living within it and wishing to move on from it. Each sphere has a *specific purpose* in cleansing and ridding that soul of the effects of the Fall so that *eventually* there is an escape from the spheres that co-exist within the same dimensions as the physical planet into the greater spheres.

The spheres of human spirituality exist within a greater sphere, and always you will see in microcosm what is happening in the greater world. In other words, if you look through a microscope, you see the same pattern as you do when you look out to the stars, and *always* it is based on a sphere. In other regions of this physical universe entry back into the greater sphere of consciousness is an easy concept – it is simply a matter of choosing not to exist physically any longer and to return to a spiritual existence in greater consciousness. However, because of the effects of the Fall, this particular area (the Earth and its surrounding space) exists as a bubble within the greater bubble and as a sphere within the greater sphere.

Within the vibration of the Earth exist the spiritual spheres of the spirit worlds that are talked about by those investigating spiritual reality. What I am trying to get across to you today (and is a difficult concept to put into words) is the fact that the spiritual spheres beyond (i.e. 'above' in terms of vibration) the Earth **are not everything.** They are not the universe of spirituality; they are not the *whole* of the greater consciousness but are simply an area around and through this planet that allows *escape* to take place. I wish to say to you that your concept (if you have investigated spirituality and accept that there are spiritual realms) has to change because those spheres only apply to *this particular journey back to God*, and beyond those spheres exist greater spheres ...and beyond *those* spheres exist even greater spheres!

You must not confine yourself (as we do not confine ourselves) with an image of the spirit worlds being all there is and being 'Heaven'. **The spirit worlds are a progression back into a greater reality,** and that progression for individual souls may take thousands or millions of years as you measure time, but they are a small part of a greater and *infinite* journey. It is also supposed that, as you progress through the spiritual realms (as you understand them, thinking they are *all*) you are progressing back to God – and, yes, you are, but only to a small portion of God. God is so much greater than the experiences you will have as you move through the successive spheres into the greater spheres.

So, you can liken your journey back to the greater sphere (where, even then, you will only have touched *minimally* the true impact of God-consciousness) to the progression from child ...to adult ...to old age ...and then moving on. Of course, you will not experience old age in the spiritual spheres but you are, nevertheless, on a journey that will *change* you. It will be a journey of growth and the experiences that you have initially as you pass over from the physical life can be likened to those of a child so that, as you reach into the greater spheres beyond the initial spheres, your understanding will be *infinitely* changed by the experiences you will have gone through. All of these experiences exist to prepare you for your re-entry into the greater consciousness – not loss of your individualisation, as you understand it, but a regaining of your concept of you being the Whole and you being the individual – untainted by the effects of the Fall, which seek to shoehorn you into a particular persona.

You grow, do you not, on Earth from childhood into adulthood and adapt and take on a persona, and you are defined by what you have grown into believing to be true: *this is you, this name is you, this family unit is you, this work is you.* One of the functions of the nested spiritual spheres is to slowly shake you out of that individual persona and to re-invest you with the spiritual persona that has always been yours but which you have forgotten about and put aside. Many people believe that when you progress to the spiritual realms you will be who you are *here.* Strictly, yes, you will be …but only as part of the sum of the personalities that you have had, and emerging through those personalities will again come the true spirit personality of **who you are.** So you will look from the vantage point of the spiritual spheres at your current personality and realise that it is just one facet or one opportunity to learn and nothing more. This may sound disturbing and frightening to you but the change is so gradual that it can again be likened to that change between childhood and adulthood that creeps up on you, that is there before you know it and is so slight and so gentle that you do not realise a change is taking place. **You are not who you appear to be today:** your name is a reference point on Earth, your personality is an aspect of the *true you* that you are utilising in physical consciousness for a purpose …and that purpose is to escape physical consciousness.

The rate at which you progress through the spiritual spheres depends on many factors. It depends on your resistance, for one thing. Many people are resistant to moving onwards because they are frightened of change, and this is an effect of the physical Field, which is saying to them, 'Don't change!' If they have lived their lives *only* on a physical level for a lifetime it is very difficult for them to change because they are used to the Field dictating their choices, even though they do not know that that is taking place.

Many people arrive in the spiritual worlds (as we have said in earlier chapters) and do not wish to change; they wish to get back to the Field and they wish to remain as they always have been – and for them progress is relatively slow. There are other souls who have investigated spiritual possibilities within and outside of themselves and there exists within those souls an *eagerness* to see what is next. With those souls the journey is far easier and they progress away from the initial physical plane much more rapidly than those souls who wish to come back and be dictated to by the Field once again. Then there are those souls who, fairly instantly upon leaving the physical plane, regain knowledge of who they were *before* they came to the Earth plane. For them it is simply a matter of remembering and re-instating their personality as an advanced soul and then gaining instant admission to the sphere from which they have come and to which they can gain entry again.

Do you have any questions regarding this concept?

Jane: Could I ask a question about the vibrations in the different spheres? On Earth the Fall occurred because we speeded up the vibration of physical matter, but then we are told that, to communicate with the inner self, we have to *slow down* in order to tune into our heart-centre, and as a result of that the soul *quickens*. I am confused because there seems to be two sorts of speed going on. When people in the spiritual spheres elevate themselves are the vibrations of their soul quickening or is it a completely different thing?

Joseph: Vibration should not be confused with speed on a physical level. If you sit in your car on a physical level and take it down the motorway at a hundred miles per hour you are going fast but your vibrational rate is not altered. Your life is *fast* but your vibrational rate is something else, is another signature of speed ('speed' is the wrong

178

word – 'oscillation' or… 'refinement of wavelengths' is a better term). The higher vibrations exist on more rapidly undulating waveforms but the experience and reality within those rapidly undulating waveforms is calmer than the reality you perceive on Earth. So, it is a different concept of speed (I wish I had another word than 'speed'); it is a more rapid vibration but a more spiritual way of life. The two are different: if you hurry through your day – if you answer the phone and answer the door and talk to people and go here, there and everywhere, you are existing within the speed of physical reality but are not altering your spiritual vibrations.

Spiritual vibrations are enhanced, evolve and oscillate more rapidly because of the experience that you bring to the vibration of your soul. The experiences of your soul are not affected by the *speed* of the Earth but by the *experience* of the Earth. How can I explain this?

…Vibrations become more refined *spiritually* as you progress and you access the more refined vibrations because they are linked to the vibrationary rate of your soul. Speed on Earth has nothing to do with those vibrations *within you* becoming refined; *experience* determines the refinement of vibrations – not *speed*. Speed is an illusion of the Earth plane and a dictate of the Field because speed on Earth prevents you from contemplating and enhancing those vibrations. You have to go fast and, as you go fast, you cannot think *inwardly*, you only think *outwardly* and that is what the Field wants. The Field does not want you to question, does not want you to become still and does not want you to go within. Do you see that?

Jane: I can understand that bit now but I just want to ask about the Fall where they speeded up the physical building blocks of life and that made things aggressive, agitated and heavier somehow – was that speeding up of the building blocks of life something different?

Joseph: This was a speeding up on a physical level and was a speeding up of *intent*, and it was the intent that created the barrier and nothing to do with the oscillation of vibrations that determine the level of consciousness of the soul. This was a Fall based on *changing physical matter* and investing in the speed and the illusion of physical matter rather than investing in God's 'speed'. It was man's speed versus God's 'speed', and so, as the effects of the experiment became apparent, there was an investment in all things physical and an abandonment of all things spiritual, and that created a barrier of vibration emanating from the souls involved in the experiment. There are two levels of consciousness, as we have always said: there is the level of consciousness of the Earth that is dictated by the Field (for the most part) and there is the level of consciousness of the soul that is to do with the oscillation of wavelengths and not physical speed. Do you see?

Jane: Yes, I understand now – we speeded up the wrong thing.

Joseph: You speeded up *the illusion* and the illusion became a trap. The illusion snapped shut around you and expelled you from your 'Garden of Eden', from your paradise of knowing that you are physical *and* spiritual – expelled from that perfect world your consciousness of also being a spiritual person, of also being a soul and of also being linked to God. It was the speed at which you attempted to evolve the physical matter around you that created the barrier and not the harmonics of your soul. One is speed and the other is harmonics and refinement. One is a hurtling forwards on a physical level and the other is quiet contemplation that results in enhanced vibrations and access to other areas of reality and creativity.

Chapter Thirteen
The Sphere of Contemplation

Joseph: What lies beyond the planes we have described thus far?

...For many souls there is that point where they wish to go onward; not back to the Earth, but *onwards*...

What lies beyond?

Contemplation is one of the things that lies beyond. It is something we often say to you: 'Be quiet. Contemplate. Think from your heart-mind. Divest yourself of the Earth experience and go within to contact *that which you really are*,' and there is a great opportunity to do this once you have left the Earth plane.

There is a sphere of contemplation, and this is a place that souls go to *simply by wanting to be there*, and return from *simply by wanting to come back from it*. It is a sphere of peace and is one of our great cleansing opportunities or places, because in this sphere there is *quiet*. In this sphere time, as you understand it, doesn't exist – it stands still and is apart from that sphere, so that spirits wishing to enter it can do so at one point in their consciousness, spend a year or a thousand years there then return to the sphere they came from *at the same point* they left it all that time ago ...you see how time does not exist in the sphere of contemplation?

The purpose of the sphere of contemplation is just that: to examine in quiet, in peace, in comfort and in *love* every aspect of the soul's existence to that point, and to examine it dispassionately and look at it slowly to appreciate fully what each experience of the soul's existence has been for. Nothing is wasted, and in the sphere of contemplation there is a great joy when you look at some aspect of your immediate past life (or previous lives before that) and realise that **there was absolute meaning to each moment** – that wonderful moment when you can say, 'That is what it was about!'

You can view those aspects of physicality by yourself or you are allowed to view them with help from other guides and elevated souls. You can view them with the 'dark glasses' taken off so, for example, if you are looking at a particularly challenging moment in your earthly life, you can view that moment again but see the influences that were around it; see the people who were advising you from the higher spheres; see the effect you were having in terms of Light-energy on other people and they on you; see the strands of karma and how they were interweaving or loosening themselves from you at that point; and also see your placement in the scheme of *all physicality* and how your choices and actions at that point affected everyone else's, both positively and negatively. The sphere of contemplation is a wonderful, *wonderful* cleansing station.

It is also somewhere where spirits go to consider what to do next and to consider their actions since they have been in the spiritual spheres, because, of course, experience and the effects of that experience go onwards far beyond the physical plane. Imagine the joy of being able to go to a place and consider your decision about what you want to do next *for as long as you want to consider it*, to make absolutely sure that that is what you do or don't want to do, and to project forwards through your own thoughts – to see the effects your decision will have on yourself and others *before* you ever take it.

The sphere of contemplation is a state of mind rather than a landscape. It is somewhere that souls can visit whilst still remaining 'corporeally' (or as an energy-body) within the sphere that they are harmonising with. In other words, if you wished to visit the sphere of contemplation, you could do so by sitting in the room you have created within the sphere that you are happy with and simply becoming quiet and giving out a message to all those who would contact you that you are now going to enter the sphere of contemplation. You then become still ...*and you are there*. You are there in an atmosphere that will allow you to view and contemplate your existence, always knowing that, whilst you are doing so, you are imbued with God-energy and that God is with you, helping you to see the effects that your consciousness and existence has had on yourself and others, and helping you to make the decisions that will next have the best effect on yourself, the others around you and those on the lower spheres that lead back to the physicality of the Earth.

The sphere of contemplation is beyond description in physical terms. It is a *state of spiritual mind*; there is no physicality to it and yet it exists. A difficult concept to transfer to you this morning that there is a sphere that exists, that is a place, and yet it is a place of perusal and of viewing that does not exist as a landscape, as a set of buildings or as an horizon. It simply exists as a sphere with *purpose* for the soul who wishes to look backwards and to go forwards.

It is a sphere that souls on the first steps of spirituality visit increasingly, once we have convinced them that there is nothing to be frightened of in visiting that place. Always, because of the Earth plane and because of the Field, we have a struggle with newcomers and those who have not revisited and taken on their spiritual identity again. Always we have a problem convincing souls that, if they go to somewhere such as the sphere of contemplation, they will not lose themselves; they will not lose consciousness; they will not lose their individuality, and that it is not an absorption or a void. That tight sense of identity and fear of losing that identity is an effect of the Field

– it is in the interests of the Field to keep you individualised in thought and dependent on maintaining that individuality. That causes a problem in the primary spiritual spheres following on from the Earth plane in that many people find it very difficult to experience greater consciousness. They fear greater consciousness; they feel that it will wipe them away; they feel that they will become a mist and disappear – and that is not the case.

Greater consciousness is *enhanced consciousness*, and enhanced consciousness puts into perspective the earthly personality. There comes a point in a soul's journey when that soul views the earthly personality for what it is and realises that it is only stripping itself temporarily of a 'suit of clothes' and that its consciousness contains that personality *and so much more* – and that is a joyous thing and not something to be frightened of.

I feel I have spoken enough about that particular sphere. It is difficult to segregate this book into chapters and sections because the spheres are interwoven and interdependent, but the sphere of contemplation is, if you like, a stepping stone to the greater spheres that we will examine on other occasions. It is a cleansing sphere but it is also a great *comforting* sphere. It heals wounds because those souls who are brave enough to visit it discover that there is nothing to fear and also discover that their darkest times on Earth amounted to something, were important, and the growth or blossoms from those darkest times can then be taken forwards. Until that time – until they have visited that sphere – they cannot because they exist as wounds within the psyche of the soul. Visits to the sphere of contemplation are essential so that souls can come to terms with those wounds that still exist within them because of the negative and painful experiences they had whilst on Earth.

The sphere of contemplation is a sphere of change because it turns everything on its head and the challenges of life are seen as the most exquisite of opportunities for growth that they actually are and were.

Do you have any questions?

David: Joseph, is the sphere of contemplation a construct for the initial spiritual planes after the physical or is it made use of by the higher planes beyond that?

Joseph: It is a sphere that has entry levels, has a middle level and has an upper level and souls (whatever their stature) have an intense and *vital* need for contemplation. As life progresses and as the cleansing process takes place, understanding increases but with none of the rush that you experience on Earth – souls do not rush to flee, via the spheres, into greater consciousness. They approach their evolution slowly because they want to get things right, because they want to take the right decisions for themselves and for everyone else around them, both on the Earth plane and in the successive spheres. At every stage when great life changes come, which they continue to do (changes in point of view, changes in capability, changes in perceived location, changes in mission, in work and in expression) then those souls retreat from whichever sphere they inhabit into an area of vibrational harmonic within the sphere of contemplation, and spend as much 'time' or experience as they wish within that sphere in order to reach a decision.

Again there are times on Earth when certain guides 'disappear' for a while or certain spiritual communicators are no longer present and have seemingly gone. They have not disappeared; they have, very often, entered the sphere of contemplation at a certain level in order to figure things out and to commune with themselves, their true desires and their God. If only on Earth people would enter into the lower levels of the sphere of contemplation, which, of course, they do, as the doorway or periphery of the sphere of contemplation opens when meditation takes place. If only there was not the rush on the Earth plane and decisions were made *after* first having meditated upon them and gained inner wisdom to understand the effects of each decision upon the individual soul wanting to make that decision (or not), the souls around that soul ...and the *whole of the Earth*. It sounds idealistic but it once was thus (and still is below the surface), and the sphere of contemplation can be viewed and a personal sphere of contemplation can be set up via meditation.

So, yes, higher or more evolved souls enter into the sphere of contemplation – in fact they do so more than the souls on the lower levels because there is more to contemplate! The glories of Creation and the wonders of physicality and spirituality are revealed more to them as they exit the experience of the Earth plane. ...A vast universe or multi-verse of opportunities! So much that can be achieved, so much that can be enjoyed, so much that can be experienced:

Which way *for now*?

What do I want to do?

Do I want to advance beyond the people that I love or wait for them to reach my level... and then we move on together?

Do I want to concentrate my abilities into observation of Creation or Creation itself?

Do I wish to experience in physicality again in another area of life on a physical level but not the Earth, or do I wish to go forwards into pure energy where I will only contemplate having a spiritual human form when I come back to visit those people I want to communicate with?

...So many decisions, but arrived at by becoming still and entering a period of contemplation.

Is there another question?

Jane: Joseph, could I ask a question about thinking in the spirit realms: do people think with both their physical mind and their heart-mind and, if so, what would they use their different minds for?

Joseph: Here is a *'secret'* that we shall now share with everyone because the secret will be in the book... and this is a further 'drip' of spiritual knowledge in the jigsaw we give to you: **originally, when you were created and were thrown forth from the Godhead, you were** *all heart-mind*.

All heart-mind!

The effect of the Fall was to pull away the two areas of mind, was to pull the spiritual away from the material and to separate your consciousness (as a means of maintaining the effects of the Fall) so that you approached, and do approach, the Earth plane from two viewpoints (actually, mostly from one viewpoint – from the viewpoint of the head-mind). And you will say: 'Did we not have heads before?' Of course you did, but the vibrational seat of understanding was the heart – the heart connected to God, the heart pervading and permeating the head so that originally your physical mind, that was designed *by you* in order for you to operate on a material level, was infused with heart-mind energy. There was no separation and the seat of the operation was your heart infusing the head-mind so that you had the point of view of materiality but the point of view of materiality *governed totally* by the heart-mind.

At the time of the Fall and after the Fall the two viewpoints became separated (because that is all that the heart-mind and the physical mind are – they are viewpoints of the spirit) and the viewpoint of the physical mind became infused not with the knowledge of the heart-mind but with the effects of the Fall and the controlling influence of negativity of the Field.

When you return to the spirit realms initially – and remember that through gradation you are cleansing yourself of the effects of the Fall – you have the two viewpoints still. As you progress through the spheres those two viewpoints become integrated once again so that there is only the viewpoint of the heart-mind. Initially on the lower levels you will operate from the viewpoint of the heart and also the viewpoint of the physical mind, as you have become used to doing. But with the prompting, education and knowledge brought to you the two will re-integrate so that you are thinking from a viewpoint of heart rather than a viewpoint of physical mind. Does that answer the question?

Jane: Yes, thank you.

Joseph: One more question, please!

Tony: Joseph, if we can experience and access the spheres of contemplation *now* through meditation, can we take individual problems, issues or sticking points in our lives into that sphere at regular intervals and can we access it at any time to contemplate those sticking points in our lives?

Joseph: It is exactly what you can do and it is *essential* that you do so because your viewpoint changes as you access the greater intelligence or the greater view of what is happening in your life.

The key, on an earthly level, to accessing greater knowledge regarding aspects of your life is to view those aspects *dispassionately* and to stand back from them in your meditation. You can take *anything* to your God and anything into a contemplative sphere but remember that when you meditate, you also *initially* take into your meditations emotional attachment to the areas that you intend to look at. That emotional attachment is a danger because the emotional attachment can *colour* what you ultimately decide about those problem areas.

You have to enter your meditation and view your problem areas as though you are an observer of someone else's problem areas. You can, for example, place the problem area as a 'film' or series of scenes in front of you and, perhaps, sit back on a 'rock' watching them in your mind's eye. By watching those scenes and problem areas and being alert for the points at which you will understand something about them or view them in a different way a pointer will come to you and a flash of inspiration will, at times, take place. You will see that scene in a *completely* different way and think: 'That is it! That is what is lacking. This is what I must do to alter things. This is what it has all been about. This is the effect it has had on me and I can now move forwards from it and treat it in a different way. I can let it go!' But the key to that is to be as dispassionate as you can – to sit back (literally) from the event and to view it and, if you need help in viewing it, to view it with a companion by your side *spiritually*. Ideally that companion should be the God-within but if you feel easier with a guide by your side ask for that guidance and ask to view that scene and those circumstances with an advisor.

...And be patient. If you initially do not see anything above and beyond what you usually see when viewing those scenes in that contemplative sphere be patient and thank God that you have the opportunity to look at and *to love* those scenes on a Monday but also the opportunity to love and look at those scenes on a Tuesday, on a Wednesday ...for however long it takes. Your detachment from those scenes and your patience when viewing those scenes will speed up your realisation of what is actually happening and what action to take. The investment of emotions into dramatic areas of your life (areas that you want to change and contemplate) slows down the outcome because you do not receive a true picture. To receive a true picture you must withdraw your emotions and look at the areas as an observer and then *all will be revealed*, as they say.

There is nothing that you should exclude from contemplation. You are a soul and, as a soul, you have the answer to every problem and to every difficulty that you come across in life but *only* when you contemplate them – not investing them with power but looking at them and asking what you really think about them and what you should do in those circumstances – then you have the answer to *everything*. If only people would contemplate, if only people would meditate, if only people would stop when they find themselves in difficulty and take those difficulties into God-consciousness and look at them and ask and think quietly and calmly what they should do next.

Each of you has all the time in the world and beyond the world and beyond that – *all the time*!

What is the hurry?

Chapter Fourteen
Spirit Society and Group Souls

Joseph: I wish to open this meeting by bringing through energy to each of you to raise the vibrations and to allow us to more accurately discuss the subject that I wish to put before you today.

I wish to speak today about spirit society, because the people who will read this book are used to a structured society and are used to being an integral part of something that they believe works in a certain way. Whilst they might make minor decisions regarding their own individual lives, the major decisions are left to government, to bodies of strength and to organisations and, for many, society works *outside* of them rather than as *part* of them.

As you would expect there has to be a structure to the spiritual spheres of reality and there has to be movement within those spheres towards certain goals. However, it is impossible to construct an Earth-like society within the spiritual spheres because to do so would infer that certain individuals were of greater importance and had greater power than others. Nevertheless, there has to be a group structure to goals within spiritual realities, and so, instead of the word 'society', I would like to use the term 'group soul'.

Each of the people reading this book belongs to a group soul – they are not aware of that fact for the most part but, nevertheless, it is true. They are part of a group or number of souls that have united in one or several of the spiritual spheres for a *specific purpose*.

As the individual soul progresses towards greater Light and greater Light-knowledge, it attracts to itself other souls who are like-minded and who share its view of reality, goal and purpose. It is rather like a snowball rolling down a hill: you start with a few flakes and then, as the snowball gathers speed, it gathers around itself more and more and more snow until it becomes quite a heavy object to be reckoned with. So it is with group souls. Originally it began with one individual (i.e. God) and then that individual 'shattered', as it were, into millions of 'sparks' and those sparks began to seek out meaning in the physical universe they found themselves in whilst having the knowledge, at that time, that they were also part of a spiritual universe – part of the One, part of the Beginning... part of the One that has no end and no beginning – God.

As individual souls (or souls given the *illusion* of individuality) recover, retrace and remember their heritage they begin to give out spiritual signals through their aura and through their being – a vibration of understanding that resonates with similar vibrations of understanding throughout the physical and spiritual realms. Those vibrations of understanding and of positioning within the evolutionary migration back towards God **seek out and gravitate towards each other**.

It happens on Earth in small ways in that you find and seek out people who are like yourselves and who have similar outlooks to you, but always pushing against that happening, because it is not in the interests of the Field, is the Field itself. It is only when vibrations become so strong and so attractive that the Field cannot interfere that true friendship, true alliances and true unification of purpose can be found on Earth. But once you are freed from that restricting vibration and restricting field of consciousness, the harmonics of your soul can be seen, sensed and felt quite clearly by all those around you if they wish to tune into you. It is, therefore, so much easier in the spiritual realms to find people who are like you. They will appear in front of you or you will appear in their realms and think: 'Why am I suddenly with this person? Why am I suddenly with this group of people?' It is because you are like them and **like attracts like** – you have a similar vibration or similar harmonic.

Long, long ago, *after* the Fall, when souls ever so slowly began to emerge from the 'soup' or thickness of the Field, in ones and twos, into the cleansing realms beyond the Earth, they began to find each other again. They once knew each other as a wholeness, as part of a complete society and as part of the completeness of God but they lost that because of the effects of the Fall. When they emerged slowly into the initial spiritual realms they found that, waiting for them there or emerging at the same time, were *similar* souls. They found that it didn't matter that their individual Earth personalities may have been different but that there was a harmonic within them that linked each to the other. That is the origin long ago of what we now describe as 'group souls'.

Eventually the whole of earthly consciousness expressed through individuality (not the Field but the earthly consciousness of the individuals that are part of God) will reunite as **one group soul emerging back into God-consciousness,** but at this present time (although 'time', as we have seen, is a misnomer) souls emerging from the Earth plane and deciding to relinquish the Earth plane for good elevate themselves to a level of reality that is suitable and comfortable for them because of their soul-vibration. They then find (having experienced that reality for a length of time and having become used to it) that they are gravitating towards souls who are just like them, and then *rediscover* that they are part of a group of souls who have a *purpose*. Group souls are the 'society' of the spiritual realms, but not a society as you would find on Earth – not a society, for example, that needs fire-engines, armies and government, but a society that works together in order to achieve a goal.

Some group souls are concerned with elevating souls on Earth and with joining together in consciousness and purpose to heal certain groups on Earth or to elevate the consciousness of group members who are at present still incarnate on Earth. They sit, become silent, and divorce themselves from their spiritual reality for sometimes a day (as we would understand it) or sometimes for years in order to contact souls on Earth and to transmit to them, through intuition, high spiritual purpose, concepts, ideas and ideals that, if grasped correctly by those souls struggling on Earth, will enable mankind to take leaps forward in *benevolent* ways – leaps forward in benevolent technology and in benevolent approach to disease. It takes a great many souls in a group to do this because, all the while, they are combating the effects of the Field and are trying to penetrate the darkness, not just of the Field, but of the individual mind. Each of you on Earth is polluted to a certain extent by the Field and the concepts you would be able to accept and open up to were it not for the Field are *beyond your imagining*. It is the Field that dampens them – or, rather, it is the individual consciousness polluted by the Field that dampens them. But certain group souls concentrate on elevating mankind through influence of the individual or influence of groups.

Indeed, individual members of a group soul can elect (after much counselling and preparation) to be the receivers of those concepts whilst they are on Earth. In other words they elect to reincarnate for the *right reasons*, which is a tremendously dangerous thing to do because the Field can envelop them and blot out their original purpose, but usually they are protected to a great extent and some measure of the concept is able to be transmitted to and though them for the good of mankind. So certain group souls are concerned with the elevation of mankind in an attempt to raise those souls out of the illusion of the Field and place them on the rungs of the spiritual spheres of evolution so that they move away from the effects of the Fall forever.

Other group souls are concerned with the maintenance of the greater realities (and by that I mean the realities created by a number of souls as opposed to the realities created by the individual souls within those groups) and they are responsible for changes in the structure of those realities. For example, in the spiritual spheres there are communal places where souls can gather – sometimes these have buildings associated with them; sometimes they are what you would describe as amphitheatres or squares, and these buildings, meeting places and edifices are maintained by the subconscious will of a number of souls for them to remain. So the individual soul creates its own reality but also group souls are responsible on a lesser conscious level (it can almost be likened to an automated process) for maintaining the overall reality of a sphere within which individuals can experience their own realities.

And because we, like you, are creatures of change, every so often we will consider changing that reality. It is then put to a 'group vote', as it were, asking all the individual souls within the group soul how they wish to change that reality, and *if* and *when* they wish to change it. Then the group soul, having received an affirmative regarding changing certain aspects of their sphere, gather together in creative heart-mind (although they do not physically have to be with each other) to construct something different. There is great joy in this and they shape the molecules, the atoms and the spirit building-blocks around them into what they wish to see and maintain for a period of time.

This also occurs on the lower levels... there are group souls responsible for changing the overall reality on the lower levels of spiritual evolution. The souls that are not part of the group soul *doing the changing* are invited to participate in that they have to, on a sub-conscious level, agree to the changes taking place **because free will reigns throughout the realities**, but the mechanics of changing and upgrading that reality rest with the group soul. If there is a majority of individual souls who say: 'We don't want change! We like things as they are,' ...then things remain as they are, which I hope explains why the Lower Astral remains the Lower Astral. ...Although there are group souls involved in trying to change the Lower Astral, their successes are linked to the change of *individuals* within the Lower Astral rather than to change of the landscape or collective reality of the Lower Astral. In other words, there are evolved souls that speak to souls in the Lower Astral to persuade them to change their own reality, move upwards and come out of the Lower Astral. However, the overwhelming desire of the *majority* of souls in the Lower Astral is to maintain it as it is (just as the Field wishes to maintain itself as it is) and so the Lower Astral remains the Lower Astral ...until such time as the majority of souls within it *wish* to change and elevate it into a more enlightened area of reality.

You can see that this is also taking place on Earth. There is no difference in terms of mechanics with the Lower Astral not changing and the Earth not changing. This is why I say in all my lectures (often to deaf ears) that the *key* to changing the reality or structure of the Earth lies in alerting, informing and elevating enough souls to make a difference. You can, as with the Lower Astral, elevate small numbers of souls and take out a soul here and a soul there, but not until enough Light has been brought into the world and into enough individuals will the world begin to change wholesale on a large scale. I digress, but this is an important point – that *the time has come* for people not to be selfish but to be spiritual-community minded ...and if they are *not* prepared to save the world then the world *will remain as it is* – until it is 'put to bed' for a period of time.

Group soul society has other purposes in the spiritual realms other than contacting the Earth plane because, as souls elevate away from the Earth plane they rediscover the joys of creation and of spiritual knowledge, and each moment of their lives is *bliss* in anticipation of new discoveries and in taking part in creating. Various group souls are involved in activities that, on the surface, are nothing to do with the Earth plane and they elevate themselves by being involved in spiritual science, in creation, and in refining their means of creating. But in doing so and by involving themselves in uplifting spiritual projects, on a subconscious level (i.e. on the level of the thread that connects all of us to God) as they elevate themselves they, to however small a degree, but as an absolute fact, also lift up the souls that have not yet reached their level, and also the souls that are beneath *them* ...and the souls beneath *them* ...and the souls beneath *them* ...and the souls beneath *them* ('beneath' is a terrible word – I cannot find the term for what I mean and I apologise for the word 'beneath'). So, although they are not actively, *consciously* involved in elevating souls on the Earth plane, they cannot help but do so as they elevate themselves through the projects they undertake because they are *linked* to the souls still incarnate on the Earth plane. As *they* elevate, *all other souls* beneath them elevate too.

Then there are group souls on the higher planes of reality who are concerned with 'condensing' the spiritual information that they have discovered. I say *condensing* because, were they to try to distribute it un-distilled to the souls that have not yet reached their position of elevation, it would not register with them. So they condense the information by stripping it of certain sequences and then, by sitting together, they transmit it 'downwards' to the souls beneath them so that those souls can grasp the beginnings of new (to them) concepts, new spiritual abilities and new spiritual knowledge.

You can see this at work in the way that we distribute knowledge to you and that, over the years I have worked with you, your knowledge has built up as we distil and condense knowledge from our level down to you in *stages* so that you can accept part of that knowledge and elevate yourselves a little through having done so. Then we give you more knowledge, which you add to the previous knowledge to build a greater picture, so that at each stage you say: 'I *understand*. This jigsaw puzzle is fitting together.' And that is what elevated group souls do to the souls beneath them ...and to the souls beneath *them* ...and to the souls beneath *them* ...to you. The group souls and the souls on different levels of reality are all learning and are all rediscovering.

When does that knowledge reach fulfilment?

Never!

There is a point where knowledge relating to the souls that were affected by the Fall reaches completion but then, at that point, the soul embarks upon a *further journey* (something that I will talk about in the future). Discovery of spiritual knowledge and spiritual capability, as far as we are aware, is *infinite*, because the souls involved in the quest for spiritual knowledge are constantly changing, adding to their own knowledge and expanding so that more knowledge can be given to them. *As above, so below* – that same process of distilling knowledge comes down to the higher souls too so they (however high and however elevated they may appear to be) are also still discovering new things, which they are passing down the chain.

Group-soul society is a vast subject but I wanted to touch upon the mechanics of it, the reasons for it and to impress upon many readers who will be used to looking at the world in a certain way the fact that there is a society within the spheres that they will become a part of. It will not be alien to them but it is, of course, nothing like society on Earth for the most part – it cannot be. They will share in companionship and in activities, pursuits and pastimes, but the society is different because it is not a society based on control and *supposed* power through control. It is a society based on the good of the whole; it is a society that requires that the majority of its members agree in order for things to change; and it is a society that is dedicated to the pursuit of knowledge and of spiritual understanding and the distillation of understanding down to the souls that have not yet reached that level of understanding. **It is a totally giving society and it is a model for society on Earth.**

If you expect, when you pass over, to be part of a society that will cater *solely* for you, you are mistaken. If you expect society in the spiritual realms to be based on the acquisition of wealth, power or materiality you are totally mistaken. You *may* exist within that bubble of requirement or need for as long as you wish but it will not bring you the joys and benefits of joining the greater spiritual society. People will come to talk to you to try and give you a greater vision of how you should be thinking but you will ultimately find yourself trapped by your expectations of spiritual society running as earthly society does …until you change your viewpoint.

I feel that I must say (one of my colleagues is reminding me) that spiritual society is based on distribution of God-knowledge. Everything that we bring to you is a distribution of God-knowledge: healing is a distribution of God-knowledge; spiritual understanding is a distribution of God-knowledge; love is a distribution of God-knowledge. It is God saying: 'I Am Everything – you are Everything. Understand as I understand and you will never be lonely, or ill, or angry, or sad, or depressed, or mistaken, or violent again because I am none of those things. Here is the knowledge of what I Am and what you are. Work to elevate yourself to accept it and the rewards are there for you and for every soul.'

I will split this information regarding group souls into two. Today's distribution of God-knowledge concerns the mechanics or the workings of the group soul but I will also talk, at a future date, about the appearance of the group soul, the experience of living as a member of a group soul and also (vitally important) about the experience of moving as a group soul from one level of reality to an elevated level of reality and how that works.

This is my *favourite* part of any communication with you, whether it is in a public hall or in this house …and I invite your questions.

David: Joseph, I was going to ask about migration of souls upwards but, as you say, you will tackle that on another day. Does a group soul always exist in a single sphere or is it interspersed between different spheres? In other words, can part of the group soul migrate upwards and then draw the rest up, or does it all happen in one leap?

Joseph: The concept of separate spheres becomes more ethereal, more gauze-like, more ...I don't want to say 'integrated' ...the steps between the spheres are steeper on the lower levels and, as you elevate yourself, the integration of the various levels becomes easier and the steps become less steep.

It is a subject that I do wish to talk about in depth and there isn't enough energy left to deliver another chapter. You must remind me because very often, from my point of view, I will talk about one subject and another and another and there are so many subjects I wish to talk about that I cannot cram them all in. But this one is vital and it is part of the discussion we shall have and the chapters we shall bring forth about living the group-soul life.

So, with your permission, I will not answer that today except to say that, as an overview, yes, group souls extend over a number of spheres. How that happens I will explain later. Also that veil that separates the various spheres becomes less of a veil so that the souls can operate within a greater range of vibrations that gives them access to a greater number of levels of reality. Is that sufficient for you? It will be spoken about and *must be* spoken about.

David: That is fine, thank you.

Joseph: Is there another question?

Jane: Joseph, can I ask a question about the Fall just to clarify something, because you have said that destruction has come to the Earth twice and you don't want a third time, but in the second book [*ref. to* **Illumination**] you said that the Fall came before Atlantis. When you were in Atlantis is that when the Fall occurred or did it happen originally before that?

Joseph: It is a repeating wave. Here is another piece of knowledge that is vitally important – we say 'the Fall' when perhaps we should say '**the Falls**' because, built into the structure of physical reality, is the *theme of the Fall*, and that theme of the Fall, which is inherent within the Field, is activated every so often when time comes to a point where enough souls have bought into it. The Fall repeats – not only does cataclysm repeat but the Fall repeats, so when we are talking about the Fall you are right to ask, 'Which Fall?'

...One of a number, unfortunately, and when you incarnate into the Earth plane you bring your soul into this quagmire but you also re-inhabit and re-inherit the faults of the Field and the faults of the past – again this phrase: 'the sins of the fathers'. A fight of the two consciousnesses – the heart-mind and the physical mind – takes place but the physical mind that has access to the Field (and vice-versa) carries within it again *the seeds of its own destruction.* It is so vitally important that we teach people a different way to cleanse the physical Field of the effects of the Fall that is like a gramophone record replaying itself every so often – once it gets enough power and enough energy.

There was the Fall at the time that I was part of Atlantean society but there has been another Fall ...and, if we are not careful, there will be a third Fall.

What happens is that the Earth lies dormant for a long time until it can support the expression of life or being that we call the human soul, but immediately the human soul comes back to the Earth plane it re-visits, on a subconscious level, those vibrations that caused its destruction before. It has to work them *out* of its system and that is part of the mechanics of evolving spiritually back to a God-level and freedom. **What has gone wrong has to be put right.** Souls grow as a society but they are not the souls they used to be... they are not the God-men they used to be. They have to come back into a physical vehicle and, in inhabiting that physical vehicle they also inherit and are immersed in the effects of what happened on a physical level before. Those effects can be eliminated by absorption of God-Light into the physical matrix so that the physical matrix changes or, if they are not, then there is a blind following of those keyed-in patterns once again, in which case the cycle is repeated. Do you see that?

Jane: Yes, and in Atlantis you got a lot further on than we have this time because you had what seems an idyllic society to us.

Joseph: An idyllic society that related to *part* of the physical world but not to all of it. The scales were weighted in a different way in those days so you had an idyllic society on part of the surface of the planet but it did not represent the entire surface of the planet. It was a joyous time in that at least we (without sounding arrogant) had got it right. At least we had got it right *for a time* and our mission was, therefore, as part of that society, to spread that information and knowledge to the rest of society. The rest of society was more materialistic than we were and, therefore, sought to smother what we were doing. Do you see?

Jane: Yes.

Tony: Joseph, can I ask a quick question?

Joseph: I am tiring Michael greatly – yes, please do, Tony.

Tony: In the group souls in the spiritual realms, do they get subjected to any negative vibration – like we have the Field that can weigh heavily on us in a negative way? Is everything positive in the group soul in the spiritual realms?

Joseph: It is positive but it is strained – and by 'strained' I mean it is as though the Light is put through a sieve before it reaches us to the extent that we can appreciate it and *exist* within it. God-Light 'burns' is the only analogy I can give. ...God-Light in its pure form is too much for the souls who are being cleansed to take on without it being muted and without it being filtered and passed down. Were you to experience God-Light here (even to the level that *we* understand it) it would – not physically blind you – but it would stop you functioning as a physical being because it is too powerful to inhabit a physical body.

The information and love that comes down is all positive. What we have to be wary of is the journey from our level *down* to the Earth plane because our experience in touching the Earth plane is one of touching negativity and we take on, even to the tiniest degree, the patterns of the materialistic world. In microcosm, as we return to the sphere that we have come from, we have to undergo a cleansing process and we have to be 'scrubbed clean' of that negativity because it weighs heavily. It would not pollute the rest of the group but, were it not taken away from us to the degree that we have taken it on (which is inevitable by visiting the Earth plane) it would prevent us, through its heaviness, reaching back to the point at which we started. It would be as though we had gone on a journey and only been able to get half way back. We are surrounded by help and by love and by Light so that we are well-protected but we, nevertheless, have to go through a cleansing experience. The way that we are cleansed is by those around us (and ourselves) bombarding the lower molecules, the physical molecules, the thought-molecules of the Earth plane with a higher level of Light than they can stand so that they cease to be in their negative form. They are *'Christed'* and are dissipated and, along with that dissipation, they lose their identity as physical molecules.

That is why Light from the highest source cannot be piped in to the physical mechanism or physical body at that intensity because the soul would lose its identity, lose its connection to certain perspectives that allow it to decide who it is and it would merge with the Godhead as a part of that Godhead but not with the individual knowledge it had. So, in order to maintain that individuality, we can only bring Light into this plane at a certain frequency. The wonderful Light that you experience in healing and in spiritual communication is only a part of the story. Were it to be the full story it would overwhelm you and would take away the reference points you have that allow you to determine who you are at this point in time. Do you see that? Does that answer your question?

Tony: It does indeed, thank you.

Joseph: I am about to take a rapid departure. I thank you and am most grateful for this opportunity to bring through knowledge in this form. God bless you and I will see you next time.

Chapter Fifteen
The Guiding Sphere

Joseph: I want to say a little about guides and to introduce you to the area where guides connect to their charges on Earth. This is a very complex idea to get across because, within the spiritual realms, there is an area that is close to the Earth, yet also close to some of the higher evolutionary realms, and guides have to 'project' themselves mentally into this area in order to communicate with their charges on Earth.

This is not a sphere so much as **a state of spiritual mind**. It is not a sphere where you would see objects, landscapes, sky, trees and bushes – it is a sphere that exists in order for communication to take place between the intuition of the person on Earth who is being guided, the intuition and will of the guide who has placed himself in this guiding area, and the influence of the Godhead and elevated beings *above* the guide, so that information can be channelled down from the higher spheres, through the guide, to the person on Earth.

Guides have lives!

It is amusing to see people's images of guides as people who walk *constantly* with a spirit on Earth and have no other aspect of life. That, of course, is not possible and would not be right. The guide spends a *portion*, not of their time, but of their consciousness, guiding a number of people on Earth... or perhaps one specific person. In order to do that they enter this area of being that divorces them from their normal sphere of consciousness so that, in effect, they become pure spiritual mind and a pure spiritual conduit for the transmission of suggestion and help on behalf of the spirit on Earth they are reaching...

...or *attempting* to reach.

...In fact, they *always* reach that spirit. **Always!** The guidance is always there. Unfortunately, in *most cases,* the outer layers of the spirit on Earth and their perception of 'reality' prevents that guidance from reaching their physical mind as their own layers of prejudice and *perceived reality* stop the transmission of help... but guidance is always given. People on Earth shake their fists (if they believe in guides and in God) and say: 'We are not guided! We are not taught or shown what to do.' Always, always, *always* you are! Unfortunately, because of your choice in coming back to Earth and because of the effects of the Field around you, you do not consciously tune into that guidance that is always there with you.

The guidance that is given is a burst of energy within the essence of each guide that manifests across the span of the life on Earth that the guide is trying to influence – or, rather, *is* influencing (that influence not always being perceived as being there from the viewpoint of the soul on Earth). That burst of energy is a constant state of spirit-mind that the guide can step in and out of. In other words, the guide sets up or uses part of their soul-consciousness to be a 'constant guide', but then steps out of that consciousness to experience their own evolution and their own perception of reality. They have a life apart from the guidance they are giving to the soul on Earth but, whenever they wish to, they can step back into that non-sphere and take up the guidance at the *exact point* at which they 'left' it, from the point of view of the soul on Earth receiving the guidance.

Oh, how difficult to explain on paper with words what actually happens within that area! But I have to try – this book concerns the workings of the spiritual realms so I have to try. When a guide is within that area of *non-projection of reality* that guide is a true conduit and gives of their life-force *totally* in order to help the soul or souls they are connected to. They have their own consciousness, yes, and in cases where they can talk to someone on Earth who is mediumistic or psychic enough to see them they will be able to have a conversation with them, but that conversation and that consciousness interaction is only *a part* of what they are accomplishing.

They act as a conduit for God-energy and for subtle tweaks to the *core* of a soul – promptings that alter the core-perception of a soul that come from souls on elevated spheres *above* the sphere of the guide. Evolution and guidance take place at a number of levels within a soul; were it not so, for most souls on Earth there would be absolutely no point in a guide *guiding* because that guidance would not be perceived by the physical senses of the soul. But guidance goes on *at many levels* and a soul exists at many levels, as you can see by my mention of the guiding area, which allows a guide to have a separate life but also, in effect, to guide at the same time.

Whilst a soul is on Earth, the future possibilities and blossoming of that soul are also being catered for, and information concerning aspects of that soul, which the soul is not even aware of whilst it is in an earthly body (or, indeed, whilst it is on the lower spheres of spiritual evolution), is sent to that soul to enhance aspects of it so that it becomes the rounded, glorious expression of God-energy that it is *...and that it will be.* We do not waste the time of that soul whilst that soul is on Earth, even though the soul itself may choose to waste its time, as we are constantly talking to it and guiding it on *many* levels.

That is also a reason why guidance from your point of view seems to be in short supply, because the soul on Earth is only looking for one type of guidance – guidance with how to deal with a relationship or pay a bill. Yes, we can say something regarding that sort of guidance, and at least attempt to show a logical path there, but that is surface, peripheral guidance only and is of little use. It is the *subtler guidance* that will expand that soul's capabilities and perceptions *once* it returns to the spiritual realms.

In concluding this part of my talk on guidance in the spiritual realms I have to say to those of you reading this book: understand that guidance from the spiritual realms is *always* there for you and is *always* sent to you but you have to look beneath and beyond your *surface* expectations of what guidance is. Any guidance that is sent to you regarding surface considerations in your life on Earth is of little value to you – it may ease the way that you feel about something but it is of little value to your eternal and infinite soul.

The true guidance you need is *spiritual* guidance – that is why they are called 'spirit guides'. You require spiritual guidance that alters your perception of the Earth plane and your physical life so that the initial guidance you have asked for suddenly becomes a silly thing because you *know what to do anyway*. Spiritual guidance reunites your earthly consciousness with your spiritual consciousness so that you begin to react to everything from the point of view of what you already know *spiritually* but which lies hidden beneath the surface. That is the sort of guidance you should ask and pray for. You get it already, but, in praying and asking for it and *expecting* it you open up your *consciousness* to it and, therefore, perceive more of it and can act on it to change your life and the lives of others around you.

I have a dual reaction to those souls who expect their car to be parked by a guide! ...A dual reaction because, if they ask for a parking space and *believe* in it, *they will get one* ...but not because a guide has spent a measure of their life-energy to create that situation. You will get one because *you* have created it; you have used God-energy in expectation and manifestation to *create* that parking space. So, I am happy that that manifestation is taking place but, on the other hand, I am appalled that guidance and direction are expected on such a *low level*.

Do you need a parking space, or do you need to escape the Earth plane and live in bliss as the God that you really are?

...My worry is that so many people out there will say, '...I need the parking space.'

Chapter Sixteen
Unlimited Potential and the Higher Spheres

Joseph: I want to talk about potential this morning – about *unlimited potential* and about changing the way that the human race looks at death, because, from the point of view of earthly life, death is a complete lack of potential and is '**the end**' – death is an end to labours, an end to experience and an end to consciousness. Of course, in this book thus far we have demonstrated that that is not so, but something else that should be considered by those of you reading this book and examining what happens after physical death is *potential* and *your nature* as a spirit as you are cleansed from the effects and memories of the Earth plane, liberated into ever more rarefied areas of consciousness and re-established as a *creator*.

'Potential' is another word for work or experience, and the spiritual life beyond the Earth is not a restful one in the sense that you do *nothing*. You are capable of doing *everything* and the time that it takes to divest yourself of the experiences of Earth is only a *small part* of what happens to you as a spirit-being and a child of God.

As you rid yourselves of the earthly vibrations – the memories of the Fall and what went wrong and the memories of your many lives attempting to put things right – you slowly become aware of your *true* nature. **Your true nature is to be a creator** and the spheres above the Earth plane exist to slowly *cleanse* you of the limiting vibrations of the Earth plane to the point where you become *free*. What I am attempting

211

to explain is that the spiritual realms leading to that freedom from the effects of the Fall exist for two purposes – one is to free you to that point where you no longer have a *need* to go back to Earth and so can re-establish your vibration as a child of God within the greater universe, and the second function is to give you back your creative powers before you *exit* this particular nest of vibrations and escape into Infinity. So the first few spheres exist to help you to *forget* your earthly life and the higher spheres above them exist to *remind* you of your spiritual heritage and of what you are capable of in terms of potential. **God is potential** – God exists as a sphere – a field or consciousness of potential. Whatever can be imagined is within God and whatever can be imagined is within you and able to be brought out of you as you progress spiritually.

The helpers that surround you in the spiritual spheres are there for two reasons. First of all, they are there to steer you away from the *need* to come back to the Earth plane and to help you through anything in your personality that you wish to cleanse yourself of as you acquire greater spiritual knowledge. They are also there to encourage you with regards to your potential; to show you that whatever you wish to do you *can* do, and to teach you how to create... or how to *re-create* – you already know how to create but you have forgotten consciously.

As we have mentioned earlier in this book, you will ally yourself with certain groups of spirits as you progress through the spiritual spheres. You will gravitate towards soul groups and those soul groups (quite apart from having a society that is unique to them and to you and which you will feel a part of) will have tasks to undertake and projects that they have decided are right for them. These are either projects that look *backwards* towards the Earth in an attempt to make a difference to earth-consciousness by bringing through concepts, healing, Light or other aspects of spirituality that will help this world out of its present dilemma, or, alternatively, group souls can choose to move *onwards* into higher spheres and will undertake tasks to understand more about the physical universe and the spiritual universes. They will find themselves working to connect to and integrate with groups of spirits from other inhabited planets in the physical universe to bring through spiritual teaching and communication to those peoples. Or, as they evolve further away from the Earth plane and through the spiritual cleansing and teaching spheres, they will actually become involved with *creation* itself.

What I mean by that is that certain groups will, first of all, concentrate on constructing the landscape within *their* area of reality and then contribute to the greater landscape of a sphere that is inhabited by a number of group souls. In other words, the creation *expands* from the group soul to a connection with other group souls so that they can influence the *greater landscape* – i.e. the shared landscape of *all* the soul groups existing within a certain band of vibrations.

Then it is explained to those souls over millennia, as you would understand it, how they can create *physicality*, how they can create spiritual reality, and how they can influence the growth of a certain sphere of reality by donating their vibrations and wishes to that sphere so that, in effect, they set up a 'society' that has their aims in mind, so they are affecting physicality from a spiritual standpoint. I am not talking here about operating in the way that group souls do when communicating with the Earth plane so that they are only perceived *dimly* through the soul's intuition whilst inhabiting a physical body. I am talking about areas of physical reality where the inhabitants of certain worlds are *consciously* connected to their group souls and so perceive those group souls as an integral part of their existence...

...This is very difficult to explain in earthly terms...

The souls living on certain other worlds are not individual as you understand individuality. They have an individual standpoint as individual children of God, yes, but they are aware (because they have not gone through the experiences of the Fall) that they are *each a part of the other*, so they experience group consciousness as well as an individual consciousness, as souls on Earth did before the Fall. It is therefore possible for those souls to also integrate with non-corporeal group souls to share a certain set of values and experiences in order to unleash greater potential within the group soul and within the souls existing in physicality on a certain world.

The original purpose of God's children inhabiting the Earth was to realise *potential* – to explore their capability within a physical framework whilst *consciously* aware of a connection to spiritual areas of life, to God and to angelic forces. The Earth was a place where possibilities were examined and, unfortunately, the wrong possibilities were embraced. But, as it was originally on the Earth, so it is still in the physical universe on certain other worlds, and those worlds are connected with the benevolent intentions for potential and for creation of group souls.

As souls progress away from the limited or 'non-potential' of the Earth plane they are made aware of their potential as beings living within the physical and spiritual universes and Infinity, and are made aware that they are working their way back to a greater communion with God that will allow them to escape from the memory of the Earth's history *completely*.

The more advanced or higher spheres – i.e. the spheres that do not solely have the purpose of cleansing the Earth's souls and yet are contained within that nest of vibrations that lead to God-consciousness again – are, therefore, concerned with *creation*. The spheres below them are concerned with the deconstruction of mistaken ideas and the deconstruction of bounds, restrictions and shackles. Once those shackles have been broken, the individual soul seeks to create and is taught to create... is taught to create by understanding more of *what it is*.

The outward manifestation of growth is creation – the inward manifestation of growth is contemplation.

The souls that reach those higher spheres spend a greater time than the souls beneath them (although that is only a relative term) in the contemplation of their connection with God, and spend a greater time viewing who they are *within* and discovering that what they are within is **everything** ...is *all* and is '*no-thing*'. There is infinite potential within each soul and that infinite potential needs to be viewed and understood as the wondrous, beautiful thing that it is. That takes place through silence, through peace and through viewing the landscape of *everything that is possible* that exists within.

We say to souls on Earth, 'Spend some time in meditation,' and souls on Earth rail against this: 'We haven't the time to meditate! It isn't important that we meditate. We have our physical lives to view.' But it is only when the landscape within is understood, contemplated and visited regularly that spiritual potential is understood. The souls in the greater spheres understand, through great amounts of time spent in contemplation and inner viewing, that whatever they believe to be true, when connected with the God-within, *creates whatever they believe to be true.*

Potential plus acknowledgement of the God-within equals activation of the God-within to produce form.

...And so it is on Earth. I am explaining an aspect of the spiritual realms, but that aspect of the spiritual realms is *vitally important* with regard to souls on Earth: **potential plus understanding and acknowledgement of the God-within activates the God-within to produce form.** The two aspects are linked and here I am giving you a word of caution because, in explaining to you how the higher spheres operate, I wish to say **that is how you operate now.**

What the soul on Earth views to be true within itself it activates via the God-within to produce form and, unfortunately, potential can be negative as well as positive on the Earth plane. You are a being of infinite, limitless potential and you create *right now* (just as much as those more evolved souls create) because you go within daily to see what you believe to be true and then bring it out into form around you. If souls on Earth understood and acknowledged it and operated under its dictates the world would change *now* because the choices that souls on Earth would make would be choices for peace, for good, for health and for spiritual evolution.

So, you must consider that in examining the greater spheres, whether it is today that you understand it, or whether it is in a million years' time in a higher sphere of understanding, you will have to come to terms with the fact that **you are limitless potential and that you create and bring forth whatever you believe to be true.**

That, to some souls on Earth, will seem to be a *frightening* prospect but, under the protective guidance of understanding and discipline, it is a wonderful prospect. What I am saying to you is that the spheres above this one are *created by the souls that live in them*. The sphere that you will go to will be created, yes, on a greater scale by the group souls inhabiting it, but on an individual scale will also be created by you so that, as you progress through the spheres, your 'reality', or the furnishings that you choose to put around you, will be *up to you*.

A soul in the Lower Astral will see grey skies, aggressive people and black thoughts because that is what that soul is bringing out of itself, and those thoughts and that creative reality link with a similar reality to create the Lower Astral. All that a soul in the Lower Astral needs to do to free itself is to bring forward Light from within to create a vibration that is higher than the shared vibration of the Lower Astral. It will then separate from the Lower Astral and find itself in another sphere, where there will be a greater reality around it, but within which will be its own individual reality, brought forward by acknowledging the God-within and by activating the God-within to bring forth form.

Each soul, upon leaving the Earth plane, is a *bubble of infinite potential*. Each soul is made in God's image and each soul is capable of what God is capable of, but for most souls the discovery of that fact takes some time. It can be as fast or as slow a process as the soul *wishes* it to be because the soul also governs the *speed* of its own spiritual evolution due to its internal belief of how quickly it can evolve, which is then coupled with the God-potential within it to bring forth the speed at which it evolves.

Every aspect of every soul's life is created by that soul from within.

Every aspect of every soul's life on Earth is created by that soul from within – the tears, the laughter, the pain, the joy ...each of these concepts is first created from within by a belief and by an activation of creative power that is the God-right of each soul.

What a long process! What a long process to come back out into the Light... because most souls believe and choose it to be a long process: 'I cannot possibly create today. I cannot possibly be a bubble of God-energy with all the aspects and all the potential of God today. It will take me a certain amount of time.' ...and so it does.

Remember there is the cleansing process to go through as well – the cleansing of the effects of the Fall. The Fall was a situation brought out of soul-potential by the soul-wishes of millions of souls who *distorted reality* by creating an alternative to God's way of doing things and to God's way of creating. But because it was through free will and was what they wished and sincerely believed in, **it took place** and was built around you. You are still suffering from it and you have to first break that idea – you have to bring forth the potential to change and to destroy that which you believe in so solidly before you can discover your potential in the greater scheme of things.

I have talked in previous books about creating a chair out of nothing and then destroying it when it is no longer needed by you. As you read this book you might think that to create a chair by thought and to see it take form in front of you *is a wonderful* thing ...but image how much greater it is to create a landscape!

...Imagine how much greater it is to create a world!

...Imagine how much greater it is to create a universe!

...Imagine how much greater it is to link into God and to see His thoughts – to channel thoughts and concepts that have been alien to you up until this point, and to create in ways that you cannot conceive of yet; and to always discover new potential, because that is the nature of God – to examine, contemplate and create greater potential and greater opportunities for existence, experience and Light ...and all these things are open to the travelling soul after physical death.

I hope I have described what is an *extremely* difficult concept in ways that you can understand. Would you like to question me and I will try my best to illuminate the higher concepts. As we become involved with the higher spheres, although I know exactly what I wish to say, it is more difficult for me to say it. As it is translated down from my viewpoint to your viewpoint it loses its 'flavour' and it loses its *multi-dimensionality* because it is being shoehorned into your dimensionality, which will not hold certain concepts. Certain concepts cannot be expressed in words – they need to be expressed in feelings, in visions and in demonstrations – and I cannot give those to you in *words*.

David: Joseph, from what you say it is important that people should realise that these cleansing spheres are there and that they can actually make a start *right now* on Earth, can't they? They can go inward and find those walls that shade the Light within and start to remove them.

Joseph: This is the extremely important point of this particular section of the book and this is why I have attempted to talk about the *length of time* it takes some souls to undertake that cleansing process. The length of time is also a product of mistaken thinking – it is potential *solidified* via the effects of the Fall.

If souls on Earth truly understood the spiritual concepts that we are bringing through, the cleansing spheres would be redundant and people would, upon physical death, find themselves instantly back as a part of God-consciousness, enjoying and undertaking a very different existence than the one that does await them. That is not to say that the experience of moving through the spiritual spheres is a limiting or a sad one – anything but, as they are glorious places of self-discovery, of Light and of joy. But they are a 'bridge' between the point of earthly 'non-existence' and the point of God-consciousness being taken up again in conscious thought.

The bridge is there – the cleansing spheres and the higher spheres are there – because the soul on Earth *gradually* understands the concept of the God-within and the potential within. It wasn't always so! Before the matrix of the Earth was changed and before the Field was changed, the Earth was visited in order for souls to realise, to contemplate and to view different potentials within physicality. Then, when they felt it was time to leave physicality, they would simply leave it and be as they were *angelically* before they visited the Earth.

You are quite right – if souls could absorb and embrace the concepts that we are bringing through *whilst on Earth* they would change the Earth instantly; they would find themselves back in the greater sea of God-consciousness instantly upon physical death and physical death would not be the traumatic experience that it is for many today. Is that making sense?

David: Yes, and as in the higher spheres where we are conscious creators, that can also start now on Earth.

Joseph: Yes, it exists now. The major problem is that God-potential is *unconsciously* tapped within the individual's soul on a daily basis and, because of the effects of mankind's Field of consciousness on Earth, souls unconsciously tap into *negative* aspects of potential.

That negative aspect of potential exists within the soul on a God-level too, so that each soul can tear down any concept that it no longer needs. For creation you have to have a positive aspect and a negative aspect but, because of the effects of the Fall, the negative aspect has been distorted and has become the 'well' from which physicality springs, rather than physicality on Earth being a 'dream' within which positive and negative are used to examine different scenarios. The Earth is *stuck*, drawing from the negative side of consciousness, but it is the same mechanism that is working. God delivers whatever the soul wishes to bring forth from the God-within, and at present the souls on Earth, for the most part, bring through creations, potentials and realities based on the negative aspect of the creative power.

So, yes, it is vitally important that souls understand that they can change *now*, that they can speed up the process *now*, that they can change the Earth *now* ...and in effect they can make us redundant in the work that we are doing at the moment, which would be a delight to us because there are other things we wish to do. But we are all part of the *original contingent* of souls that visited the Earth and so we wait, and help, and look forward to the day when we can *all* escape 'the play that went wrong', the potential that was misused and the creation that locked us in ...and still locks in souls on Earth.

Jane: Joseph, can I ask a question about the Fall concerning what would have happened if we had taken the experiment the other way and slowed down the physical building blocks of life, ending up with too much positivity as a result? What would life have been like and would we still have become cut off from God?

Joseph: This is something that I will discuss in the account of the Fall [*ref. to book on the Fall*]. It is not a matter of too much negative energy or too much positive energy – it was a skewed way of thinking that only allowed potential on the lower vibrations to be drawn from the negative side of things. You would have to ask God what the result of too much positivity would be and, for all I know, there may be areas where that experiment took place and the consequences of that are still being examined.

Positive and negative are tools; they are aspects of the same thing. It is *this particular experiment* that we have been locked into. It may be that experiments do not take place outside of this area of reality. It is only when we escape and completely relinquish this area of reality that we are open to new potentials. That does not mean that we cannot use potential in a positive way to bring Light and balance back to the equation whilst we are here within this nest of spheres. Other potentials exist beyond this nest of spheres but we can only report on what actually happened here and not on what *could have* happened. Do you see that?

Jane: Yes, I do. If this is an area of mainly negativity that is sealed off from the God-energies, how is there any positivity in this world at all? Why don't things just go wrong or decay immediately?

Joseph: Because you have a *mixture* of souls visiting the Earth at any one time. Each soul, in its viewpoint of the world, is a mixture of positive and negative, and because each soul *at its core* knows subconsciously that it is part of God those aspects of God-consciousness leach and seep through every time there is a good deed, every time there is compassion for someone, every time there is an attempt to help on a physical level. Also, despite the Field operating on negative energy, each soul is still a user of positive and negative – that is built into each soul. You cannot destroy the positive; you can only mask it with dire consequences – those consequences being that the negative continues to produce a specific scenario until such time as the souls balance themselves. You cannot destroy the positive within a soul.

I also have to say to you that positive and negative are *aspects* of each soul but are not the soul. The soul is not negative; the soul is not positive. The soul uses those tools and those aspects of God to bring forth reality, but they are 'limbs' or appendages. You could say that souls on Earth at present have one arm in a sling and are working with just the other arm but you wouldn't say (knowing, as you do, that you are spiritual beings) that the arms are the soul. Positive and negative are not the soul – they are the 'limbs', tools or creative forces within the soul.

The soul is beyond positive and negative, as God is beyond positive and negative, and God has other aspects of Himself to reveal once the escape from the spheres is made. Do you see that?

Jane: Yes, thank you.

Joseph: We have talked about very interesting concepts today and each of those concepts could be defined to a greater extent and would take up a sizeable book on its own. I am trying to give you an 'overview' but, as we revisit this book as you put it together, if there are aspects you wish me to talk about and try and explain, I will attempt to do so to knit together a coherent view of the spiritual spheres and how they relate to man and to God.

At this point, much as Michael needs a rest, I, too, need a rest, because I am conveying information regarding a certain 'viewpoint' of reality and am conveying abstracts into words. This is difficult on Earth and it becomes more difficult as we begin to examine the higher spheres, but my intention this morning was twofold:

First of all to explain to souls reading this book that they are filled with potential and that potential is their *reward*. You talk of Heaven:

'I am going to Heaven. I am going to my reward.' **Heaven isn't a place, it is a realisation of potential.** Although the cleansing spheres beyond this one are *extremely* light, pleasant, delightful and filled with love, 'Heaven' comes at the point where the Earth is relinquished and the soul goes forward. Heaven is *within* in infinite potential, as each soul discovers that it is everything and is capable of creating everything and is capable of creating far more things than it imagined up until that point. So, I am saying that, yes, Heaven awaits, but it awaits through *construction*, through *application*, through realisation of the God-within and through greater alignment with the God-within.

I also wanted to point out today that the souls on Earth are exactly the same as we are and exactly the same as the souls 'above' us in terms of potential. That potential exists within souls on Earth – it is simply a matter of changing one's mind and changing one's viewpoint and bringing through, from within, the world that one wants for oneself and for others around the Earth.

Chapter Seventeen
The Sphere of Communication with God

Joseph: When we begin to work with you, we take down the 'rush of vibration' of the Earth plane to a point of silence. That point of silence is so important here on Earth, but particularly important in the next levels of existence, where we teach spirits who are progressing to exclude everything from their consciousness for periods of time in order to listen to the *rhythm of their soul*. It is such a mistake on Earth at the moment to have this cacophony of different sounds and sensations around you all the time because, in approaching silence and in becoming silent, you let in that part of your consciousness which **knows where you are going and what you need to do next.**

There is a plane – although 'plane', I suppose, is the wrong word... there is a 'gathering place in consciousness' that spirits from various levels of existence can go to *at will* in order to become silent and in order to share. The silence I am talking about is not just a silence that excludes noise, it is a silence that excludes surface thinking, surface intentions and any constructs that may be around that soul which are masking the *intent* of that soul's voice. At any given time on any *elevated* level (because, of course, on the Lower Astral level there is too much clamour for this to take place) a soul may choose to go into the realm of silence, and it is like flicking a switch or moving from one state of being into another.

It is difficult to explain what happens next, but once that state has been reached all the constructs around that soul disappear. The environment that they have placed themselves in temporarily disappears; the conversations they are having with their own heart-mind disappear ...and they simply become **a vessel waiting to be filled**.

In that state the beat, vibration, and intention of God can filter into that soul. In that state the soul itself can reach out beyond the bounds of the constructs of the spiritual realms into a greater reality. In that state the purpose of the soul as an individual – and the purpose of that soul relating to every other soul and every other piece of Creation – can be revealed, step by step.

Also, in that silence the soul can heal itself, and one of the first things we do when we are dealing with souls who have been hospitalised when they come over (once we have healed the apparent outer problems and outer manifestations of the believed illness) is to instruct them as to how to go into the silence. In the silence the flow of God-energy takes away their perceptions of the illness. A soul that has divested itself of the physical manifestations of an illness that it believed in before it left the Earth plane can be trained to go into the silence to let go of the belief or circumstances from the *core* of its soul that manifested the illness in the first place.

As souls progress through the spiritual levels, the 'commune of silence' is visited more readily and more often but with different views in mind because, as the soul progresses, it wants and needs the silence in order to experience the bliss of communing with God. It goes into the silence to ask God for instruction – instruction that doesn't come from the outer layers of the vehicle housing the essence of God but instruction that speaks directly from the soul-core *outwards* and, in conjunction with the plan of God for His evolving Creation, instructs the soul as to the best thing to do in any circumstances.

For example, an elevated soul may go to God and say: 'I wish to deal with a situation on Earth. I wish to inject my persona and my wishes into a situation on Earth to heal it. Should I do this, Father, and *how* should I do this, Father?' That soul enters the silence and listens to the rhythm of God. At that point in a soul's existence the voice of God is heard not as a voice but as a pulse – a pulse of energy that harmonises with the core of that spirit's soul and instructs that soul by aligning its core *magnetically*, as it were, with the wishes of God. This is the meaning of: 'Ask and you shall receive.' It is not 'ask for a house and you shall receive a house' or 'ask for a car and you shall receive a car', but ask within yourself, within the silence, to be aligned with God, and you will receive that connection from God and God's wishes will be manifest in your soul and will emanate from you to help yourself and those around you.

Longer periods of contemplation in the silence are part of a soul's existence as that soul climbs the ladder of spiritual evolution that leads to freedom, away from the effects of the Field and away from the cleansing levels that are nested within and around the Earth and that eventually lead to escape.

More and more time is spent in silence.

This may seem, from your point of view, a very alien thing to do: to spend so much of your existence listening, but 'listening' is so small a word for what I am trying to put across... it is *receiving* and *accepting*. You eat food on this level and there is a joy to it; you need that energy and you take in food that you enjoy, or you feel you need music or stimulants – all these things give you a sense of wellbeing. Imagine how much greater is the experience of tuning into God as a receptacle and feeling as an individual that you are receiving *directly and just to you* the influence of the God-voice, a voice that says: 'I love you. You are My child and this is what I have in store for you in conjunction with your wishes.' You must understand that it is *always* in conjunction with the soul's wishes. The soul *by volition* has gone to God; therefore, the soul's free will is in operation and, through free will, the soul has chosen to go to God and say: 'Feed me! Direct me! Be one with me! Commune with me! Fill me!' So there is no corruption of the law of free will that operates throughout God's universe.

I also have to tell you that in the silence the soul increasingly becomes aware of the community of souls around it. The soul becomes aware that it is one vessel in a vast hall of other vessels and that each vessel is vibrating at the same rate, each vessel is receiving communication from God, and each vessel touches every other vessel. Each soul touches each other soul and is in a state of bliss because of the sharing of awareness, the sharing of purpose, the sharing of *community* and the sharing of the knowledge that we are one and yet separate, and that God runs through each of us and has a purpose for each of us.

If only souls on Earth would realise that they have a purpose – each of them has a purpose. So much trouble is caused on Earth by souls reacting violently or obsessively because they feel that they have no purpose in life. From their point of view they are born into this existence, they exit this existence and there is nothing more. There is no purpose! If only we could impress upon souls today the importance of going into the silence, even at your level, because *as above, so below*. Just as the soul receives information and direction on the higher levels of consciousness from God, so does the soul on Earth. Yes, that information is filtered by the soul's heavy physical and mental perceptions through being in a region of heavy matter, but, nevertheless, that instruction comes to the soul; that peace comes to the soul; that sense of oneness and purpose comes to the soul... And the soul begins its climb out of the well of darkness that we could describe your existence as – the well of darkness that you were sucked into at the time of the Fall.

So, where does this community of souls exist on the spiritual levels? *Where?* Where is this specific sphere of communication with God?

It is everywhere!

A soul on one of the initial levels of consciousness can be trained to go into the quiet and a soul on one of the many elevated levels of consciousness (who is part of a group soul engaged in specific purposes to further the cause of Creation or to further the cause of Light on Earth) also will go into the silence. The experience is universal throughout the spiritual spheres.

Also on Earth, when you go into the silence, although your physical and mental senses *mask* it you are, in fact, connected to all those souls who at that time are entering into the silence for reception of God-energy. So it is not a *place* as you understand it, it is a *state*, and that state is *universal*. Whenever you go into the silence on Earth you join all those souls who are experiencing the bliss of communication from the God-pulse.

In saying that I must try and make you understand that, when communicating with God, you will not necessarily hear a voice. God is a purpose, God is a movement, and that purpose and movement will *resonate* with the purpose and movement of the soul that you really are. You may well translate that pulse into a voice but it is not experienced as such by the souls in the spiritual realms. It is experienced as a *knowing*, because when you connect with God there is a knowing of what to do next; there is a knowing of when to move and when to stand still; there is a knowing of when to put things into operation singly; there is a knowing of when to put things into operation as a group, and there is a knowing of what things to put into operation and when. That *knowing* is the purpose of God becoming manifest in a soul because that soul has chosen to harmonise with the God-within.

There are many books that talk about the landscape of the spiritual realms but the landscape of the spiritual realms is *ever changing* and the landscape of the spiritual realms, as I have explained earlier in this book, is created by the souls that are in those realms. What I am trying to express is the *abstract quality* of life in the spiritual realms. Yes, there is coherence – coherence of landscape, coherence of companions as long as you want that – but, within that coherence of landscape and personalities there is also the ability to *transmute* that landscape into what you want it to be, second by second, but also to visit other areas of being, one of which I have just described – which is the ability to consciously become one with God.

On Earth you may travel to different destinations, and you go to different destinations to experience different aspects of what the Earth has to offer. In the spirit worlds you travel to different areas of *being* to experience what those different areas of being have to offer, but all *at the same time* as you are travelling through the outward manifestations of the actual spiritual planes. You are on several journeys at once, as you are now if only you realised it, because on Earth you have the ability to travel to different areas but you also have the ability to *travel inwards* to look at things from an ever-changing mindscape or heartscape. You are again being taught, if you will look for the signs on Earth, how the future of your journey will manifest itself, and you are being shown in microcosm how things are in the spiritual realms.

The realm of oneness, of silence, of peace and of quiet, is one that I have attempted to describe today in order to tell you about your connection with God and how important it is, but also to illustrate, as best I can in words, how your landscape in the spiritual realms shifts and changes according to where you want to be. Existing within the levels of consciousness there is a universal level... there are actually *several* universal levels, depending on your purpose and intent, and one of these is the area of oneness, the area of silence, the area of communication with God.

I also have to say (I am vacillating between the two themes today) that, whilst you are in this area of oneness and of silence, you will be able to experience more of the God-heart. As you give yourself to God as a receptacle you become aware of His intention for you and for your group and companions, but you also become aware of **the vastness and greatness of God.** For a time your spirit and your perceptions are expanded because they are linked with the intent of God so, not only will you be aware of the spiritual realms that you have visited thus far, and not only will you be aware of your oneness with all souls through the sphere of silence and of becoming one, you will also be aware of *other* spheres beyond your immediate perception because you will be connected to God at all points of God-consciousness.

As part of the experience of oneness before you return to your respective sphere you can, if you so choose and following your instruction being successfully received from the Godhead and the God-heart, expand along those points of consciousness to contact other points of God's Creation. You can, for a time, as you climb higher in evolution and perception, **see beyond the veil.** Not the veil between the Earth and the spiritual realms but the veil between the most elevated spiritual realm and *Infinity*. Infinity becomes something that you can experience in small doses. You can also experience other aspects of physical Creation, visit other constructs of Creation, view other civilisations and other souls and communicate with them (if that is your wish and if that is their wish), because within that sphere of oneness you are connected to all things. The experience is blissful in that you are a receptacle for God's wishes, power and energies, but also because you can experience the wonder and infinite diversity of God's Creation along your line of communication with Him. Then, gently, you come back into the level of Creation that you were at before you joined the oneness.

I wished to get across these points with some eagerness this morning whilst Michael was in the correct 'condition' to receive them. The energies are retreating now, unfortunately, but I have so much more that I want to say and so many areas I want to cover. One of my exercises in oneness is to pray to God that the 'building blocks' or the means for you to do this will be put into place so that, whilst we are set up as we are at the moment (with me in my particular realm and you on the Earth plane), we can connect, through the oneness, to bring through as much information as possible for the benefit of souls around the Earth. It is a gigantic task but it is one that I approach with *great* enthusiasm and *great* love because there is so much that can be revealed and so much that **hasn't been revealed before** due to the Earth plane having polluted the communication or the communicators.

I must now push for your questions whilst there is still energy available in which to answer them.

Tony: Joseph, are we living an illusion by being too busy in our lives – thinking, possibly, that we are carrying out our purpose here on Earth but actually (from what you are saying) perhaps missing that purpose by being too busy and not tuning into the silence?

Joseph: When you are growing up there are parents there (for the most part) and those parents *guide you*, and it is a good and secure thing to be able to go to your parents and say: 'I don't understand this situation – what do I do?' ...and the knowledge of the parent is passed down to the child. What you do by being busy is to disconnect yourself from your heavenly 'Parent' and from the purpose and advice that your heavenly Parent can give to you regarding your life. Therefore, by being busy, you *do mask* your true purpose. It may be that your true purpose and the purpose that you have within your busyness are the same thing ...**but you don't know that.** You, therefore, need to connect as often as you can to the oneness, to the silence and to the advice of the Parent so that the Parent can gently reveal your true purpose. Do you see that?

It is simple – a simple equation to reconnect to the Parent to say: '*I do not know everything, but You do. What do You want me to do?*' – and please realise that **what God wants you to do is also what you, as a soul, really want to do.**

Remember the busyness of the Earth plane is a mask that souls put around themselves as a result of the Fall to give them the purpose that they no longer had because they had disconnected from the Parent. Therefore, in order to give their existence some meaning and to exist without the total upset of being disconnected from God (and remember, they did it, not God) they invested their time in pursuits that were designed to take the place of the God they had 'lost'.

Society is still doing that: investing time in pursuits that are there to take the place, in race memory, of a God they feel they have lost.

Another question, please!

Mark: Joseph, would it be right to say that reliance on five-sensory perception is a big part of the trap for souls and, to help ourselves and other souls, would it be true that encouraging them away from reliance on the five senses and into the stillness would help to free that aspect of themselves?

Joseph: The five senses are so shallow – the five senses are tendrils that you put out into the illusion that you have created. You are attempting to console yourself and to propel yourself through that journey by only using the shallowest of senses and the most peripheral of perceptive 'devices'. It is always amusing to watch your scientists, your medical people, and those who are *totally* involved with the five senses arrogantly claiming that they have made sense of what is an illusion. How can you make sense of an illusion? If you watch a programme on the television are you part of that programme? Only if you project yourself into that programme …but it is still an illusion.

So, yes, it is *vitally* important and it is something that people shy away from and you will see it said by advanced cultures and by mediums and communicators with the spirit realms that you must go into the silence and *you must learn to meditate*. Of course, the Field doesn't want you to do that, the Field wants you to be immersed in the attractions and distractions of the illusion, but it is vitally important because that oneness heals you, that oneness gives you motivation, that oneness strengthens you and guides you.

All the things that you are looking for from the illusion are available *within* and are available to you *personally* – not through the dictates of a doctor, or a politician, or a scientist, but *directly to you* so that you know from within *exactly* what to do. There is a great reliance by people on figureheads within the illusion: on someone being able to take care of your health; someone being able to take care of your finances; someone being able to take care of your destiny; someone being able to take care of you in your retirement, and very rarely do souls want to approach the oneness within to say: '*I* will take care of these things.' It is easier through the senses to invest in the Field, in the illusion and in the *need*.

What each of you need is not the illusion and the false gods of the illusion, but the God-within. Once you find the God-within you need nothing – you need only to connect with the God-within. The time spent with the God-within will change and enrich your physical senses so that **you will see the truth behind the illusion**. In your approach to the world you will see the truth, in your dealings with people you will see the *underlying* schemes and insecurities behind people, because your senses will be showing you the God-within them and how the God-within them is being distorted.

You have no choice but to use the physical senses whilst you are here, but you have a choice as to how those physical senses are tuned. Your physical senses can be tuned to a *greater degree* of sensitivity by approaching the God-within and by allowing that energy to flood the physical mind, to flood the physical body and to tune the physical senses so that they operate differently than they do for most of the people around this planet. Is that a sufficient answer?

Mark: You have been very helpful, thank you.

Jane: Joseph, when people are learning to go into the silence in the spiritual realms do they ever make the mistake that we do on Earth when we are starting to meditate when it is really coming from our head and not our heart? Do people make that mistake or are they trained so that they don't?

Joseph: In the spiritual realms they are trained to *think* from the heart as a matter of course. They are trained to *project* from the heart; they are trained to *remember* that they can project from the heart and that they are *creating* from the heart.

It is not a matter of mistakes as much as a matter of: 'Today I can connect with God,' or, 'Today there is too much interference from my own mind and my own circumstances to allow me to do so' ...and, slowly, that tendency is filtered out.

There are greater problems on Earth because souls on Earth have to be trained to operate from the heart-mind. If they operate in meditation from the physical mind then the physical mind (unless that physical mind is completely protected from the effects of the Field) is homing in on aspects of the Field. That is when some of the nonsense on Earth that is spoken in the name of the spiritual realms comes out. That is when connections are made to those souls who are close to the Earth plane who would cause mischief and mayhem wherever they could if they could get onto someone's wavelength ...and they do so very, very frequently.

It is not a matter of mistakes, it is a matter of knowing where you are going and knowing where you are coming from. It is a matter of preparing yourself *correctly* here before you go into the silence; of asking for the all-pervading love and purpose of God to surround you during your time in meditation; of having the presence of heart-mind to let go of the thought process that you are used to during your conscious moments and of listening to the different thought process of the heart-mind.

This is something that only comes with practice and, again, **motivation is vitally important** when you are going into the silence. It is no use approaching God if your motivation is to manipulate people and circumstances with regard to your position of importance within the Field. If you do that then you do not actually approach or connect with God – you approach and connect with those pockets of like-minded vibration from within the Field that will fuel your desires to manipulate it. Then, in such circumstances, the communication that you are possibly getting, which will tell you that you are such an important being, that your message is so important and that people should come *only* to you, those messages are coming from the illusion and not from the God-within. The God-within will simply move you to be all that you can be in His name and to express yourself according to the steps that He puts in front of you for you to mount and to climb.

So, purpose is important. If you are approaching the oneness, *why* do you want to approach the oneness? If you want to approach the oneness because you wish to become one with God and God's purpose then you are protected. If you wish to approach the oneness from the point of view of ego in order to elevate yourself and give power to your desires within the illusion, then you will not approach God, but you will approach pockets of energy within the illusion that will allow you, to some extent, to indulge in your fantasies – in other words, to take yourself further away from God.

There is danger in approaching God from the wrong point of view. It has to be a point of view of: 'Father, guide me from the heart, protect me without and within during my time of oneness with you and give me the spiritual sense to filter out anything that comes into my head-consciousness that I feel is not right for my journey.' Do you see that?

Jane: Yes, thank you.

Joseph: I must leave you at this point as the connection is going.

Chapter Eighteen
The Second Transition

Joseph: I want to talk today about where we are going. You would imagine that a book on life after death would be about where you go to immediately after physical death. However, I want to talk today about where we are *ultimately* going.

One of the principle concepts of this book is that life after death is not a 'finishing post', is not the place you are ultimately going to, but is a journey through a number of spheres or dimensions that exist in order to *cleanse* you from the effects of the Earth plane so that you can reclaim your heritage as the being you were before you were trapped in the effects of the Fall.

For us, life is not a constant but is a constantly changing and evolving viewpoint, and for us the spheres that we inhabit are only *temporary*, however long we may inhabit them for, because there is a great movement away from earthly thinking back towards the thinking that we had as the beings we were *before* we became trapped.

We may seem unmoving, unchanging and settled to you but we are anything but – we are engaged in ever more complex and beautiful acts of creation and we are also engaged in a 'journey'. It is not a journey as you would understand the term – a journey for you means actually *physically* taking yourself somewhere. For us it is a journey of changing circumstance around us, and of changing viewpoint – a transitional experience involved in and sited within cleansing spheres that eventually leads *somewhere else.*

...And there is an end to that journey through those spheres of cleansing, in that there comes a time when the material that houses the soul becomes of a vibration that is equal to the vibration of the higher side of Creation and, having attained that vibration, the soul within is then free to harmonise with, to merge and to return to the rest of higher Creation from whence it came.

I have looked at much of the literature concerning *life after death* that has been handed down to you over the years from different communication sources, and there is talk here and there of 'a second death' – as though you have to go through that experience again in order to escape from the spheres of spiritual cleansing. I do not like or *agree* with that term 'death'. On Earth, death implies a loss of consciousness, a loss of individuality – and these things are not so, as you will see when *you* eventually make your transition from this area. At the end of your journey through the spheres of cleansing there comes a time for *transition*, not death. It is not an absolute, it is not a climactic event, but rather a simple movement or change, as though you have come to a crossroads and decided which road to take. You are still you, you are still on a journey, but you have simply turned left or turned right or gone straight on.

As you approach the end of the cleansing period and you become aware that your vibrations are harmonising with a different set of circumstances you are allowed to determine how long you wish to remain within the spheres of cleansing. In terms of earthly time this can be years, centuries, millennia... or you may choose to go on as soon as that vibrational awareness comes to you. At that point it is simply a change of spiritual mind that takes you onwards, nothing more. It is not as though you have to die to make a major transition a second time – you simply decide that you wish to be somewhere that you are not now; somewhere that calls to you from within; somewhere that is harmonious according to how you feel at that time. Then, having decided a hundred percent within your soul that you wish to move onwards, you *have* moved onwards.

The only aspect of you that 'dies away' – to give you an allegory – is the last vestiges of your humanity. That, again, seems to be a strange comment, and you see the worthlessness of words when trying to describe something from the higher realms. Here is something for you to think about: you regard yourselves as 'human beings' and that you travel onwards in a human form, and that is true – your physical make-up is that of a human being. **But you are not actually human – you are a spirit inhabiting a human form.** Because you are used to that human form, and also because that human form has trapped you to a great extent because of the effects of the Fall, you have to move onwards through the spheres of cleansing in an approximation of that human form, although that becomes looser as you approach the end of your journey through the spheres.

When you move onwards to regain your angelic status it is natural that the last vestiges of that 'assumed form' (*assumed form* in that you assume that is what you are) has to be left behind because, in acknowledging that you harmonise with the higher creative force, you assume another form. You assume the form that you once had and have always had, crushed, restricted and imprisoned within your assumed human form ...and that is the **angelic form.**

What I am saying is that there will come a day when you remember *totally* who you are, when you harmonise with the Creation that you came from and when you finally divest yourself of 'humanity' in the sense of a *human* form.

Of course, you associate humanity on Earth with a certain set of values, but those values are *spiritual* – they are nothing to do with humanity – and you take those values with you. You could not have climbed so high had you not had those values, practised those values, believed those values and *been* those values. You take with you your spiritual values – those spiritual aspects of humanity – but you leave behind the need to be recognised within a human form.

This brings me to the next interesting point: just as we visit you to impart our advanced spiritual knowledge ('advanced' in the sense that we have furthered our spiritual knowledge through our trials and our work to climb through the spheres), are *we* visited by those brothers and sisters who have gone *home*? The books I have studied, which talk about a second death, also talk about an 'absence', as though spiritual beings reach a certain point, move onwards through a second death and then their influence is not made available to those that are left behind. To use one of the words I am very fond of – *nonsense*! **We are visited by those we love.** How could a loving God allow separation between those who love each other? Separation occurs on Earth because of the barrier that death creates and that wall of death is created from your side and not from the spiritual side. There was a time when death or transition was acknowledged and understood, and communication took place as a matter of course between those that were discarnate and those in physical matter, so there wasn't the sense of bereavement that you now experience.

God does not seek to separate His children – He seeks to *unify* His children and, once the second transition has taken place, of course those spirits who have moved on into angelic form can come back to visit us. They also impart their knowledge from beyond the spheres of the Earth plane to us and we can then distill it and bring it down to you.

When those brethren that have returned 'home' communicate with us they can choose the manner in which they do so. Sometimes we perceive them as a light – as a light we feel in our heads, in our souls and in our auras. Sometimes they revisit the form that they had and are able to assemble that form *at will* so we see them as we did before they made that second transition, although in a lighter, more etheric way.

I want to touch on the subject of *individuality* and I know this is something that vexed Michael many years ago when he read in accounts of life after death that, at the point of second death, individuality is *given up* to merge with the Godhead. In a scientific way (or as close to earthly science as I can put it) **you are one with God at this point and there is no separation,** so there is nothing for you to do in order to merge with God. You are already merged with God. It is only your earthly mind that puts barriers up and assumes that you are separate and individual. And yet you have, and you reflect, unique qualities of God – you are identified by the way that you use the God-qualities within and the way that you react to the Field on an outer level. You are, to all intents and purposes, an individual, and yet at the same time you are one with God and are merged with God. It is only your perception and your vibration that we seek to change so that you can escape from the prison of the Earth plane.

If you are already one with God and merged with God why, at a point of second transition, would you need to merge with God *again*? Why, if you have existed as a facet of God and a delight to God by being who and what you are, would you have to relinquish that and become absorbed by Universal Intelligence at the cost of that individuality that contributes to the uniqueness, flavour and structure of the universes and of Creation?

I want to reassure you that, at the time of second transition, you *retain your individuality* ...although I have to tell you that, at that point, your individuality is not what it was on Earth. As you read this book you will be associated within with a personality: you will have a particular name, a particular job and a particular set of circumstances. You will regard yourself in a certain way – as a father or mother, or a son or daughter, or a husband or wife, or a worker, and always with the name that you have been given – and you look in the mirror and identify yourself with that particular personality. That changes almost the instant that you move into the spiritual cleansing realms because, from that point onwards, you become aware that you are a greater being than that, you are a more *whole* being than that; and that you have had earthly personalities in the past that are *facets* of who you really are, just as you are a facet of who God really is. So your perception of individuality changes throughout your progression through the spiritual cleansing spheres.

The person that you find you are, as you make that second transition, is a very different person, in terms of understanding individuality, than the person you were when you left the Earth plane at the point of earthly transition. In fact, you will regard individuality as a nonsense... but yet will be individual. ...If I can explain that a little better: you will acknowledge that you are a unique viewpoint through which God experiences His universe, but at the same time you will acknowledge that you are God; that you are part of the Whole; that there is no merging necessary; that merging has always been there. The illusion of separateness will fall away and yet maintain itself so that you can continue to contribute to the growth of Divine Intelligence through *your* input.

Here, again, is something that is a joy to turn around in your thinking... many people on Earth seek input from God. They seek input in their daily lives and they seek their daily lives to be changed as they want them to be changed through God's intervention. They see God as contributing something to their existence and as a necessary Contributor, day after day, to shape things into how they want them to be. By the time you reach the second transition you realise that **you input God** and you realise that it is a joy and a wondrous gift that *you are bringing something to God*. At that point you do not say, 'God, do this for me! God, do that for me!' You say, 'God, I am bringing this to You. I hope this is an exciting aspect of Yourself that I deliver to You as only I can.'

In the second transition away from the spiritual cleansing spheres you become, if anything, far more individual in spiritual terms than you have ever been on Earth, and yet far more of the Whole. You exit into *bliss* and you exit into adventures that we cannot comment on because we are only given tiny glimpses as to what those adventures are, but we can say that the adventure goes on ...and on ...and on in wonderful, exciting, creative, blissful, harmonious and loving ways.

This, of course, shakes up your conventional religions' view of Heaven, where Heaven is a stopping point. **Heaven is a starting point!** Heaven is an ongoing situation that you contribute to and create in millions and millions of different ways. At the point of second transition your final burdens with regard to restriction are abandoned and you exist in a joyous state of freedom, finally freed from the effects of the confining situation I have referred to time and time again, called *the Fall*.

I feel that succinctly wraps up what I wanted to say today but, of course, if I am able to, I will answer any questions that you have.

Jane: Joseph, with those people that have finally escaped the cleansing area and are free, I thought they couldn't be totally free until *all mankind* was free of the effects of the Fall?

Joseph: There is, as I have said, communication with these beings and they come back to teach us, but you cannot confine higher-level vibration within a prison. The effect of the cleansing spheres is to gradually release that prison. Their consciousness is still available to us, *they* are still available to us, and they will connect to us until each soul has been extricated from the effects of the Fall, but there comes a time when their vibration *links with everything*. They remain our helpers and servers and we are connected, because that connection and concern for the Earth plane goes on, but those individuals are better suited to serve that 'cause' as part of a higher intelligence. Part of their consciousness is always connected, and will be until the last soul emerges in the quest to extricate souls from the trap of Earth.

I will speak more about angelic tendencies and the angelic way of life, which is so different, even, from *our* way of life, that it is extremely difficult to put into words (which is why I need the connection to other advisors)... I will talk about 'angelic being' (as opposed to *angelic beings*) in the book on the Fall. Does that make sense to you?

Jane: Yes, it does. Thank you.

Joseph: There is no abandonment at God-level of the people who are trapped on Earth; there is no abandonment in the cleansing spheres of those spirits and there is certainly no abandonment from those who have moved on. In moving on they are still with us, are still connected and they are still part of that force, and what better way of being able to serve the cause than by bringing through higher concepts that infuse the nesting of the spheres down to the Earth plane (although it has to be distilled because the brilliance of it would not be absorbable by people within earthly bodies)? What better way than to bring through more knowledge of higher consciousness to free those on Earth by making that knowledge available to them, enabling them to see further?

Another question, please!

David: Joseph, you mentioned individuality but, in going up through these cleansing spheres, you have soul groups that I assume amalgamate and share knowledge and so forth. Is that right?

Joseph: I am part of a soul group and, yes, that is correct. As an analogy you could see a soul group as a circle and that circle becomes bigger, of course, as the evolution through the spheres takes place. In effect, what is happening in the soul group happens at the time of the second transition, because soul groups are brought together by that same principle of vibration attracting a similar vibration. And, yes, individuals move on as soul groups, so at times you have momentous, joyous occasions when a complete group will move up. In fact it is rarely the individual that moves up – the individual moves up within part of its soul group.

A soul group is a call to a similar vibration. All transition through spiritual realms is a call to a similar vibration and is a harmony of similar vibration. The soul elevates itself through experience and understanding, and in elevating itself gives out a signal which harmonises with equal signals and brings that equal signal back to itself, pulling itself towards that signal. Soul groups are selected by vibrational signature and by the will within to be a *part of more of the same*.

The eventual transition from the last sphere of cleansing into the area beyond is a call to a similar vibration, and it is a call to a similar vibration that can be heeded slowly or quickly. Sometimes it takes a great deal of time for the souls to decide to relinquish the last vestiges of their humanity. **One of the great factors that hold souls back is fear,** and fear has to be gradually erased and cleansed from the human system. One of the great, great fears that you have on Earth is *fear of the unknown* – and that fear of the unknown is so deeply ingrained that, even in us, we have to filter it out step ...by step ...by step. Fear of accident and incident is very quickly quelled when you arrive in the spiritual cleansing spheres because there is nothing that can happen to you once you have moved higher than the Lower Astral, but there is still that ingrained fear of the unknown. At each step God asks you to step out into the unknown and embrace it – then it becomes known, it becomes joyous, and it becomes better than that which you have experienced before.

So, even in the highest spiritual cleansing sphere there is often that fear of the next step – not fear as you would understand it but a reticence to make that final change. That is why I say that you have to divest yourself of the last vestiges of humanity at that point ...and *very often* the last to go is fear, which is replaced by an acceptance that what lies beyond that fear is better and more exciting for you. There always comes a time when the pull of the harmonious vibration is *stronger* than the fear and, at that point, the decision is made and the individuals in that group move onwards.

Is that sufficient?

David: Yes, that was what I was getting at – whether it was the soul group making the transition rather than the individual.

Joseph: I have to address the mind-set and experience of the people who will be reading the book, and it is quite a shock to some people to be confronted with the prospect of an ongoing journey rather than a Heaven; or to be confronted with the prospect of continuing life rather than oblivion, let alone the prospect that they will merge in thought, purpose and dedication with other souls and then continue to move onwards to another plateau. So, we must take our example of an individual given this morning as an *illustration* rather than the reality of a single soul approaching a door on a certain day and deciding to go through that door.

Is there anything else?

Mark: Joseph, in relation to the cleansing spheres and the effects of the trap resulting from the Fall, is it that the spheres have always been in place for spiritual evolution and now the purpose is even more significant in terms of a rescue mission for souls from Earth? Has that changed in any way, or has that always been the case?

Joseph: That is an excellent question because, according to most spiritual literature, the emphasis is on the spheres being the path of evolution ...and a *confined* path of evolution. Some mention seven levels of evolution, some mention other numbers, and some literature I have seen states that those spheres are nested around the Earth (which they *are* in comparative terms) and that, when you reach the pinnacle, that is where you reside. I want to suggest to you that that information brought through has been *skewed* by the Field and, again, limits, in terms of what the soul feels it is capable of, its view of what it should be achieving.

The spheres came about as a result of the Fall – prior to the Fall they were not necessary. Prior to the Fall the angelic inheritance of mankind was fully realised in consciousness and people were able to visit this area to experience, but also return to the greater consciousness *at will* without death and without fear. There was no need for a path of evolution. I would turn that term 'evolution' on its head and say 'cleansing'. After the first great cataclysm it became necessary, as the trapped souls on Earth could not be reached by *direct* contact with higher Creation because they were encased in a heavier field of matter than that Creation could make an impact on. It would be like trying to describe a motor car to an insect – the two do not connect. So there had to be put in place, over millennia, a mechanism whereby communication could be distilled down to the souls on Earth so that they would begin their quest to look beyond the Field they were trapped in. This, again, is a topic that will be covered at length in the communications on the Fall.

But, in answer to your question, the spiritual spheres of evolution are really the spiritual spheres of *cleansing* and it is *now* time to make people aware of that fact ...**whilst there is *still time* to make them aware of that fact.** Before the first cataclysm those spheres were not there and were not necessary. They are a means of communication; they are a means of cleansing; they are a means of restoring. You could call them 'restoration spheres' if you like – 'cleansing' seems very clinical. They *restore* the heritage of each soul back to that soul through a series of events that change thinking, perception, outlook and viewpoint to the point where they emerge into the 'sunlight'.

Does that make sense?

Mark: It does indeed, thank you.

Is there one final question?

Jane: Joseph, could I just ask about something that goes back to a previous chapter, where people are advised that they have passed over and that they can move on in the spiritual realms, but they are drawn back to the Earth because they might have some issue that they haven't resolved or they might be attracted to fast food, fast cars ...or whatever. Do those people get any say in what life they are going to lead? Will they have a life with fast food or fast cars, or could they be born as an AIDS orphan in Africa? Who is it that *chooses* the life of an AIDS orphan in Africa?

Joseph: Always, as we have explained, the choice is made by the soul to return to Earth. But, because the soul is linked to a number of souls, that choice is linked, through the line of restoration, cleansing or evolution, to a number of souls above that soul who desperately want to illuminate that soul's consciousness to the dilemma that it finds itself in. Therefore, through request, permission is given to those who are in a position, through experience, to organise certain events along the life-course of a soul. Permission is given for them to work, in conjunction with the wishes of that soul, to divert that soul into situations that are likely (but not guaranteed) to illuminate it.

The soul says: 'I want to come back!' and the soul is then born into *a different era*. The world has changed within the Field since the soul last visited it so the soul will try and seek out *similar experiences* to those that it feels it is missing. Again, the fast food is only an illustration and is a symbol of some deeper desire. To see the fast food, or the fast car, or the cola as something that the soul is coming back for is a little bit misleading – those are the end points of what the soul finds gratifying. But there is a desire for certain *types of experience* again, which may manifest as a desire for the food, or the cola, or the car, or the sex, or whatever. But it is really the desire that is manifesting in the soul and it is the desire for more of the complexity and instant gratification of the Field that draws the soul back.

Once that soul has been drawn back, yes, it will find those things along the path of the new life, but it is the wish of the souls working out that soul's life-path to draw that soul into experiences where the desire of the soul to return to the Field is *lessened*. It is a collaborative effort and the amazing thing is that, *at heart* within the soul, **there is a desire to escape from the Field.** No matter that the soul has drawn itself into physicality again – at that point of connection with God there is a desire to be extricated. That is why it is allowed and permitted, for those with more knowledge, to influence that life into situations that increase the desire to escape and diminish the desire to remain. Do you see that?

Jane: Yes. I just wondered about the people who come back into terrible lives – such as the AIDS orphan or people in war zones. How have they chosen to come back there?

Joseph: Let me tell you – *every* life is a terrible life! **Every life on Earth is a terrible life because it is not the life you are supposed to be living** and we have to examine the functions of the Lords of Karma at great length (at greater length than I can today) to understand the placing of souls.

At each moment in each life souls are placed in an opportunity to grow. With certain souls that opportunity to grow has to be more *explicit* – has to be more of a 'shake' and more of a dramatic occurrence on a physical level, otherwise they would never stop the repetition of life ... after life ...after life ...after life. Also, because of the complexity of being linked to everything else, you have to understand that the souls who appear to be having worse lives than other souls are also shining as beacons to those other souls who need to take notice of that life to shake themselves out of their *own* complacency.

Souls are placed where it is considered most fitting for them to do the most good to themselves and to others. There are many lines or vibrations that run through a soul's life: there is an intuitive level; there is a purpose level; there is a level of past experience; there is a desire level. All these things have to be projected, looked at and woven together with the end result of the soul that has reincarnated and the souls that it is touching getting the most benefit *spiritually* out of that life.

Remember that the physical is an illusion. The physical is a combination of two things – the pull of the Field and the unseen quest to extricate souls from the Field. Whenever you are looking at a soul in matter you are looking at a soul that is a representation *physically* of the Field pulling on that soul and that soul seeking, at core-level, to pull itself out of the Field. You are looking at a projection in matter that is designed to evolve that soul ...but also to evolve you and to evolve the souls that touch that soul. It is a complex matrix of energy and probabilities and the life on Earth that is lived exists *never just for the individual*.

Your life does not exist for you – it exists for you at one level but it also exists for everyone else. **Everyone's life on Earth exists for them and also for everyone else.** It cannot be otherwise – you cannot be part of the Whole without influencing the Whole and the Whole influencing you.

So, the positioning of a soul in a certain type of life is to allow that soul to grow away from the Field but also to allow the others that connect with that soul to grow too: to grow in compassion, to grow in understanding and to grow in the need to change things. Always we are combating the Field and, for every soul that comes back, it is not our wish that they come back but it is our wish that that soul's life is not wasted, so we take the opportunity (most times without the soul knowing this on a *conscious* level) to change as much as we can, not just for that soul but for everyone. Do you see?

Jane: Yes, thank you.

Joseph: I am always happy when I feel that we have taken a step forward and have changed things during a communication, and today I feel particularly that we have got a number of concepts across as I wish to – as *we* wish to. I thank you for that and I wish you to know that we are involved in your lives (How could we be otherwise than involved in your lives?) and are helping to make those lives as tolerable as they can be as you deliver the communication we are bringing to you.

Chapter Nineteen
Needs in the Higher Spheres

Joseph: I begin with a good morning ...and it *is* a *good* morning! It is *always* a good morning – it is only the *perception* of that morning by individuals that makes it anything other than a good morning.

We don't waste any information and we sometimes try to integrate a message before we actually deliver it, so what you have been talking about [*ref. to members of the circle discussing what they want for lunch*] is relevant, because I begin this morning by bringing in a loaf of bread. It is a beautiful loaf of baked bread – there is a smell with it, and a texture to it, and it is something that every man, woman and child across this globe will recognise as something that they desire and want. If you place that bread in front of them, they *want* it – whether or not their physical framework *needs* it they feel in their mind that they want it because it sets off certain signals within them.

It is the same, to a lesser or greater extent, with a great many things for people. People are surrounded by *things* from birth to physical death ...things they feel they want and feel they need. They *must have* certain clothes; they *must have* a certain car; they *must have* holidays; they *must have* a type of house; they *must have* certain types of food; they *must* live in a certain political climate; they *must* live in a particular area of the world; they *must* see that others share their values so that they are being fed back their own values, projected onto others and projected back to themselves. It is a world of *need* and

253

desire you find yourselves in from cradle to grave, with needs being met many times each day in order that you feel satisfied *for a short time* ...and then you have to address another need, another desire, and another 'requisite' just down the road, that you *have to have*.

What has this got to do with life after death?

Everything!

Everything – because, to a lesser or greater extent, the need for things is carried over by the soul into the next stage of existence. The soul arrives and feels that it still *needs*: it needs to eat; it needs to sleep; it needs the comfort of others; it needs ...it needs ...it wants ...it *wants*! This is a *barrier* to the development of the soul because the soul, at any point in its existence (even on Earth), always has everything that it needs – because it needs *nothing*. It is part of the Divine and the Divine is infinite supply and, therefore, at any stage in its existence *it has everything*. The need to *need* is the effect of the Field, and it is an effect that you have to transmute when you arrive in higher spheres of consciousness.

When souls arrive in the initial realms they feel hungry and, because they feel hungry, they think of a specific type of food ...and that food *appears* in front of them. They eat it and feel its effects – its taste and its texture – and they drink, they eat and they smoke. Would it surprise you that certain souls actually take drugs for a while? But none of these things are 'real', just as the needs *here* on Earth are not real. The person who has eaten frequently, smoked frequently or taken drugs frequently can eat, take those drugs and indulge in whatever *needs* they want, until a certain time comes when those things lose their substance and their effectiveness and the soul has to look beyond them and discard them.

One of the greatest lessons that a soul has to learn in the initial spheres of consciousness after physical death is that there is no need and that every need is met. It is a difficult thing to explain because, in saying that every need is met, you imply that there is a need... and **there is no need.** If you confront a soul in the initial spheres of consciousness and say, 'What does God need? What does the Divine need? Eventually that soul has to admit that God needs nothing.

How could it be otherwise?

If God is everything and everything is contained within God, how can there be a need? How can God have any need? You could say that God needs His children back ...but they *are* back. They are already part of God – it is only within *their* perception that there is a need to be back. In God's perception they have not gone anywhere that is separate from Him because there is no separation from Him.

And so, by trial and error, the soul that is evolving eventually finds that it does not need food – that the food is an illusion. It does not need drugs – the drugs are an illusion. It does not need anything *material* because the material things are illusion. It then has to take the step past *needing the Earth*, which returns us to an earlier part of the book when we were talking about the desire of souls to return to the Earth plane again ...and again ...and again. That return is because of the need within the soul that the soul has generated for itself: 'I need to experience this again or that again. I need to tie up loose ends. I need to build something new. I need to taste that. I need to have that sensation again. I need the Earth!'

You need nothing, and part of the experience of progressing through the cleansing realms is to divest oneself of that need and to understand that *the soul needs nothing.*

Actually the soul does need something: the soul needs to *be.*

But that is not a need; it is a recollection; it is a remembrance; it is an awakening. You talk of 'awakening' on Earth and you don't understand the term. Awakening means remembering and understanding the integration that you have, the remarkable power of the Divine that flows through you, that remarkable power that instantly chases away all your perceptions of need. If you are ill, you are perceiving a need – a need to be well. You have no need to be well – you cannot be otherwise. What you need to understand to get rid of the illness is that the illness is not there.

So many needs!

There comes a point in the spheres of progression and cleansing when need is recognised as being something that does not exist. At that point the landscape around the soul changes dramatically because, until that point, to a lesser or greater degree, the soul creates around itself memories of that which it is used to and of that which it perceives it needs. From the spiritual mind there is a mental need for a familiar landscape that is linked to the Earth, and so, at first, there is a need for the buildings and trappings of the earthly life. As the soul progresses, these change to more classical and timeless styles of building but they are still buildings. In some of the initial spheres of being there are buildings that are very like those that you see on Earth at the moment – they are contemporary to the time-scale of the soul that has moved on. The soul that moves on today (if that soul has not progressed far, spiritually) will find itself in a setting very similar to the one it has left on Earth, with buildings and streets that seem familiar.

As the soul progresses there is a gradual refining of landscape and environment, with souls *choosing* a habitat for themselves because they need a point of reference, but it is not a need based on the need to constantly be in a particular time-scale. My colleague, the *Persian Gentleman*, has chosen for himself a tower that overlooks the boundary between two dimensions or areas of 'reality'. That is not a need but a *familiarity* that enables him to project his essence onto the universe in a particular way. That tower can be there and gone at a moment's notice, dependent on what he feels he wants to project at any particular time (although 'time', as we have discussed at length, is a relative term).

Souls progress, initially, through a series of circumstances around them that are very similar to those they have encountered on the Earth but then, as the desire for earthly things diminishes, the landscape around that soul (and those souls as they group together) changes. Here, we come to an exploration of territory that cannot be explored *effectively* through earthly words because the landscape becomes more creative and more sensitive to the dictates of the spiritual mind. In other words, it is more malleable and easier to shape than the levels below, but also the landscape is becoming more God-infused and more aware of its God-heritage. The landscape in the higher spheres exhibits more of the potential and infinite variety of form that is contained within the Godhead. The landscape reflects the power of God to a *greater extent* than the lower spheres do – and certainly more than the Earth plane does. The Earth plane's features are locked by the effects of the Field and the effects of millions of souls expecting to get up, morning after morning, and look out of their window onto the *same* scene. You are locked into a certain *limited* display of created potential but, as you move away from the Earth plane and the need to view things in that way, then other potentials reveal themselves around the travelling soul. By 'potentials' I mean aspects of God-creativity and aspects of what God can bring into form if He wishes and if the souls travelling through those regions wish too.

The landscapes that I am trying to describe (and I include the emergence of *my* soul group into one of those landscapes as well) are places where creativity, potential and the desire to integrate into certain projects all mesh into one. There is a changing landscape around each individual soul, depending on its desires, and there is a changing landscape around the group soul, depending on its desires, projects, aims and intentions.

What do these landscapes look like?

Indescribable in earthly terms!

I can tell you that we have a colour spectrum that is vastly different to yours – vastly enhanced. I can tell you that we can *feel* the energy from the atmosphere to a far greater extent than you can; that we are enthused with a sense of wellbeing, of bliss, of strength, of youth and of capability that is far beyond anything that you experience when encased in flesh whilst on Earth.

As group souls we have an 'anchored landscape' – in other words we have a landscape that is a reference point within which we can communicate and live but we know that, if we are involved in a project or if we want to experience something else (either individually or as a group soul), then we can let go of that landscape for however long we wish to without fear that we will *lose* it.

Back to another aspect of need – you need on Earth because you fear that there is going to be a lack, so you keep having to top things up: 'I have food now but I will need food tomorrow. I have love now but I will need love tomorrow' – and always you are reluctant to let go of the constructs that you have put around yourself. We know (and this is not arrogance – I am trying to explain something) that there is no lack and no need, so we can let go of something and instantly bring it back without fearing that it will disintegrate and without putting part of our energies into maintaining that need.

We can let go of the anchored landscape of our group soul to experience other aspects of being. Sometimes we exist in a formless state so that we can share concepts better without any barriers and hindrance of form. Sometimes we exist in a creative joined-state so that we can bring forth *new* form, and that is a blissful state to exist in – to see your thoughts and intentions being constructed. Sometimes we exist to *observe* and we find ourselves overlooking and integrating with other aspects of universal Creation simply to experience them, not to interfere or to adjust but to simply experience – to experience life on other planets, to experience the landscape of space, the landscape of planets and the various options in the physical universe.

Consider yourselves on Earth and how limited you are at this stage in your existence. You exist in a need society, which prevents you from experiencing in full the beauty of the Earth, and you have not yet reached out to experience the beauty of other worlds. For the most part you maintain that there is only yourselves in the physical universe because you need the security of feeling that you are the only constructive and intelligent beings in this universe. Were you to consider that there are other beings that would make you feel insecure (more insecure than you are at the moment) so you are locked in. You study other planets and space *darkly* – always from the perspective of need: 'I need the universe to work in a certain way and I will not look beyond that.' From our vantage point (and remember this is not the end for us because we have not reached an 'end') we can see so many things and can experience Creation in so many ways ...and that is what we exist to do as the *angelic beings* that we really are. **We exist to experience Creation – to be one with it, to create it and to experience it.**

That is the secret of 'individuality' (that really doesn't exist): to know that you are One, to know that you are a participant in that Creation and to know that you can actually step back from it to experience what you are from a distance. That is all individuality is – nothing more!

I must tie into this chapter a little section concerning the end of things because it ties into need and what I have said about always wanting and thinking that there will eventually be a lack and an end to supply. There is no end to supply and, as far as we can see (and I have a twinkle in my eye as I say that because we can see pretty far), *there is no end*.

There is no end!

There is only a new experience; there is only a passage from one experience to another. You do not end as you know (or I *hope* you know in reading this book) when you reach the point of physical death. You do not end when you move from one sphere to another. You do not end when you escape the cleansing spheres and emerge into Infinity.

End is a human term. I wish you to understand that – end is a human term and has no meaning beyond your physical life. In fact, it has no meaning within your physical life from a *spiritual* perspective. There is no such thing as an end – nor is there such a thing as a *beginning*. The journey that I am describing within this book is not a journey that begins and ends – it is simply a journey or series of experiences and those experiences go on. You are entering worlds without end, and they only 'end' in the sense that you pass through them into another sphere, into another world and into another energy-matrix.

There is no end!

...And I wanted to say that because it may free some souls from the *need to return to Earth*. There is no end to your endeavours; there is no end to your creativity; there is no end to the people you have loved. You cannot return to the Earth simply because you fear that there will be an end to things if you do not come back, *and I would ask you to think about that*. Whatever you feel that you want to continue and that the Earth plane has to offer can be continued in far greater and more satisfying terms outside of the sphere of the Earth. You can continue with your creativity; you can continue to explore aspects of your own spirituality and aspects of your own emotional and mental self; you can continue with your voyage of self-discovery, if you so wish, far more easily *after* you have left the physical cradle of the Earth.

Nothing is ever lost – no thought you have had is ever lost; no person you have ever met is ever lost; no situation you have moved through is ever lost. Far better, after some time of rest, to consider the true meaning of the situations that have come to you on Earth from a *spiritual* vantage point than by returning to Earth and immersing yourself once again in a situation that robs you of your spiritual memory and power.

We are growing close to an end to this book. It is a vast subject but I think we will have contained within the covers enough information for you, the reader, to gain some insight into what lies ahead for you. Just one further chapter and I will close this book, but this morning, before I do so, of course, there are *questions*... and I invite those questions.

Tony: Joseph, can I ask a question on *need*? I can relate what you have been saying to stages in my own life where I have had need (particularly in the wrong directions), experienced it and then relinquished that need. I have a concern that I am now trying to work very hard in the way God's thoughts would wish for me but can that also be a need? Have I transferred the need to another area? Is it possible to need in a spiritual sense equal to a material sense?

Joseph: First of all, you must understand that when we come through sometimes we sound very harsh and very strict, and it is because we love you that we have to shepherd you as much as we are allowed to within the time that we have for communication. We don't... pity you... 'pity' is the wrong word... we are *sorry* and *worried* that you are in physical matter. We are worried for *all* souls in physical matter... In your question you have highlighted one of the problems of the filter of the physical mind, because **the physical mind loves nothing more than to indulge itself in a loop or a spiral of thought.**

In order to work spiritually to your best ability each day all you have to do is *surrender* to the Divine (which is also you) and to demand of that *divine-you* the instruction that will allow you to work in the optimum way spiritually each day.

261

Your goals are known by the universe and by you – the inner-you. Therefore, there is no need to worry *beyond* the day that you have, and there is no need to worry *for* the day that you have. If your intention is to elevate souls and elevate yourself so that you can further elevate souls in a cycle, there is no need to worry. You are doing *what you can do* according to the energies that you are able to draw to yourself and we are able to put around you. Remember, you are working from within the Field. Remember that, for hundreds, thousands and millions of souls the question that you have asked would *never* occur to them and that should answer for you the fact that you have reached a certain level of *remembrance* of spiritual awareness.

We ask nothing and everything. God asks nothing and everything. In other words, God does not expect you to push yourself to incredible limits in trying to define what you should be doing spiritually. We ask everything, however, because what you have chosen is a life of intense sacrifice that requires you to think differently, to go against the crowd and to put aside some of the things that the Earth will tell you that you need, in order to determine and address what other people need.

As a friend (because I am a friend, I hope, and an advisor and an equal) I would say: please do not become too engrossed in what to do next. Please do not become too engrossed in feeling that you are failing (*especially* in feeling that you are failing to do what you should do next) because in becoming engrossed remember you are a creative being and the mind, therefore, creates a further feeling of failing and a further disruption in the way that you feel you are progressing spiritually. Rather, walk hand-in-hand with God and, whatever you are tasked to do on a daily basis, accept that God-energy is flowing through you to allow you to make the right decisions. Accept that there is a plan for you, and that plan will only be seen by you stepping back from it after a period of time and not now. Accept that you are a worker in a war situation and you have to fight the good fight today …and today …and today, with no worries for *tomorrow*.

Do not become over analytical or critical within your own physical mind or you will paralyse yourself. In order to work effectively for God and for yourself, forget the self. If there is a straying from the path, you will be brought up short and you will be told that there is a straying from the path, and the endeavours that you put your energies into will not bear fruit. If there is no straying from the path and you are correct in what you feel you should be doing, that path will open up. Remember that you have been placed within a community that you sit with today so that other information can be *dispassionately* given to you to ensure that you stay on the right path and that every member of this little group also stays on the right path. Gosh, what a long answer! Do you understand that?

Tony: Yes, thank you, I do.

Joseph: We do not come critically to you – we come amazed at your steadfastness. I mustn't say too much or I will make you bigheaded, but we come thankful for the link because without you we have no link with the Earth plane. So we do not come to criticise; we come to point out that which you already know and we have to do that strictly in the form of communication that we give to other souls to shake them out of their complacency and to shake them out of their world mind-set. But we come with love, with patience and with thanks – and love, patience and thanks are what you should also give to yourself in doing this work, and the work is progressing as it should progress.

Don't make things complicated because if you make things complicated, you are projecting complications around you. It is simple: 'I am doing what God wants me to do. I am instructed by God. I know what to do' ...that is all.

Is there another question, please?

Jane: Joseph, we are coming to the end of the trilogy[1] and I wondered if you could summarise the advice of what we can do on Earth, and

263

also when we get to the initial levels, to enhance our spiritual development? I get the impression that, for people in the cleansing spheres, it can take them a million years to move up or they can do it quite quickly. Similarly, our development on Earth can be very slow, so I wondered if you could give readers a summary of how to best progress on Earth and in the spiritual realms?

Joseph: What you don't have at the moment is a read-through of the book that we are coming to an end with and you also don't have the last chapter of the book. I would rather that we built up the picture of reality beyond this Earth *gradually* through the course of the book. You have to understand that for many years you have understood what we are talking about but, for many people, it is like trying to describe a flavour to them. These concepts are new and we are aware of having to put as much information into the communications as we can whilst also having to *tailor* that communication to the fact that people are, for the most part, new to it. For you, with accepting minds and the evidence of years of communication through spiritual contact, you are used to certain concepts and you have taken them on board. You could say it is like trying to teach a baby to drive a car; for you who have driven for years it is second nature but for the baby it is an alien landscape. So, gradually, we will build up communication.

I have not yet fully decided on the final chapter and I have not yet decided which fork in the road to take after this book has been delivered. For me it is important to deliver the rest of the information on *life after death* but it is also important to deliver information on the Fall. Those two things are in my being at the same time and I can switch the switch and go from one subject to another. Would that I could use Michael to deliver two strings of information, which I *can* do spiritually, as many streams of information can be delivered simultaneously, but not through one physical channel.

If I were to choose, I would be delighted to deliver the information on the Fall next. I feel it is time! I feel it is something that Michael wishes to be involved in and I also wish to use the medium whilst he is at the prime of his ability. That is not to say there is not a lot of time left – there is, *relatively speaking*, but I would rather deliver that information at a point where it is easiest, before the Earth plane eventually builds up (even with Michael) a layer that is harder and harder to penetrate as his earthly energies begin to wane. But that has not happened yet and is not to happen for some time... So, I suppose, I have talked myself into the Fall, and I hope I have talked *you* into the Fall.

Would that we could manipulate your Field globally! Would that we could make it all right, make it easy and make it so simple for you to sit back and deliver this information, but we are only allowed to influence your own auras and your own pieces of the world. Yes, we can bring like-minded people to you because they are ready to make that connection but we cannot influence the whole world, unfortunately, because that is to do with free will and to do with the Field.

We become frustrated at times because this information is ready to deliver *now* but I can't deliver it today because you do not have the means for me to deliver it today – financially, materially, or through the channel. The channel could not sustain communication for the length of time it would take me to deliver the book. If he could we would deliver it *now*. So we, like you, are fighting circumstances, but we, like you, are doing the very best we can and saying: 'Yes, God, that is what You want and that is what we will do.'

A final question, please!

David: Joseph, which part of us does need arise from – is it the physical side or is it within the soul?

Joseph: And that is the reason why I want to write the Fall next, because that is a very pertinent question and it is a question that needs to be answered *at length*.

In brief (and very briefly and sketchily) the soul on Earth has a need and that need is to remember who it is and to be reunited with God and to go 'home' – that is the soul's need.

That need is then layered by aspects of physicality – by mental fields, physical fields and material fields – and is perverted and translated into a *perceived need* for things on this level: money which will make me happy; sex which will make me happy; buildings which will make me happy; control over other people which will make me happy; the need to put down roots and to accumulate things that will be mine forever (but obviously won't) which will make me happy... All those needs go back to the *basic need* to be reunited with God and take away the barrier because, of course, you *are* united with God – it is the barrier that you have built up since the time of the Fall that makes you believe that you have needs.

It is a soul-need that is not a 'need' at all. It is an absolute yearning that, were you to experience the core of each soul on Earth and translate it, you would be overwhelmed by – a cry for reunification with God. It is a sad and heart-rending thing to hear because, irrespective of what the soul is doing physically or mentally, there is that cry from its core to be reunited with God. Everything that the soul does on Earth (whether correctly in line with God, or mistakenly and thereby causing harm to others) is as a result of that prime need. *There is no other need!*

You have no other need, and the irony is that you do not actually have that prime need either because you are part of God. Your *real* need is to take away the scales, the darkness or the veil. You describe us as 'being beyond the veil', as though you lift a veil and there is the spirit world! It is *you* who are wearing the veil, not us. **You need to lift the veil!** This is why we bring though the communication – so that you can lift the veil, recognise who you are and then restore harmony, progress to this level and escape this level ...to go on to be the creative being that you were before the time of the Fall.

I must relinquish my post and must relinquish the driving seat in order to give Michael time to recover. Tell him that all is well – I know he is troubled.

[1] A reference to **Revelation, Illumination** and **Your Life After Death**.

Chapter Twenty
Love – A Different View of Life After Death

Joseph: It is my intention to close this book by giving readers a different view of life after death. We have covered many topics in the preceding chapters and the whole process may look incredibly complicated, incredibly deep and incredibly varied as to the worlds you can visit inside yourself and around yourself. There are seemingly infinite possibilities as you leave behind the earthly body, but there is one word that has to be re-introduced at the end of this book into everything I have said about the spiritual realms ...and that word is **love**.

Everything that happens to you when you cross over the threshold into the spiritual realms happens out of love – happens out of love for yourself, the love of others for you, and the love of God for you and for everything. Indeed, everything that happens to you whilst you are in the *mud and mire* of the Field happens to you out of God's love and God's desire to extricate you from that mess of thought you find yourself in because you have chosen to place yourself in it, time and again.

The choices that are open to you on the spiritual side of life, as on Earth, are presented to you out of love and out of the 'need' to get you back to your original status and grandeur; the need to rid you of the illusions that have plagued you for millennia and the need to restore your heavenly and spiritual memories. What you regard as the 'be all and end all' – i.e. your earthly life – and what you may regard, if you are spiritually aware, as another encapsulation of experience – i.e. the spirit worlds – are only a *fraction* of your true perception.

You are operating mentally, physically and spiritually at this moment on a very narrow waveband. You are capable of operating on an infinitely far, *far* greater waveband but you have *chosen*, through your beliefs and actions in the past and through your beliefs now, to only see through a little slit into the outside world, into reality, into greater reality ...and at times even that slit is closed off to you.

Your passage through earthly life and your passage through heavenly or spiritual life, as you understand it with regard to the spheres we have talked about thus far, is intended to set you *free*. **Love and freedom are the same thing!** God has not imprisoned you, you have imprisoned yourself. The first step in releasing yourself from that prison is to look back at the earthly life and see it for what it is and what it was, a series of happenings that only present you with a dulled-down, compacted and restrictive experience of being. Once you are able to see that you set yourself free from the earthly life and are free to take great strides in spiritual evolution in the cleansing nest of spheres that lead to Infinity.

You then have to constantly seek freedom in *those* spheres – freedom from thoughts and concepts you hold on to, believe to be true and take with you on your journey as 'travelling companions'. The purpose or function of the spheres beyond the Earth – between the Earth and Infinity – is to cleanse you and make you free. This freedom begins when you turn your back on the earthly life. *Begins*, not ends! You make yourself increasingly free through the experiences that come to you as you travel through the greater spheres.

I want you to remember, too, that your journey does not end with your reaching the most elevated state that you are able to within the cleansing spheres, because that state, too, is an ending... and a *beginning. Life continues.* In fact, it *starts* in all its God-glory, potential and creative power with your attainment of 'be-ing' in the final sphere and your decision to step through that door into Infinity and into the glorious concept-possibilities and infinite joy of God-creativity that exist beyond the confinement of the Earth and the spiritual cleansing spheres. It is a confinement that gradually lessens, to be sure, but it is still confinement and is *necessary*. It is necessary, as you will discover when we discuss the effects of the Fall on your ability to perceive, because the Fall restricted perception, spiritual ambition and the creativity and freedom of the soul. All were taken away and, because this is what you are left with, this narrow field of perception, you believe it to be everything, you believe it to be your world and many of you refuse to see beyond that narrow perception.

...And where do I, *Joseph*, fit into all of this? If Infinity beckons, why have I decided to remain in the cleansing spheres of spirituality that exist beyond the Earth plane?

The answer to that lies in the word 'freedom', as I have said, because as we progress through the spheres we make choices, through freedom and because of our increased vision spiritually. We see that, as we are 'be-ing' in the elevated spheres, we are also residing in the lower spheres, because we reside in each of you and you reside in each of us. As we regain spiritual freedom we become more aware of our 'oneness', a oneness that means every person you encounter is *you* and that that oneness of you and them is God. For certain of us it then becomes a matter of conscience and a matter of needing everyone – every aspect of me, *Joseph*, and every aspect of you – to be free from the effects of the Fall and free from the effects of the Field. In other words **we imprison ourselves in love;** we imprison ourselves by saying, 'Not until *everyone* is free will we move on.'

There are those of us who do move on but they remain *linked*. We do not perceive them as we perceive each other because they are on a different level of consciousness and manifestation of matter but the link is still there. And we encourage them. We say, 'Go! Be free! Leave these wonderful spheres (because they *are* wonderful; they are beautiful, they are fulfilling and they sustain us); leave them because we know that you are going to greater glory. We will make choices on your behalf and we will send you messages to report on our progress in taking out by the roots those souls on Earth and in the lower spheres as part of the plan to return those *facets of God* back to God and return this area of Creation – the Earth and its surrounding matter – back to its original concept.'

We have been here a very long time in your terms – *a very long time*. We have seen civilisation on Earth rise and fall and the same mistake being made as souls encrust and entrap themselves deeper into physical concepts of matter. And then we wait. We have to have patience. We wait …and we wait …and we *wait*, until such time as those souls can be re-installed within a framework that they are familiar with and can be gradually approached so that their concept of matter can be changed and they can slowly elevate themselves.

This is what we mean when we say it is difficult for you but it is more difficult for us. We have waited for a long, *long* time, but we cannot do anything else. It is not as though we are doing anything noble; we are doing what we *must* in order to have any peace, and we are doing what we must because we love each other and we love you. We do not make gradations in that love – we do not say that we love this spirit ten percent and that spirit eighty percent of the whole. We cannot do that because we have reached a point where we realise that love is equal for all things and must be sent to all things equally. **All things must be regarded as equal**, no matter what they have instigated in the Field of heavy matter on Earth. That doesn't matter; there is no judgement from us, only judgement *from the souls themselves* as they try to regain freedom.

The journey for us is not over and will not be over until we have extricated every last soul that still believes in the old ways, still believes in the old illusion and still pours power into the old illusion. The old illusion must end and, if you have read my other books (and also if you have not) there is a warning: **civilisation is reaching a point where it is about to make the same mistake again.**

My purpose in delivering this book is to open your eyes, to open your ears and to open your heart to something different, to a better way to approach yourself and others *before it is too late*. Actually, it is never too late in the Infinite scheme of things, but unless there is change it will be too late, in this instance, to prevent the souls who are trapped at the moment on Earth from entrenching themselves *even deeper* into their reliance on the Field and thereby placing themselves in an area of 'non-consciousness' until they can be re-installed into a *similar* vibration to the one they will have left (a cleansed, but *similar* vibration, because their souls could not endure a higher level of vibration).

There is still time **...but not much!**

There is still time to look at your life and the lives of others; to ask God, the Father, to show you on a certain day – not a day that you dictate but the day that He dictates – to show you things *as they really* are and to open your eyes from morning 'til night to the *reality* of the sphere you are so reliant upon. During that day you will experience terror and horrors as you see the effects of the Field of consciousness of mankind upon souls living on the Earth; the effects of the Field on the Earth; the effects of the Field on you; the effects of the Field on everyone: on children, on animals, on the planet itself. *Ask to be shown.*

Then, when your eyes have been opened, you will approach your life in a different way and you will be working towards the day when the knowledge that I have given you in this book is with people from birth; when the book will be redundant; when you will *know* what is ahead of you, *know* who you are and *know* how to react *correctly* with others in your environment to restore to yourself and to others the spiritual heritage that is yours.

You have 'slept' for thousands of years. You fear what comes next. You fear death but death is a doorway to greater life. The spheres that exist beyond the Earth plane are a further doorway to a greater life, a doorway back to a life that is yours, that cannot be destroyed but is inaccessible to you at the moment because of the choices you made so long ago and continue to buy into now.

If I can take away your fear of life after death then other influences – others of my group and other groups in my sphere and the spheres beyond – will have greater success in influencing you through your intuition, through your instincts and, in certain cases, by appearing to you and talking to you, as I appear and talk to this little group.

We *will* meet again because I have more to say. I am not going to let this opportunity pass without delivering all the information I can on what is wrong and how to put it right. My next collection of information in a book, or however it is presented, will be on the Fall, which I have spoken about for years to Michael and his friends. It will explain *in precise detail* how you placed yourself at such a perceived distance from God, what went wrong and how that event millennia ago, on a very different Earth than you now see, is still holding you in its thrall.

Until that time please consider what is written in this book – not for my sake but for yours, and for the sake of the brothers and sisters around you. May God bless you and keep you in your efforts to shake yourself free from what is only a tiny portion of your true heavenly, infinite and glorious life.

[*Addressing the circle*] It is always with some amusement (after what I have said about us being linked) that you feel I cannot hear what you are saying, that your conversations are private, that when you say something regarding *Joseph* that *Joseph* doesn't pick up that information, and that when you joke I don't pick up those jokes [*reference to Jane joking to Michael the evening before that she imagined Joseph to be like an accountant*]. How could I not? The minute you think about me you are linked to me; you have 'made the call' and I pick up the 'phone' and I hear and see.

I feel that there is enough energy for Michael to continue and, therefore, I am going to invite questions. What would you like to ask me?

Jane: Joseph, you mentioned that if we don't change the world will close down again and that the souls who are still trapped will go into a state of unconsciousness for a time. When that happened last time, were the *borderline* people able to escape into the cleansing spheres? By that I mean those people where you advise them not to come back but they still choose to return to Earth. In that situation are those people then forced to move on into the cleansing spheres because there is nowhere else to go?

Joseph: Each time this has happened there has been the same result but a different set of circumstances that led up to it. It is a good question but it is a question that needs to be answered in the next book. There is always a certain amount of souls who have seen beyond the illusion and those souls are free.

What you have to understand (and it is a difficult 'pill' for readers to swallow) is that souls *by volition* place themselves in harm's way, in cataclysm, in the end of things and in stasis. If you choose not to be part of that *then you are not a part of that* – and you will say: 'Well, if the skyscrapers came crashing down and the waves were hitting the land, people would be screaming not to be a part of that situation!' But you have to remember that people operate on a number of levels, and *subconsciously* the soul is only able to perceive a vibration harmonious to itself. It chooses a range of vibrations at any one time that it is comfortable with and, if that range of vibrations does not extend into greater worlds and greater perceptions, then that soul cannot escape its own creation and its own illusion.

So, what I am saying is that the souls who remain within the effects of a cataclysm or end of civilisation have no choice but to be within it because they are operating within their waveband of perception and could not operate anywhere else. That is the whole point of raising consciousness – to make them aware of a greater waveband so that they *do* escape that entrapment and imprisonment, which is *inevitable* if they don't expand their spiritual senses.

Any soul that has gained a *degree* of spiritual freedom will be able to escape the pull of the Earth.

That soul will still have to traverse the cleansing spheres but will be away from the non-conscious state or stasis that other souls will have to be placed in because to do otherwise for them would place them in constant terror. Where would they go? Again, this is the point I am making – **where would they go?** They can only be within their own perception-band and, if that perception-band is in a physicality that is no longer there, where do they go? They cannot perceive because there is nothing for them to perceive! They are not capable of perceiving outside of that 'envelope' they have placed themselves in and, if there is no physicality that matches that envelope, they have to be withdrawn. We then have to wait until there is a level of physicality that can accept them once again, so that they can be re-introduced into that same old cycle with the hope that *this time* we can reach them to break that cycle. Do you see that?

Jane: Yes.

Joseph: Are you sure?

Jane: When they are in that stasis-state, isn't that a bit of a respite for the rest of Creation because it is stopping the Field and all that negativity and suffering for a while?

Joseph: It is not a good thing. Our hearts, minds and souls *ache* because part of us is restricted, part of us is not operating as it should. **Those people are us!** They are us – we are them and, as I mentioned this morning, it is our nature, as spirits, to change. That is how information and evolution comes to us, through *change*. If a part of us is unchanging, imagine how frustrating and... I... can't think of a word in earthly language – you would have to experience how we feel. It is against the nature of God for things to remain static but part of us is remaining static.

So we must wait and prepare for a time when we can re-introduce movement into the stasis and **it is a great frustration to us!** It is a great frustration that vexes our minds – the fact that the people in stasis should be moving and *would be* moving if they had the *perception* but aren't. They have placed themselves into an 'impossibility' – it is a paradox and yet it exists. This, again, is to do with the Fall – you cannot have a *full stop* in nature, yet twice you have come to a full stop and a position where you cannot move, you cannot evolve – not because God has prevented you from evolving or because we have prevented you from evolving but because *you* have prevented yourselves from evolving because you cannot see spiritual reality as it is. You cannot see that reality at all most times, and the glimpses you get are distorted too. Do you see?

Jane: Yes, thank you.

Joseph: Tony, is there a question?

Tony: Can we turn it round, Joseph? Are we going to avoid that dreadful stop? Can we do it?

Joseph: As we graduate through these books it becomes increasingly difficult to focus my concepts into concepts that you, with your limited view, can understand. That sounds so pompous, and yet I don't mean it in that way – I have to translate concepts.

You cannot destroy yourselves. You can destroy the surface of the Earth and you can destroy your physical bodies but you cannot destroy yourselves because you are indestructible. You are spirits; you are a part of God and that part of you cannot be destroyed. Therefore, there has to be a point where that point of view, that is greater than what you feel you are on the Earth, stirs and *remembers*. That is all we are trying to make you do – *remember*.

...And at that point mankind will come out of the darkness.

So, the information that we bring is (with hope, prayer and work) to make the end go away *this time*; to make the end dissipate, but that information, *should* the end come again, will be made available again ...and again ...and again ...and again ...until such time as the consciousness of mankind is raised.

The cataclysm or end (however it comes – whether it comes quietly or with a bang) does not concern us as much as the waste of 'time' or waste of *experience of being* that happens after that cataclysm – the waste, again, of people having to be held within a field of their own creation until such time as we can reach them again.

I haven't answered your question because, minute by minute, the answer *changes*.

There is nothing more powerful on Earth than one soul who has seen the Light, seen the *lighter side* and seen the truth, because that soul becomes both the vessel and the beacon – a vessel for information and a beacon for Light that is transmitted out into the darkness of the Field. The Field is terrified of the Light. As I have said before, the Field is a child but a child, unlike your children, not terrified of the *dark* but terrified of the *Light*; terrified of the truth; terrified of letting go and terrified of allowing God to permeate its atoms and its consciousness.

We have to bring in souls here and there who can transmit that Light and it is intended (if the change comes and if the end of physicality *for the time being* is to be avoided), and we are working towards, a time when there are so many souls transmitting the Light that, at a certain point, that Light *unifies* and effectively 'blows out' the Field and puts out the negative aspects of the Field. The Field will remain conscious but will be filled with God-Light and that is what 'ascension' means. It is a term that annoys me because it is talked about glibly as though: *at three o'clock on one afternoon Mr. Jones will ascend and then the following day somebody on a different continent will ascend and physically fly up to Heaven!* No! Ascension comes at the point where there is enough Light put into the Field to change the balance, and that is what we are working towards.

So, it is a question I cannot answer; it is a question that I would love to say, 'Yes, certainly, we are coming through and the end will not come.' However, things can change in an instant and, as we have said before, each soul that carries the Light actually prevents the end from coming and, in effect, buys us time. Remember that not just I and my group are working but there are groups contacting souls around the globe at this time with a similar purpose, night and day, and as you sleep someone else is receiving information – someone else is changing their mind with regard to the Light.

Would that I could transfer the urgency of the need to absorb and transmit Light to the readers. There is a feeling – and this is again an effect of the Field – that *it will be all right, it will never happen!*

I am sorry ...but it won't be all right and it will!

There is urgency and there is a need for personal responsibility.

I hope that we do not find ourselves (all of us in this room and all of us here) giving this information to another set of communicators. I hope that the communication can end here *with this cycle*, because if it ends with this cycle then it has gone into the consciousness of the souls on Earth ...and the change has been made.

Also available in **The Joseph Communications** series:

Revelation

who you are, why you're here

Second Edition

...a book to change your world.

In this first book of the series, Joseph invites you to understand who and what you really are, where you came from, why you are here and the miraculous things you are capable of achieving. Joseph reveals the amazing potential of the human spirit and provides a plan for changing the future of this planet before it's too late.

Intelligent, thought-provoking, non-religious and written in direct, concise language, this book will revolutionise your views through its challenging revelations about life and the nature of reality itself.

Revelation will empower you through a new awareness of the active part you play in creation and inspire you to look at your world in a whole new light.

'WOW! All I can say is I will never view my existence in the same way after reading this.' Ronaldo (Amazon).

'Joseph answers so many of the questions I have always wanted to know about the nature of reality.' Julia Seymour.

'I've read every metaphysical book I could get my hands on for years but there is information in this book that I've not come across anywhere before. I would wholeheartedly recommend this series to anyone seeking answers and the inspiration to finding wisdom within.' jmj4 (Amazon).

'Whatever your religion Revelation will inspire and help you to understand why we are here on this planet and make you think about the way you are living your life.' Joy (Amazon).

'The most direct and compelling book on spirituality I have ever read.' G. R. Munro-Hall (Amazon).

£13.95

ISBN: 978-1-906625-07-8

Available from good bookshops, Amazon or direct from www.josephspeaks.com

e-Book format also available for Kindle, iPad and other platforms.

Also available in **The Joseph Communications** series:

Illumination
change yourself, change the world

...A powerful spiritual manual for personal and global transformation.

Time is running out – Earth is heading for cataclysm. This vitally important book reveals how each of us can literally save the world ...before it's too late.

We need to change and accept personal responsibility now – or Joseph warns there are only three generations left. The Field has become so polluted by mankind's negative energy that the planet cannot sustain itself much longer ...unless radical changes are made to the way we think.

It is our responsibility to renew the Field by infusing it with sufficient Light to redress the balance and return the planet to the paradise it originally was. Illumination provides all the 'tools' to achieve personal and global enlightenment empowering the reader to direct Light and transmute our negativity into harmony, joy, love, peace and spiritual progression.

There is a great urgency to Joseph's words - we do not have an infinite number of tomorrows in which to put things right.

'Read the book, adopt its practices and discover a new life of spiritual harmony and lasting fulfilment.' Jan Quigley.

'A masterpiece of spiritual work! What is very clever is the way Joseph builds up his case throughout this book with possibilities to test his meditations as you go – this is not dry theory! I will certainly continue the daily Light-work which I now regard as essential.' Tony Cross.

'If you wish to bring peace, joy and abundance to yourself and those you love then this book gives you means.' Mr. C. Fraser-Malcolm (Amazon)

'Joseph's chapter on religion couldn't have been closer to my own thoughts!' Liz House.

£12.95
ISBN: 978-1-906625-01-6
Available from good bookshops, Amazon or direct from www.josephspeaks.com
e-Book format also available for Kindle, iPad and other platforms.

Also available in **The Joseph Communications** series:

Trance Mission

Over a period of three years Joseph was asked more than 150 questions 'live' by those attending twelve remarkable public trance demonstrations.

His illuminating, eloquent answers are reproduced word-for-word in this double-sized, 448-page book, in which Joseph focuses on and expands our understanding of a wide range of spiritual topics, including:

pre-destiny and choice • the nature of time • natural disasters • Indigo children • meditation techniques • God • the future of the planet • aliens • reincarnation • angels • past-life baggage • sexual energy • healing • the Bible • animals • infant mortality • ascension • the reason for accidents ...and many more.

As with each Joseph title, **Trance Mission**'s contents are shot through with his refreshingly no-nonsense approach to spirituality. Highly illuminating, deeply spiritual and presenting practical information on every page, **Trance Mission** also gives a unique insight into Joseph's background and relationship with his 'instrument' Michael, immersing all who read it in the unique, irresistible atmosphere of his public trance appearances.

'I can't say how satisfying it is to read someone's question that exactly mirrors my own, and what deep and thought-provoking answers Joseph provides.' Eugenie Heraty.

'It is such an extraordinary book - so many new perspectives on old ideas.' Peter Wallace.

'Rarely do you read any "channeled" material that answers questions directly and sensibly. This is the book that does and I highly recommend it to anyone on their spiritual journey.' Meria Heller.

'Wonderful - many of the additional questions I had been asking after reading the other four books have been answered.' Rowen Harris.

'Truly, it's fabulous! I'm finding it to be a real page-turner. I love it!' Ian Davison.

'Trance Mission is a magnificent read - so many answers to questions that spiritual truth-seekers yearn to know.' Joanna Eden.

'Anyone seeking to be uplifted from this negative world view should read Trance Mission – much Love and Light and hope on every page.' Christine Wood.

£19.95

ISBN: 978-1-906625-06-1

Available from good bookshops, Amazon or direct from www.josephspeaks.com

e-Book format also available for Kindle, iPad and other platforms.

Also available in **The Joseph Communications** series:

From Here to Infinity

...In this sixth book in the acclaimed series Joseph clarifies, demystifies and redefines – from a spiritual perspective – many of the major earthly concepts we take for granted and find ourselves immersed in including: Time, Space, Energy, Perception, Memory and Infinity.

Joseph also offers further insights into the nature of the Divine and, by exploring and enhancing our creative potential, he reveals advanced ways of transforming and elevating our inner and outer worlds and infusing our lives and the matrix of this entire planet with the highest expression of Light.

As a reader of the Joseph Communications, this 288-page volume is set to expand your ability to live in the Light and to give out the Light, offering new methods and meditations that will further empower you to make a real difference in this world by – literally – illuminating yourself, those around you, and the physical landscape you are currently a part of.

'Oh boy, Joseph really seems to have lifted the tempo this time.'
Kate Wrigglesworth.

'Joseph REALLY gets into the nuts and bolts of what's NEEDED for us Warriors of the Light! I'm so humbled by this information.'
Jorge Castaneda.

'I don't mind admitting that the last chapter moved me to tears. This book has made me more determined than ever to meditate daily to send Light out to the world.'
Tracy Dewick.

'I wish it were required reading in every school, library and institution, so important is the message.'
Jeannie Judd.

£16.95

ISBN: 978-1-906625-08-5

Available from good bookshops, Amazon or direct from www.josephspeaks.com

e-Book format also available for Kindle, iPad and other platforms.

www.josephspeaks.com